Week by Week

Insights into the Riches of the Old Testament

Winfried Balke

Impressum

Title of the German original version: Woche um Woche
D 75378 Bad Liebenzell, Germany
Copyright of the German version 2010
English Translation: Winfried Balke
Cover layout: Hallerwedemarketing e.K.

Copyright: 2014 Winfried Balke
Production and Publication: BoD – Books on Demand, Norderstedt
ISBN 978-3-7357-5656-5

Acknowledgments

I would like to extend my thanks to Karl-Hans Fuchs for his encouragement in editing this English version of the book.
I am especially thankful to Dr. Wayne Becker for his thorough proof-reading. Without his manifold corrections and suggestions, his patience and his compassion, a text would likely have been published that would have been understandable but with occasional wording identifiable as that of a non-native speaker and without its pleasing readability.

Preface

"That which God loves, I want to love as well!"

With these simple words a certain very involved leader of one of the larger Free-Churches of Germany answered the question of why he was willing to invest so much of himself in Israel. Winfried Balke´s simple answer at that time impressed me for many years. Both of us could recognize jointly how the blessings that God allowed to rain upon our Assembly came from varied sources: It was the love for the biblical Word of God, and a willingness and openness to the activity of the Holy Spirit, as well as being inwardly firmly committed to God's beloved Nation – the Jews.

No one will be able to understand the history of this World or that of the Christian Church, or even that of the local Church, who ignores God's inextinguishable faithfulness and love for Israel. God's heart moves with a love that touches both Jews and Christians. The ingathering of a people from the Diaspora evolves in parallel with the ingathering of those who confess Jesus as Lord and follow Him. Nowadays we also speak of the "Ecumenicalism of the Heart". Yes, God leads people together who belong together. At the same time it seems significant to me that what is important in this place is not a bi-lateral kindness, but rather a kind of common fate, which Christians and Jews share. Both live off the love and election of the Grace of God.

Nowadays there are many Christians who possess a certain sympathy for Israel (an "Israel-Sympathy") They invest themselves on behalf of the Jewish people. Some of them are even quite zealous. Yet one could get the impression that they are partly also somewhat blind to the rough reality of history, in which the people of Israel found themselves in all those centuries and still find themselves even today. In Winfried Balke I see and esteem highly a clarity of understanding and also determination. His love of God is seen not only in enthusiasm, but rather at the same time also in determined action. He invests himself intensively with the people of Israel and has supported them in many ways. He promotes contacts with Jews and seeks them out, and above all he deals intensively with the Old Testament Scriptures.

From his exegesis of the biblical texts that follow the weekly "Haftarah"-Readings, we can learn a lot about Judaism. It often seems that we are looking more accurately at the Jewish roots that underlie Christianity (Romans 11:18). The author regards biblical texts from both the Jewish and the Christian perspectives - "with both eyes" so to speak. Some of his remarks refer also to the current situation of Israel. Even if a reader does not accept his exegesis of specific details, he might nonetheless be motivated to do further research on his own. Throughout, the book resonates with a love of God for His Chosen Nation of the Jews. At the same time, God´s love flashes forth anew, as is seen in Jesus and is open to all men.

My desire is that this book may not only lead to a blessed time of devotion, but also to a new and deeper understanding of God's history of salvation that is well founded both biblically and historically. It is my prayer that by means of this exegesis the love of God and of His People, the Jews, may be newly aroused in the hearts of the readers of this book and may lead to resolute action.

Dr. Heinrich Christian Rust
Pastor of the Church of Peace of Braunschweig

Introduction

The purpose of this book

It's important to read the Bible daily. But to be maximally fruitful, we ought not to content ourselves with a few verses, but rather to read longer passages, also even whole chapters. It is a special blessing to focus on a certain text in prayer, with a sincere heartfelt desire to receive from it specific guidance for one's own life of faith and spiritual growth.

But here's an important question: Do we devote ourselves to the first two-thirds of the Bible just as intensely and joyfully as to the latter third? Do we discover the treasure of the so-called Old Testament as the guiding principle of our daily life, as Paul instructs us in 2 Timothy 3:16-17[1] "All Scripture is God-breathed and is useful for teaching, rebuking, correcting and training in righteousness, so that the man of God may be thoroughly equipped for every good work"? We're not likely to do so if we:
- regard whole passages of the Old Testament as historically interesting, yet without relevance to our Christian life;
- pick out a few favourite passages;
- attribute the statements of the O.T. primarily to ourselves without asking what the words, addressed originally to Israel, may have to say about our relation to the Jewish people and the present-day State of Israel.

Oh how little connection our worship services, prayer meetings and Christian celebrations of feasts have with our spiritual

---

[1] All quotations according to the New International Version unless mentioned otherwise

roots! It's sad – maybe even frightening – to observe how Christianity simply runs alongside Judaism, usually without establishing any concrete connections. We celebrate Easter and fail to remind ourselves of what happened at Passover; we celebrate Pentecost fifty days after the Feast of Resurrection, yet do not see any connection between it and the Jewish Feast of Weeks, Shavuot, which is intended to remind us of the giving of the Torah at Sinai; we read in the Bible about the Day of Atonement, Yom Kippur, and about the Feast of Tabernacles, and all too often we regard these celebration as "something for the Jews", with little realization of their relevance for us. We seem not to notice that our Lord Jesus celebrated the Feast of Dedication of the Temple (John 10:22) and we don't pay much attention to the fact that the Feast of Chanukah is still celebrated today. Now and then one can even hear the question being asked: "How do the Jews celebrate Christmas?" What an important difference it would make in our preaching and teaching if we were to emphasize the connections between the Jewish and the Christian Faiths!

I know from my own experience, that it can be a great help if we are willing to relate our own reading of the Scriptures to that of the Jewish People, at least in part.. In the synagogues, the whole Torah (the five Books of Moses) is read through once a year, with several chapters being read, rather chanted, each week. The liturgical reading in the Synagogue from the Books of Moses is called Parascha. To complete and deepen the reading, a passage from the Prophetic Writings or from the historical books of the Bible, the so-called Haftarah[2], is added. The selection may be a little surprising for us -- our division of these books into chapters was undertaken only later- some

---

[2] „Haftarah" means something like „conclusion, ending". The plural form is "Haftarot".

chapters that we might find more "central" according to Christian understanding may be missing, some readings seem to deal with completely diverse ideas and do not cover just one major topic. But this is exactly what makes it challenging. As far as I am concerned, it motivated me to work out for myself which "sermon" is somehow contained in a particular Haftarah. And what I noticed was, that without this more intensive Bible study I would have passed over the verses many times quickly and superficially. It is my hope that the following interpretations will also be a help to others and will lead to an enrichment of understanding.

I find it also helpful to know that the Hebrew name of Jesus is Jeshua which in fact is a proclamation: it means salvation!

A Few Practical Tips

A few comments regarding the Jewish calendar are likely to be helpful for the practical use of this book:

The Jewish calendar (as fixed by Hillel, 330-365 C.E.) is adjusted to the cycle of the moon and not to the solar year, as the Gregorian calendar is. The cycle of the moon is about 29 1/2 days, so the months have either 29 or 30 (never 31) days. The Jewish year therefore consists of 354 days, which makes it 10-11 days shorter than the solar year.

As a result, the Jewish feasts would move forward every year by 11 days, were a special adjustment not made. This was necessary precisely because the feasts are connected with phases in agriculture and seasonal happenings in nature. For instance, the Lord ordained that the "Feast of Weeks" (Shavuot) was to be celebrated as the "Feast of the Firstfruits of the Wheat-Harvest" (Exodus 34:22), which links the feast firmly to the harvest season. Similarly, Succoth (the Feast of Ingathering or, literally, the Feast of Tabernacles or Booths) must not be moved in time, since it is to be celebrated "after you have gathered the produce of your threshing floor and your wine-press"" (Deut.16:13). And as to the Feast of Passover, it is written: "Observe the month of Abib and celebrate the Passover of the LORD your God" (Deut. 16:1). "Abib" means "Spring". In order for Passover to be celebrated in spring each year, a leap year is installed according to a certain rhythm, which contains an additional month (the second Adar). As a result, the Jewish calendar does not correspond directly with our calendar, which means that a certain weekly portion of the Bible cannot be attributed every year to the same date on our calendar.

Furthermore, the Jewish year does not start in January, but rather in autumn, with the feast called "Rosh Hashanah" (the "head", or "top" of the year). The reading in this book entitled "Week no.1" applies to this beginning of the year. According to Jewish tradition each weekly section possesses a Hebrew name, which we have not included here in general. In some sections, however, we have inserted the Hebrew term in form of a footnote, since a certain portion of the Bible cannot be ascribed each year to the same week especially toward the end of the Jewish year.. In connection with important feasts or dates of remembrance there are additional Haftarot. A few examples of such are added at the end of this book.

Two important remarks should be added here:
From the weekly Haftarah only a few verses are actually cited for each interpretation, which makes it is especially important to read the whole biblical text previously.
And keep in mind that the interpretations compiled here can only supply preliminary thoughts which should be examined along with the Scriptures, with the hope that it will stimulate a deeper Bible study of one's own. I would be most happy if

there would grow from these studies a more intensive relationship between the roots of our faith and the faith of our Jewish brethren.

Winfried Balke   Summer 2014

Week 1

Isaiah 42:5 - 43:10

This week's portion of the Torah-Reading is Genesis 1:1 – 6:8. Here we find the great tension between the wonderful account of Creation and the declaration that "the Lord saw that the wickedness of man was great in the earth..." (Gen. 6:5). The Haftarah picks up a thread from here, in that it deals with God the Creator and His plan to raise up righteousness and to save His people

1) The Almighty One introduces Himself

"This is what God says – He who created the heavens and stretched them out, who spread out the earth and all that comes out of it, who gives breath to its people, and life to those who walk on it" (Isaiah 42:5).
"I am the LORD, that is My name! I will not give My glory to another or My praise to idols"(42.8).
"Sing to the LORD a new song, His praise from the ends of the earth..." (42,10).
"Let them give glory to the LORD and proclaim His praise in the islands."
"For I am the LORD, your God, the Holy One of Israel, your Savior..."(43:3).

All honor is due to the almighty Creator of heaven and earth, to the Creator of all life, for what He did and what He is doing. His glory shall span the whole world. "From the rising of the sun to the place where it sets, the name of the LORD is to be praised" (Ps. 113:3).

declares the LORD, 'will the descendants of Israel ever cease to be a nation before Me" (Jer. 31:35-36).

The measure of how closely the Almighty wants to be united with His people Israel is described wonderfully in the picture of the "husband". Similar pictures underline this too: "In that day, declares the LORD, you will call Me 'my husband', ...I will betroth you to Me forever; I will betroth you in righteousness and justice, in love and compassion. I will betroth you in faithfulness, and you will acknowledge the Lord." (Hosea 2:16+19-20) Righteousness, justice, love, compassion and faithfulness for all eternity!

Israel is so near to the heart of the living God, that He has bound Himself to this people with the Holiness of His name. When Moses received the assignment to lead the people of Israel out of Egypt, he was told to say to the people specifically: "...The LORD, the God of your fathers - the God of Abraham, the God of Isaac and the God of Jacob - has sent me to you. This is My name forever, the name by which I am to be remembered from generation to generation"(Ex. 3:15). Jesus recalls this when he says concerning the question of His resurrection: "...Have you not read what God said to you, 'I am the God of Abraham and the God of Isaac and the God of Jacob? He is not the God of the dead but of the living." (Mt. 22:31-32).

We believe in this eternal, unchangeable "God of Israel" (Mt. 15:31), the Holy One of Israel.
Thus we can join in with the song of the writer of the Psalms: "I will praise You with the harp for Your faithfulness, O my God; I will sing praise to You with the lyre, O Holy One of Israel" (Ps.71:22). And the Jewish people too have every reason to rejoice: "Shout aloud and sing for joy, people of

Zion, for great is the Holy One of Israel among you" (Isa. 12:6).

"The LORD Almighty is His Name". The LORD "Zebaoth". What do we read in the account of the birth of the Savior? "Suddenly a great company of the heavenly host appeared with the angel, praising God..." (Luke 2:13). And what was the objection that Jesus raised when speaking to one of His disciples, who wanted to defend Him with the sword, when He was taken prisoner? "Do you think I cannot call on My Father, and He will at once put at My disposal more than twelve legions of angels?" (Mt. 26:53)

With this "LORD Almighty, the God of the armies of Israel", whom David expressly refers to in the fight with Goliath (1 Sam. 17:45), Israel is safe and secure: "The LORD Almighty is with us; the God of Jacob is our fortress" (Ps. 46:7). Why is it so? "The vineyard of the LORD Almighty is the house of Israel, and the men of Judah are the garden of His delight..." (Isa. 5:7). The garden of His delight! Of Zion the LORD says: "...You will be called Hephzibah ("I delight in her"), and your land Be'ulah ("married") – literally: "one that has a husband or "lord"); for the LORD will take delight in you, and your land will be married" (Isa. 62:4).

This has a wonderful consequence: "...The Lord has redeemed Jacob; He displays His glory in Israel" (Isa. 44:23)

2) **The divine measurement of time"**

"For a brief moment I abandoned you, but with deep compassion I will bring you back. In a surge of anger I hid My face from you for a moment; but with everlasting kindness I

will have compassion on you, says the Lord your Redeemer...Though the mountains be shaken and the hills be removed; yet My unfailing love for you will not be shaken nor My covenant of peace be removed, says the LORD who has compassion on you." (54:7-10).

The LORD is a just God. That is why He must punish us from time to time, "because the LORD disciplines those He loves, and He punishes everyone He accepts as a son" (Heb. 12:6). But we experience this also: "The Lord is compassionate and gracious, slow to anger, abounding in love. He will not always accuse, nor will He harbor His anger forever" (Ps. 103:8-9). His purpose is to straighten us out, that we might reach the goal.

The tension between a short-term sadness and the occasion of everlasting joy is brought before us with a few words, so that we might gain the right perspective: "And the God of all grace, who called you to His eternal glory in Christ, after you have suffered a little while, will Himself restore you and make you strong, firm and steadfast. To Him be the power for ever and ever. Amen!" (1 Pt. 5:10-11) Paul writes: "I consider that our present sufferings are not worth comparing with the glory that will be revealed in us." (Rom. 8:18)

With regard to the promised salvation this is what is written in Peter's letter: "In this you greatly rejoice, though now for a little while you may have had to suffer grief in all kinds of trials. These have come so that your faith – of greater worth than gold ... - may be proved genuine and may result in praise..." (1 Pt. 1:6-7).

Week 3

Isaiah 40: 27 – 41:16

The Torah Portion comprises Genesis 12 – 17, an account that includes the calling of Abram, the covenant with Abram, the changing of his name and the promises made to him. What then might be the connection with the prophetic text in the book of Isaiah? Just as Abram needed the promise "...Do not be afraid, I am your shield..." (Genesis 15: 1) to ensure that his service would be a blessing, in the same way -- and even more so -- Israel needs the encouragement of the LORD in her time of distress and captivity in order to hold fast to her calling to be an instrument of God.

1) Against Despondency

In this portion of Scripture it becomes clear that God knows very well about fearful hearts, for isn't He the One "...who knows the heart..." (Acts 15:8) and the "God of Knowledge" (1 Samuel 2:3).
"Why do you say, O Jacob, and complain, O Israel, 'My way is hidden from the LORD, my cause is disregarded by my God?" *(40:27)* How many Jews there are, who, after the incomprehensible experiences of the Holocaust, cannot rid themselves of the tormenting question: Where was God at that time? O, that the miracle would happen that in spite of this, they may turn to the Holy One of Israel!

We can find three helps against discouragement in our text.

a) HE is eternally the same

"Do you not know? Have you not heard? The LORD is the everlasting God, the Creator of the ends of the earth. He will not grow tired or weary..."(40:28)
"Who has done this and carried it through, calling forth the generations from the beginning? I, the LORD – with the first of them and with the last – I am He." (41, 4)

We recollect how God revealed Himself to Moses with the words: "...I AM who I AM..." or "I shall be that I shall be" in Hebrew: "ehyeh asher ehye" (Ex.3:14) "I am the Alpha and the Omega, says the LORD God, who is and who was and who is to come, the Almighty" (Rev. 1:8)

Unchangeable is this LORD, "...who does not change like shifting shadows..." and of whom it can therefore be said in James 1:17: "Every good and perfect gift is from above, coming down from the Father of the heavenly lights...". When is it that there is no change in the shadow? When the sun stands in the zenith. God, "the Sun of righteousness" is every day afresh in the zenith of His power, in the zenith of His love!
What a precious perspective when we are about to be discouraged!

b) God has acted with power

"Who has stirred up one from the east, calling Him in righteousness to His service? He hands nations over to Him and subdues kings before Him....Who has done this and carried it through...?" (41:2 – 4)

God appears to the 99 year old Abraham and says to him:

"I AM God Almighty", "El shaddai" in Hebrew, and promises to make this elderly man very, very fruitful. (Gen.17:1+6)
Everything was created by His Word (John 1:1-3). With ever new amazement we hear: "And the Word became flesh and dwelt among us." Of this LORD Jesus we are told: "For by Him all things were created: things in heaven and on earth, visible and invisible, whether thrones or powers or rulers or authorities..." (Col. 1:16). Therefore everything is subjected to Him. He "...is head over every power and authority" (Col. 2:10).
Based on this authority He sets up kings and removes them (Dan. 2:21), "...there is no authority except that which God has established..." (Rom. 13:1)
Therefore David can pray: "The LORD is my light and my salvation - whom shall I fear?" (Ps. 27:1) And we can hold fast to Jesus Christ "...who has destroyed death..." (2 Tim.1:10). "Who shall separate us from the love of Christ? Shall trouble or hardship or persecution or famine or nakedness or danger or sword?" (Rom. 8:35)

c) He also strengthens the one whom He has chosen

" HE gives strength to the weary and increases the power of the weak. Even youths grow tired and weary, and young men stumble and fall; but those who hope in the LORD will renew their strength. They will soar on wings like eagles; they will run and not grow weary, they will walk and not be faint." (40:29-31).
"So do not fear, for I am with you; do not be dismayed, for I am your God. I will strengthen you and help you; I will uphold you with My righteous right hand" (41:10).

We human beings can and should help and encourage each other. "...each helps the other and says to his brother, ´ Be *strong!'" (41:6).* But in the end we urgently need the help of God. So the thought here in the text from Isaiah continues with the words: *"But you, O Israel, ...do not fear, for I am with you!" (41:8+10)*

Jesus promises his disciples: "You will receive power when the Holy Spirit comes on you..." (Acts 1:8). Therefore we may know: "For God did not give us a spirit of timidity, but a spirit of power..."(2 Tim.1:7). We are sometimes in danger of forgetting this. That is why Paul continues in prayer that we may know "...His incomparably great power for us who believe. That power is like the working of His mighty strength" (Eph. 1:19). "His divine power has given us everything we need for life and godliness through our knowledge of Him who has called us..."
(2 Pt. 1:3).

How gloriously is this precious "Yes" of our LORD repeated forcefully here in the words of Isaiah to those that belong to Him, in order to write it into our hearts and into the hearts of Israel : *"...I will strengthen thee; yea, I will help thee; yea, I will uphold thee..."! (41:10, King James Version)*

2) For Israel this has special consequences

a) The destruction of the enemies

"All who rage against you will surely be ashamed and disgraced; those who oppose you will be as nothing and perish. Though you search for your enemies, you will not find them. Those who wage war against you will be as nothing at all" (41:11-12).

What a mighty promise! When we consider how in our days the Jews and the State of Israel are being pressed hard from all sides, -- how Iran, Hamas, Hisbollah and Fatah want to extinguish Israel! Antisemitism breaks out again and again in Germany, Europe and many other lands. And lately even the "friends" of Israel, (such as the U.S.A.) are involved, when, for instance, they maintain that it isn't right that Israel build "settlements" in Judea and Samaria. To hear the promise of God with this background can only cause us to be overwhelmed by amazement and worship. The enemies will not only be overcome, they will not only be made weak, no – they *"will be as nothing"!*

b) An instrument of God

"See, I will make you into a threshing sledge, new and sharp, with many teeth. You will thresh the mountains and crush them, and reduce the hills to chaff." (41:15)

People who are set against the Jews, will take up these verses gladly, as a "proof" that Israel is to blame for all the conflicts in the world and that it treats its Arabic neighbours disproportionately harshly or even brutally --something which, if examined conscientiously, turns out to be completely untenable. How then are we to understand the words "threshing sledge" and "crush them"?

We read in another place in the Old Testament that God uses Israel as His instrument against godless nations: "I will bend Judah as I bend My bow and fill it with Ephraim. I will rouse your sons, O Zion, against your sons, O Greece, and make you like a warrior´s sword" (Zech. 9:13). "I will take vengeance on Edom by the hand of My people Israel; and they will deal with

Edom in accordance with My anger and My wrath...(Ezek.25:14). Israel is being used as a tool, in order to assuage the fury of God. "You are My war club, My weapon for battle – with you I shatter nations, with you I destroy kingdoms" (Jer. 51:20). The words with which this is being described may sound strange to our ears, but God's Word is after all "...sharper than any double-edged sword, it penetrates even to dividing soul and spirit..." (Hebr. 4:12).

Since the LORD is interested in the building of His Kingdom and in the establishment of His honor, Israel is to serve Him to *"thresh the mountains"*, which represent spiritual strongholds. Interestingly, as we continue reading in the above cited chapter, Jeremiah 51, we encounter the threat of judgment against Babylon: "I am against you, O destroying mountain, you who destroy the whole earth, declares the LORD..." (Jer. 51:25): Do the "sons of Greece" (Zech.9:13) perhaps represent the champions of hellenism and humanism?
"The Light of Israel will become a fire, their Holy One a flame" (Isa.10:17).

Week 4

2 Kings 4 : 1-37

Just as in Genesis 18:22 (the Torah Portion for this week) Sarah experiences in her life a work of God that sets aside natural laws, so also the Shunemite woman, who is in the center of the Haftarah record, experiences in a mighty way the miracles of the LORD in her family.

Tests of faith

From this account at the time of the prophet Elisha, we can learn a few things about tests of faith, which can happen to us too.

1) **"Is this a just God?"**

"The wife of a man from the company of the prophets cried out to Elisha, 'Your servant my husband is dead, and you know that he revered the LORD; but now his creditor is coming to take my two boys as his slaves" (v. 1).

Here we have a man who had been pious, belonged to the disciples of a prophet, evidently had been zealous in the study of the Torah, had listened intently to the words of his teacher with avid spiritual hunger – and then such a man as he ... died. On top of all this, his death triggered a financial crisis. Although not voiced per se, a question arises: Is that a just God? Is there no reward for being pious?

Perhaps we have had a similar experience; perhaps we too have asked ourselves: Why is it that this good man, of all people, was taken away, while that apparently unscrupulous other person continues to live on cheerfully? Even the writer of the psalm has to confess: "But as for me, my feet had almost slipped, I had nearly lost my foothold. For I envied the arrogant when I saw the prosperity of the wicked." (Ps. 73:2-3).

From the Scriptures we know of other examples where people could not understand the ways of God. When the prodigal son is being received home by his father with a banquet, his brother rebels against it: "...Look, all these years I have been slaving for you and never disobeyed your orders. Yet you never gave me even a young goat so I could celebrate with my friends" (Luke 15:29).
Or consider the parable of the workers in the vineyard: All receive the same wages, without regard to the number of hours they worked. Not surprisingly, those who had served for the longest time grumbled the most. (Mt. 20:10-12).

The question: "is this fair?" clearly lies near to our hearts, and it is incumbent on us to press through to the right answer. Here are several promises of God that may be a help to us in this:
"God is not unjust; He will not forget your work and the love you have shown Him as you have helped His people and continue to help them" (Heb. 6:10) "...each will be rewarded according to his own labor." (1 Cor.:3:8) "For evil men will be cut off; but those who hope in the Lord will inherit the land" (Ps.37:9). In Ps.73 the praying person recognizes a significant truth: He couldn't understand God's dealing with the evil-doers, "till I entered the sanctuary of God; then I understand their final destiny" (Ps.73:17).

But it is also important that we make it clear to ourselves again and again: Our LORD is the Almighty God, sovereign in His decisions. "…He causes His sun to rise on the evil and the good, and sends rain on the righteous and the unrighteous" (Mt.5:45) Jesus asked: "Don't I have the right to do what I want with My own…?" (Mt.20:15) "Woe to him who quarrels with his Maker, to him who is but a potsherd among the potsherds on the ground. Does the clay say to the potter, 'What are you making?'… (Isa. 45:9)
In Revelations we read a song of jubilation: "…Great and marvellous are your deeds, LORD God Almighty! Just and true are your ways, King of the ages" (Rev. 15:3).

2) "Isn't this too audacious?"

"Elisha replied to her, 'How can I help you? Tell me, what do you have in your house? ' 'Your servant has nothing there at all', she said, 'except a little oil'. Elisha said, 'Go around and ask all your neighbors for empty jars. Don't ask for just a few… Pour oil into all the jars, and as each is filled, put it to one side.' She left him…" (v. 2-5).

We read here how the widow obeyed the order of Elisha without critical questioning and without "if"s and "but"s. How would we have reacted? "But I have only one jug of oil", "why so many vessels?", "and if the neighbors ask me, what this means…?"
What confidence the widow had! She was richly rewarded for it. *"When all the jars were full, she said to her son, 'Bring me another one'. But he replied, 'There is not a jar left'. Then the oil stopped flowing" (V.6).*

Again and again circumstances happen in our lives that test our faith and we probably think (yes, we "think"), that what we wish from the Lord is too big, that the request is too daring. What does the Lord call out to us? "...Open wide your mouth and I will fill it!" (Ps. 81:10) "...My people will be filled with My bounty, declares the LORD" (Jer. 31:14). In the letter to the Corinthians we read about the "surpassing grace of God" and of "His indescribable gift". (2 Cor.9:14-15). It is our God, who is able to do "...immeasurably more than all we ask or imagine..." (Eph. 3:20) We may ask of Him the greatest, most important, most beautiful thing that enters our mind. "For in Christ all the fullness of the Deity lives in bodily form, and you have been given fullness in Christ..." (Col.2:9).

The jug of oil is a beautiful picture of the Anointing with the Holy Spirit. If we reach out for it we can pray together with David: "...You anoint my head with oil; my cup overflows" (Ps.23, 5). (When "the Kiddush", the blessing of the wine, is pronounced in Jewish households and the head of the house fills the cup with wine, he fills it to overflowing on purpose, as a sign of this gift.)

3) **"Could this apply to me?"**

"...Well, she has no son and her husband is old... 'About this time next year', Elisha said, 'you will hold a son in your arms'. 'No, my lord', she objected, 'Don't mislead your servant, O man of God!" (v. 15-16).

You can probably think of a similar situation in connection with Abraham: "....he laughed and said to himself, 'Will a son be born to a man a hundred years old? Will Sarah bear a child at the age of ninety?" (Gen. 17:17)
The answer given to Abraham and to Sarah, who also doubted in her heart, was: "Is anything too hard for the LORD?..."

(Gen. 18:14) Also Jesus confirms: "…all things are possible with God" (Mark 10:27).

Sometimes the challenge comes to us in the fact that, though we utter these promises and believe them in principle as being true, we still find it difficult to apply them in our actual present situation. For instance: The LORD can heal wonderfully, and He has healed many of my acquaintances, but can He and will He also do that for me now?

"…The LORD bestows favor and honor, no good thing does He withhold from those whose walk is blameless" (Ps. 84:11).

4) "Why?"

"But the woman became pregnant, and the next year about the same time she gave birth to a son, just as Elisha had told her. The child grew, and one day he went out to his father, who was with the reapers. 'My head, my head!', he said to his father. His father told a servant, 'Carry him to his mother'. After the servant had lifted him up and carried him to his mother, the boy sat on her lap until noon, and then he died"(v.17-20).

The widow had received an unhoped-for blessing, and all of a sudden this blessing is taken away from her again. The grief over the loss of her son causes her to accuse Elisha and thereby to become angry at the Giver of all gifts. Wouldn't it have been easier not to have had a son in the first place? "Why did God act like this?"

In the Psalms we come across this question several times: "…Why have You forgotten me? Why must I go about mourning…?" (Ps. 42:9). "Why, O LORD, do You reject me and hide Your face from me?" (Ps. 88:14) We even find the question: "…Why do You sleep?…" (Ps.44:23) Indeed, the

Bible does not hesitate to reveal what it sometimes looks like in our hearts.

Peter gives us an answer as to why we are sad in temptations of our faith: "…that your faith - of greater worth than gold, which perishes even though refined by fire – may be proved genuine…" (1 Pt. 1:7). In those crises the enemy intends to tear us away from trusting God, but if we hold fast to our confidence in God, we may expect a precious reward: "Blessed is the man who perseveres under trial, because when he has stood the test, he will receive the crown of life that God has promised to those who love Him" (James 1:12).

5) "May it be that God does not want, after all?"

"Elisha said to Gehazi: Tuck your cloak into your belt, take my staff in your hand und run…Lay my staff on the boy's face! … Gehazi went on ahead and laid the staff on the boy's face, but there was no sound or response. So Gehazi went back to meet Elisha and told him, 'The boy has not awakened´. When Elisha reached the house, there was the boy lying dead on his couch" (v. 29-32.) "

Evidently Elisha had expected from the LORD that by laying his staff on the lad, he would awake. Now the question arose: Give up, as perhaps God did not wish to grant the miracle, or persevere? Again – a trial of faith. Elisha remains in prayer and in so doing is able to witness, as a tool of the Almighty, that the lad comes to life. (v. 33 – 35).

"…Put your hope in God, for I will yet praise Him, my Savior and my God" (Psalm 42:11)

"We want each of you to show this same diligence to the very end, in order to make your hope sure" (Hebr. 6:11).

"Consider it pure joy, my Brothers, whenever you face trials of many kinds, because you know that the testing of your faith develops perseverance. Perseverance must finish its work so that you may be mature and complete, not lacking anything" (James 1:2-4).

Week 5

1 Kings 1 : 1 - 31

This Haftarah has probably been chosen as a supplement for the Torah portion (Genesis 23:1 - 25:18), because on the one hand through the finding of the right wife for Isaac the House of Israel would be kept free from foreign influence, and on the other hand it would ensure the right successor for King David.

The section indicates the challenge that existed in the anointing of the right person as king.

What lesson can we learn for our own situation?

1) "I" on the throne

"Now Adonjiah, whose mother was Haggith, put himself forward and said, 'I will be king" (v. 5)

Here we have someone who does not want anyone to rule over him, but wants rather to have everything under his rule. As the Bible reveals to us forcefully, this is also a significant problem of spiritual life. Already the Serpent, in the Garden of Eden, whispered to Eve that man could become like God (Gen.3) The Prince of Tyre who had been blessed in many ways was cast down to earth. "In the pride of your heart you say; I sit on a throne of a god...´, Because you think you are wise, as wise as a god..." (Ezek. 28:1+ 6).

We are in danger of wanting to decide everything ourselves and to keep ourselves from being underneath someone else's yoke. Yet our loving Master says to us: "Take My yoke upon you and learn from Me, for I am gentle and humble in heart, and you will find rest for your souls. For My yoke is easy and My burden is light." (Mt.11:29-30).

The Scriptures bring different pictures before our eyes, to show how we can be seduced into lifting our "I" upon the throne: "If anyone thinks he is something, when he is nothing, he deceives himself." (Gal.6:3) "Let us not become conceited, provoking and envying each other" (Gal. 5:26). "For everyone looks out for his own interests, not those of Jesus Christ" (Phil 2:21). Gal.5:20 and 2 Cor.12:20 warn us against "selfish ambition" and "factions", Phil. 2:3 against " vain conceit". But the main concern is that we rebel consciously or unconsciously against being led by our eternally loving Father. "God opposes the proud, but gives grace to the humble. Humble yourselves, therefore, under God´s mighty hand..." (1 Pt.5:5-6).

HE belongs on the throne of our life!

2)   Beware of deceivers!

"...So he got chariots and horses ready, with fifty men to run ahead of him" (v. 5).
"Adonijah conferred with Joab son of Zeruiah and with Abiathar the priest; and they gave him their support" (v. 7).
"...He invited all his brothers, the king´s sons, and all the men of Judah who were royal officials. But he did not invite Nathan the prophet or Benaiah or the special guard or his brother Solomon" (v. 9-10).

So Adonijah then succeeds in drawing many men on to his side. He makes his appointments in order to achieve his selfish goal. We do not read what arguments and crafty tricks he used to keep people from following the true king. But we do read in the Bible urgent warnings not to let anything draw us away from the King of Kings:

"Let no one deceive you with empty words; for because of such things God´s wrath comes on those who are disobedient" (Eph. 5:6) "See to it that no one takes you captive through hollow and deceptive philosophy, which depends on human tradition and the basic principles of this world rather than on Christ." (Col.2:8). "Do not be carried away by all kinds of strange teachings…" (Hebr.13:9).

.3) The succession to the throne has been fixed

"The king then took an oath: "As surely as the Lord lives, who has delivered me out of every trouble, I will surely carry out today what I swore to you by the LORD, the God of Israel: Solomon your son shall be king after me, and he will sit on my throne in my place"(v.29-30).

The Lord had exhorted Israel: "Be sure to appoint over you the king the LORD your God chooses…" (Deut.17:15). David had received the promise from God that from his lineage would ensue an eternal Kingdom: "When your days are over and you rest with your fathers, I will raise up your offspring to succeed you, who will come from your own body, and I will establish his kingdom forever… Your house and your kingdom will be established forever" (2 Sam.7:12-16). The immediate follower of David on his throne was to come from his house, but it could not be Adonijah, since it was Solomon who built a house for the LORD according to the will of God. David confirmed the decision of God before the elders of the people with the words: "Of all my sons - and the Lord has given me many - He has chosen my son Solomon to sit on the throne of the kingdom of the LORD over Israel." (1 Chr. 28:5).

But the promise transcended this by far! What do we read in Jeremiah? "The days are coming, declares the LORD, when I will raise up to David a righteous Branch, a King who will reign wisely and do what is just and right in the land…This is the name by which he will be called: The LORD our Righteousness" (Jer. 23:5-6). This is none other than the One who has become "our Righteousness" (1 Cor. 1:30), Yeshua, the Messiah. "For to us a child is born, to us a son is given, and the government will be on his shoulders…" (Isa. 9:6) The Register of Genealogy given in Mt. 1 makes it clear, that Jesus is a follower of David, the son of Jesse, "A shoot will come up from the stump of Jesse; from its roots a Branch will bear fruit. The Spirit of the LORD will rest on Him…" (Isa.11:1-2). The "Son of David" (Mt.1:1) will reign over a united Kingdom of Israel: " I will make them o n e nation in the land, on the mountains of Israel…My servant David will be king over them, and they will all have o n e shepherd…" (Ezek. 37: 22-24). As "King of Kings" (1 Tim. 5:15) He will reign over all the world. Referring to Isaiah, Paul writes: "The Root of Jesse will spring up, one who will arise to rule over the nations; the Gentiles will hope in Him" (15:12). Our LORD is set "far above all rule and authority, power and dominion, and every title that can be given, not only in the present age but also in the one to come" (Eph.1;21). Halleluiah!

Week 6

Malachi 1:1 – 2:7

The beginning of the Haftarah for this week refers to the story of Jacob and Esau in the Torah-Portion of this week (Gen. 25:19 – 28:9)

1) God's Almighty power over Israel and the nations

"An oracle: The word of the LORD to Israel through Malachi. 'I have loved you´, says the LORD. 'But you ask, 'How have You loved us?´ 'Was not Esau Jacob's brother? 'the LORD says: Yet you say: Wherein have you loved us? Was not Esau Jacob's brother?´ the LORD says. 'Yet I have loved Jacob, but Esau I have hated... Edom may say, 'Though we have been crushed, we will rebuild the ruins´. But this is what the LORD Almighty says: 'They may build, but I will demolish. They will be called the Wicked Land, a people always under the wrath of the LORD. You will see it with your own eyes and say, 'Great is the LORD – even beyond the borders of Israel!" (v. 1-5)

In manifold and wonderful ways God has manifested His love for Israel, and yet He receives this critical response of the people, to which He responds by pointing out the contrast to Esau and Edom. Are we not also at times thus - that we recognize the goodness of the LORD afresh only when it becomes clear to us what people miss who are without God?

The Holy One of Israel has sworn eternal faithfulness to His Jewish people, whom He had led out of the slavery in Egypt, has promised them land and given it to them, has smitten their enemies before them and gave them a most astounding promise for the end-time: "I will bring Judah and Israel back from captivity and will rebuild them as they were before. I will cleanse them from all the sin they have committed against Me and will forgive all their sins of rebellion against Me. Then this city will bring Me renown, joy, praise and honor before all nations that hear of all the good things I do for it; and they will be in awe and will tremble at the abundant prosperity and peace I provide for it" (Jer. 33: 7 – 9).

Already the Lord is magnified "beyond the borders of Israel" by the fact that the world recognizes God's deeds of lovingkindness to Israel. But His Almighty power also extends – and in the most diverse manners – to all the nations: Since God "...wants all men to be saved and to come to a knowledge of the truth" (1 Timothy 2:4), He has shown His power and grace through the fact that "...the gift of the Holy Spirit had been poured out even on the Gentiles" (Acts 10:45).

At the end of time, "He will judge among the nations and will settle disputes for many peoples. They will beat their swords into ploughshares and their spears into pruning hooks. Nation will not take up sword against nation, nor will they train for war anymore" (Isa. 2:4). What a divine intervention!

And the LORD will judge the nations according to their attitude to His beloved people Israel: "All the nations will be gathered before Him, and He will separate the people one from another as a shepherd separates the sheep from the goats. He will put the sheep on His right and the goats on His left. Then the King will say to those on His right, ´Come, you who are blessed by My Father, take your inheritance, the kingdom..." (Mt. 25:32 – 34). "...I tell you the truth, whatever you did for one of the least of these brothers of Mine´(the Jews), ´you did for Me." (Mt. 25:40) The power of Jesus, which extends *"beyond the borders of Israel"* is also revealed in the statement

"...that He is the One whom God appointed as judge of the living and the dead" (Acts 10:42).

2) An unclean, and a correct sacrifice

"A son honors his father, and a servant his master. If I am a father, where is the honor due Me? If I am a master, where is the respect due Me? says the LORD Almighty .It is you, O priests, who show contempt for My name. But you ask, 'How have we shown contempt for Your name?' You place defiled food on My altar. But you ask, 'How have we defiled You?' ...When you bring blind animals for sacrifice, is that not wrong? When you sacrifice crippled or diseased animals, is that not wrong? Try offering them to your governor! Would he be pleased with you?..." (1:6–8) "...I am not pleased with you, says the LORD Almighty, and I will accept no offering from your hands."(1:10).

There had been times in the past when the people erroneously thought that they could appease God with the sacrifices that they offered. The verses ring harshly in our ears: "I hate, I despise your religious feasts, I cannot stand your assemblies. Even though you bring Me burnt offerings ...I will not accept them. Though you bring choice fellowship offerings, I will have no regard for them. Away with the noise of your songs! ...(Amos 5:21-23). What is this weekly portion supposed to say to us? How do we think we can "offer" to the Almighty God something that we would not dare offer to a worldly personality? How do we allow the respect due to our Creator to be missing?

We want to pursue two questions: How are we to give our sacrifice to the LORD, and what is designated as a sacrifice in the New Testament.

First of all Yeshua exhorts us: "Therefore, if you are offering your gift at the altar and there remember that your brother has something against you, leave your gift there in front of the altar. First go and be reconciled to your brother..." (Mt.5:23-24). It is also important that a financial offering be only a matter between us and the Lord and that we are not to seek recognition from men: "Be careful not to do your ´acts of righteousness´ before men, to be seen by them. If you do, you will have no reward from your Father in heaven" (Mt.6:1). And we are warned to keep from giving in a calculating manner: "But when you give to the needy, do not let your left hand know what your right hand is doing." (Mt.6:3) Let us remember also the widow, who gave not from her surplus, but rather "...out of her poverty put in all she had to live on" (Luke 21:4). "Each man should give what he has decided in his heart to give, not reluctantly or under compulsions, for God loves a cheerful giver" (2 Cor. 9:7). And God will even bestow gifts upon us richly: "Bring the whole tithe into the storehouse, that there may be food in My house. Test Me in this, says the Lord Almighty, and see if I will not throw open the floodgates of heaven and pour out so much blessing that you will not have room enough for it" (Mal.3: 10). Besides, we often forget that because of our spiritual roots we should also remember Israel with our gifts: "For if the Gentiles have shared in the Jews´ spiritual blessings, they owe it to the Jews to share with them their material blessings" (Rom. 15:27).

But not only financial and practical allocations are to be considered. "Through Jesus, therefore, let us continually offer to God a sacrifice of praise – the fruit of lips that confess His name. And do not forget to do good and to share with others, for with such sacrifices God is pleased" (Hebr.13:15-16). And Paul exhorts us "...to offer your bodies as living sacrifices, holy and pleasing to God – this is your spiritual act of worship" (Rom. 12:1). In this sense it is also written: "You also, like living stones, are being built into a spiritual house to be a holy priesthood, offering spiritual sacrifices acceptable to God through Jesus Christ" (1 Pt. 2:5).

Along with all this we should remember, that Jesus "…gave Himself up for us as a fragrant offering and sacrifice to God" (Eph. 5:2). "Because by one offering He has made perfect forever those who are being made holy" (Hebr. 10:14).

3) Responsiblity of spiritual leaders

"And now, this admonition is for you, O priests. If you do not listen, and if you do not set your heart to honor My name…" (2:1)

"…that My covenant with Levi may continue…He revered Me and stood in awe of My name. True instruction was in his mouth and nothing false was found on his lips. He walked with Me in peace and uprightness, and turned many from sin" (2:4-6)

Here criteria are given by which we can measure true leaders. But much of this applies just as much to every single believer, since we are "a kingdom of priests" (1 Pt. 2:9). Certainly we are inclined to say that we honor the name of our LORD, both in our prayers as also in testimony. But many times we do not confess that we belong to the "Holy One of Israel" (Ps. 71:22), to the "Son of David" (Mt. 21:9), to "Immanuel" (Isa. 7:14 + Mt. 1:23). He desires to be honored as the God of Abraham, Isaac and Jacob. For "…this is My name forever, the name by which I am to be remembered from generation to generation" (Ex.3:15).

Of Levi it is said: *"He walked with Me in peace"*. What a mighty gift, to be able to live in peace with the Almighty God!

"Therefore, since we have been justified through faith, we have peace with God through our LORD Jesus Christ" (Rom.5:1). Jesus Himself says: "Peace I leave with you; My peace I give you. I do not give to you as the world gives..." (John 15:27). Timothy´s letter makes clear what it means to live in peace and godliness: "I urge, then, first of all, that requests, prayers, intercession and thanksgiving be made for everyone – for kings and all those in authority, that we may live peaceful and quiet lives, in all godliness and holiness" (1 Tim. 2:1-2).

The concept of *uprightness* is also taken up in the New Testament: "Do your best to present yourself to God as one approved, a workman who does not need to be ashamed and who correctly handles the word of truth" (2 Tim.2:15).
And the exhortation is addressed to leaders especially: "Preach the Word, be prepared in season and out of season; correct, rebuke and encourage – with great patience and careful instruction" (2 Tim. 4:2). So it may possible through the Grace of God, to *"turn many from sin"*.

Week 7

Hosea 12:13 - 14:10[4]

In the first verses of our text Hosea reminds us of James, of whom the Parascha deals (Gen.28:10 – 32:3), and of the fact that the LORD had led Israel out of Egypt.

1) Known

"But I am the Lord your God, who brought you out of Egypt. You shall acknowledge no God but Me, no Savior except Me. I cared for you in the desert, in the land of burning heat" (13:4-5).

God heard the cry of His people Israel, when they were being oppressed by Pharaoh and were forced to do slave labor. He had compassion for them and saved them out of it. There is nothing that is hid from Him, and His own are anything but a matter of indifference to Him. The Creator has known His creatures from the beginning and loves them.

Together with David we too may be sure: "My frame was not hidden from You when I was made in the secret place. When I was woven together in the depth of the earth, Your eyes saw my unformed body. All the days ordained for me were written in Your book before one of them came to be" (Ps. 139:15-16). Nothing that has happened to us or will ever happen to us surprises our Creator. "The LORD is good, a refuge in times of trouble. He cares for those who trust in Him" (Nahum 1:7). He

---

[4] See exegesis of Hosea 14:2-10, week "50 b"

Who knows all the stars by name (Isa. 40:26), calls out to Israel: "...I have summoned you by name, you are Mine" (Isa.43:1). And when we have obeyed His call, we too may be sure of this: We belong to Him. What a gift! It was from God that the initiative went forth. At a time when we as yet did not want to know anything of Him and were yet "enemies", Yeshua already died for us on the Cross (Rom. 5:10).

"The Lord knows those who are His..." (2 Tim. 2:9). "O LORD, You have searched me and You know me. You know when I sit and when I rise; You perceive my thoughts from afar. You discern my going out and my lying down; You are familiar with all my ways" (Ps. 139:1–3). When David is being oppressed by enemies he can pray with confidence: "Record my lament; list my tears on Your scroll – are they not in Your record?" (Ps. 56:8) Thus our Savior also knows all about the many situations in which we personally feel we´re in the *"burning heat"* described in Hos. 13:5. He calls out to us: "...In this world you will have trouble. But take heart! I have overcome the world." (John 16:33). Yes, "...the LORD knows how to rescue godly men from trials..."(2 Pt. 2:9).We may lean on the promise: "...And God is faithful; He will not let you be tempted beyond what you can bear. But when you are tempted, He will also provide a way out so that you can stand up under it" (1 Cor. 10:13). "Who shall separate us from the love of Christ? Shall trouble or hardship or persecution or famine or nakedness or danger or sword?" (Rom. 8:35)

2)   Forgetful

"When I fed them, they were satisfied; when they were satisfied, they became proud; then they forgot Me"(13:6).

All things are revealed to the LORD: our troubles and cares, the times of our "heat", but also the situations in which we have forgotten him! "If we had forgotten the name of our God or spread out our hands to a foreign god, would not God have discovered it, since He knows the secrets of the heart?" (Ps.44:20-21).

How many times may we have forgotten to thank our faithful Shepherd for what He has given us whether "we asked for it or not"? The exhortation that Moses passed on to the people in that day is valid and important to be heard today as well: "When you have eaten and are satisfied, praise the LORD your God for the good land He has given you. Be careful that you do not forget the LORD your God, failing to observe His commands, His laws and His decrees that I am giving you this day. Otherwise, when you eat and are satisfied, when you build fine houses and settle down... and your silver and gold increase and all you have is multiplied, then your heart will become proud and you will forget the LORD your God who brought you ... out of the land of slavery" (Deut.8:10-14)

Solomon evidently knew about the lurking dangers: "...Give me neither poverty nor riches, but give me only my daily bread. Otherwise I may have too much and disown You and say, ´Who is the LORD?´ Or I may become poor and steal, and so dishonor the name of My God" (Prov. 30:8-9).

We also read about forgetting in the story of Joseph: Joseph in prison informs the chief butler of Pharaoh about the release of this servant from prison and begs of him: "But when all goes well with you, remember me and show me kindness; mention me to the Pharaoh and get me out of this prison" (Gen. 40:14) The butler is indeed set free, and then the story continues: "The chief cupbearer, however, did not remember Joseph; he forgot him" (Gen.40:23).

Doesn't this point to the danger in which we Christians stand?: To be set free by a Jew and then not to connect this unfathomable good deed with this King of the Jews, i.e. to forget that "...Salvation is from the Jews" (John 4:22)?

"Praise the LORD, O my soul; all my inmost being, praise His holy name. Praise the LORD, O my soul, and forget not all His benefits- who forgives all your sins and heals all your diseases, who redeems your life from the pit and crowns you with love and compassion" (Ps. 103 : 1-4) .

Week 8
Obadiah 1: 1-21

Genesis 32:4 – 36:43 is the Parascha for this week in which we are dealing with Jacob's fear of Esau. Obadiah's vision is concerned with the judgment-threat against Edom (which, as a nation, is descended from Esau), but that, however, must constitute an urgent warning for all those who are guilty of acting towards Israel in like manner.

1)   **Precisely you !**

"Because of the violence against your brother Jacob, you will be covered with shame; you will be destroyed forever. On the day you stood aloof while strangers carried off his wealth and foreigners entered his gates and cast lots for Jerusalem, you were like one of them. You should not look down on your brother in the day of his misfortune, nor rejoice over the people of Judah in the day of their destruction, nor boast so much in the day of their trouble. You should not march through the gates of My people in the day of their disaster, nor look down on them in their calamity in the day of their disaster, nor seize their wealth in the day of their disaster. You should not wait at the crossroads to cut down their fugitives, nor hand over their survivors in the day of their trouble" (10-14).

It is with great seriousness and urgency that the Lord names here the manifold failure to come to the help of His beloved people Israel! Doesn't it make us uneasy when we recognize how tangibly these verses apply to our recent past?

Here we are discussing first of all the matter of *violence*, and we are bound to remember with shame the more than 6 million

Jews, who were driven to their death by Germans, and also by so-called Christians. How was it possible to miss hearing millions of times the commandment "You shall not murder!" (Exodus 20:13) whilst our Lord Jesus has shown us that killing starts already with being angry with our neighbor (Mt.5:21-22)! And the brutal and perfidious murdering was preceded by a whole chain of dreadful oppressions and mean, despicable deprivations of rights. We must be willing to face the accusation: "He who oppresses the poor shows contempt for their Maker..." (Prov. 14:31).

At this point many of us could raise the objection: "I wasn't present at the time". How then do we regard the guilt of our fathers and forefathers? Neither shaking one's head nor shrugging one's shoulder nor accusations are the proper reaction, especially since it isn't known how the ones "born later" would have behaved at that time...We can receive a helpful orientation from Daniel's attitude, who, with regard to the destruction of Jerusalem, prayed to God with the words: "...We have sinned and done wrong... (Dan.9, 5). He, who had lived before God in such an unimpeachable way that he was saved even from out of the lion's cave, includes himself in the sin of his people: "We have sinned".

"On the day you stood aloof...". As it is written at the crucifixion of the King of the Jews: "The people stood watching..." (Luke 23:35), just in that same way millions of people – at the time of the Nazi-regime – stood idly by, beholding, how the Jews were being derided, tormented and expelled. And they could have interfered then! But, how is it today? Do we each one proceed to our own agenda, when injustice is done in our land, in our professional or private spheres, to our Jewish fellow citizens; when Jewish cemeteries are being desecrated; when slogans of hate are being shouted on the streets? Do we then raise our voices?

When they *"...cast lots for Jerusalem, you were like one of them"*. Nowadays, when lots are cast, we leave the outcome to coincidence, to one's "destiny"; in other words, no importance is attributed to one result or the other. What importance do we attribute to the future of Jerusalem? In our days it is not only the power-wielders in the Middle East, but also in the USA, in Europe and beyond, who are contending about the future of Jerusalem. What do we do regarding this matter? Are we indifferent to the intentions to divide the Holy City? Do we retreat to the position that "God will attain His purposes in any case"? While politicians intend, as it were, to give parts of Jerusalem away, are we then "*like one of them*"? Do we remember that our Lord has said: "But now I have chosen Jerusalem for My name to be there..." (2 Chr. 6:6)!

"Pray for the peace of Jerusalem...!" (Ps. 122: 6) Why, in what you might call an incomprehensible way, are we being called upon as in the words of Isaiah: "...You who call on the LORD, give yourselves no rest, and give Him no rest till He establishes Jerusalem and makes her the praise of the earth.!" (Isa. 62:6-7)

"You should not wait at the crossroads to cut down their fugitives...". In the years from 1930 onwards there were again and again situations that resembled such crossroads, in which people said Yes or No to the future of Jewish co-citizens and in which it was far too often the case that they were cast out as strangers. Jesus said: "I was a stranger, and you did not invite Me in" (Mt.25: 43). This is how Jesus identifies with "the least of His brethren", the Jews, that he applies the help that was denied to them, to having been denied to Himself. Nowadays there live amongst us such as *"survivors"* of the gas-chambers. Do we do good unto them? "Accept one another, just as Christ accepted you..." (Rom. 15:7). Our service should be a "comforting"-service. (Isa. 40:1)

You should not *"...look down on them in their calamity..."* When Israel is being oppressed so severely in our time, when again and again enemy-fire is raining down on the land, suicide attacks are being perpetrated and Israel is being accused by the UN, then think how often we read in the newspapers completely distorted reports and malicious commentaries. I hope this does not set off in us a reaction that "the Jews should not be surprised about it, for after all...."! Malicious glee can at times play itself out very quietly..."You, of all people" is what out text means. Precisely the Germans and precisely we Christians have every reason to examine our attitude towards the Jews critically!

You should not *"...seize their wealth..."*. How many dispossessions of Jewish property are part of our horrific past and hence our frightful guilt! "You shall not covet your neighbor´s house...or anything that belongs to your neighbor!" (Ex.20:17) Turning to Israel the Lord says: "But all who devour you will be devoured...all who make spoil of you I will despoil" (Jer.30: 16).

An especially wicked way to deprive the Jewish people of something that is their due lies within the spiritual sphere: Many times it is taught in churches that the Church has displaced the Jews in the plan of God, that the Jews are discarded. And all the while we are the ones, who "... were separate from Christ, excluded from citizenship in Israel and foreigners to the covenants of the promise,,," have become – only through the grace of our LORD, "...fellow citizens with God´s people and members of God´s household" (Eph.2:12 + 19)! How then can we deny the Jews their title to being household-owners!

2) **Nevertheless!**

"But on Mount Zion will be deliverance, it will be holy, and the house of Jacob will possess its inheritance" (v.17).

"All the kingdom will be the Lord´s" (v. 21).

However great the failings of mankind may be towards the Jewish people - God will receive His due in connection with the people of His First Love. He keeps His promises and shall be glorified in Israel.

Week 9

Amos 2:6 – 3:8

The Parascha (Gen. 37:1 – 40:23) tells us, amongst other things, about Joseph's dreams, in which important future developments are revealed. That the LORD reveals His purposes to His servants is also a message of the Haftarah.

1) Nothing through one's own proper strength

"Now then, I will crush you as a cart crushes when loaded with grain. The swift will not escape, the strong will not muster their strength, and the warrior will not save his life. The archer will not stand his ground, the fleet-footed soldier will not get away, and the horseman will not save his life" (2:13-15).

These words are preceded by verses which point out how Israel had rejected the law of the LORD. Oftentimes we have to be punished because of our failings before we appreciate that we are unable to manage without God. When, as it were, the ground under our feet is pulled away, our apparent security is no longer present, then we start to think and reach out for help from above.

"...Apart from Me you can do nothing" (John 15:5) says Yeshua. How often we think we can manage most things ourselves, and ask the LORD to do only the "remainder" that we do not manage! But listen to how it stated in the song of Martin Luther that we sing, "A firm foundation is our God"? : "Did we in our own strength confide, our striving would be losing; Were not the right Man on our side, the Man of God's own choosing: Dost ask who that may be? Christ Jesus, it is He."

Paul writes: "I can do everything through Him who gives me strength" (Phil. 4:13). If we trust in our own ability, we belong to those who possess a form of godliness but deny the power thereof. (2 Tim.3:5). But if we reach out to the Lord, it becomes true that: "...those who hope in the Lord will renew their strength..."(Isa. 40: 31) and this is the strength of God. Solomon instructs us with these words: "Trust in the Lord with all your heart and lean not on you own understanding!" (Prov.3:5)

Our Creator knows all about our limitations. "...I know that you have little strength..." (Rev. 3:8), but the LORD desires that we commit ourselves to Him just as we are, in order that He might be able to act in us and through us – to His glory. Then it is that the secret unfolds which He revealed to Paul "My grace is sufficient for you: for My power is made perfect in weakness" (2 Cor. 12:9). In the same way, David is able to call out in adoration: "I love You, O LORD, my strength!" (Ps. 18 :1) and to realize with amazement: "...with my God I can scale a wall" (Ps. 18 : 29).

In his intercession Paul declares: "I pray also that the eyes of your heart may be enlightened in order that you may know ...His incomparably great power for us who believe..." (Eph. 1:18-19)

What is most important in this has been summed up wonderfully by John the Baptist, thus: "He must become greater; I must become less." (John 3:30).

2) Nothing without revelation

"Surely the Sovereign LORD does nothing without revealing His plan to His servants the prophets" (3:7).

What an amazing realization! The Almighty takes us, human beings, so seriously that He reveals His plans to us! He informs us in the Bible of what is going to happen to the nations, to Israel and to the Church in the end of days. We can assess what a mighty privilege this is by comparing it with the custom prevalent among us humans: As employees of a firm we must generally be grateful if the employer reveals in advance just a few of the changes planned for the near future.

How very rich the Scriptures are in prophetic books! In them God speaks via illustrations, dreams, visions and instructions. Ezekiel writes: "...the heavens were opened and I saw visions of God." (Ezek. 1:1). In Isaiah we read: "The LORD Almighty has revealed this in my hearing..." (Isa. 22:14). When Jeremiah was concerned about why Israel was in such bad circumstances, he was able to say: "...I knew it, for at that time He showed me what they were doing" (Jer. 11:18). "He reveals deep and hidden things.." prays Daniel, when he saw in a night vision the interpretation of Nebuchadnezzar's dream and therewith the future of diverse kingdoms (Dan. 2:22). Amos sees in advance the coming judgment in several visions (Amos 7 – 9). And we could continue with additional accounts such as these.

Often the recipient of God's message is led in wonderful ways, e.g. Ezekiel: "The Spirit lifted me up and brought me to the exiles in Babylonia in the vision given by the Spirit of God. Then the vision I had seen went up from me, and I told the exiles everything the LORD had shown me" (Ezek. 11:24-25).

Or, think about what happened to John: "After this I looked, and there before me was a door standing open in heaven. And the voice I had first heard speaking to me like a trumpet said, 'Come up here, and I will show you what must take place after this.' At once I was in the Spirit, and there before me was a throne in heaven with someone sitting on it" (Rev. 4:1-2). "And he carried me away in the Spirit to a mountain great and high, and showed me the Holy City, Jerusalem, coming down out of heaven from God. It shone with the glory of God…" (Rev. 21:10-11).

With regard to the prophetic word Peter advises us: "And we have the word of the prophets made more certain, and you will do well to pay attention to it, as to a light shining in a dark place, until the day dawns and the morning star rises in your hearts" (2 Pt. 1:19). For: "All scripture is God-breathed and is useful for teaching, rebuking, correcting and training in righteousness, so that the man of God may be thoroughly equipped for every good work" (2 Tim. 3:16-17). Likewise also Paul writes that the secret of God is "… now revealed and made known through the prophetic writings by the command of the eternal God, so that all nations might believe and obey Him…" (Rom. 16:26).

"The word became flesh and made His dwelling among us…" (John 1:14). God had manifested Himself in His Son. "In the past God spoke to our forefathers through the prophets at many times and in various ways, but in these last days He has spoken to us by His Son…" (Hebr. 1:1-2). Yeshua has come and He will come again, to set up His kingdom in Jerusalem. The way that God will then reveal Himself has already been revealed to us by Isaiah with the words: "The Lord will lay bare His holy arm in the sight of all the nations, and all the ends of the earth will see the salvation of our God" (Isa. 52:10).

Week 10

1 Kings 3:15 – 4:1

Wisdom from God is the central theme for this week, in the one case (Parascha Gen.41:1 – 44:17), Joseph's wisdom in the interpretation of dreams, measures undertaken against famine and dealings with his brothers; in the other case, Solomon's wise judgment in the strife between two mothers.

1) The gift of wisdom

"When all Israel heard the verdict the king had given, they held the king in awe, because they saw that he had wisdom from God to administer justice" (3:28)

We read the moving story of two mothers who both claim the same child as belonging rightfully to them and into which Solomon brings clarity in an astonishing way. The whole nation recognizes that this wisdom can only come from God.

"For lack of guidance a nation falls…" (Prov. 11:14). Some of us will perhaps heave a sigh with regard to many a plight that they feel in the political conduct of their own country. But let us look more at ourselves, the believers!

It will often be the case that we long for more wisdom. "If any of you lacks wisdom, he should ask God, who gives generously to all without finding fault, and he will be given to him. But when he asks he must believe and not doubt…" (James 1:5-6).

Our faith too "…might not rest on men´s wisdom, but on God´s power" (1 Cor. 2:5). For "…Has not God made foolish the wisdom of this world?" (1 Cor.1:20). Solomon had asked the LORD to give him a "hearing heart", "...to distinguish between right and wrong..." (1 Kings 3:9). How is it possible for us to be able to distinguish in this way? The Epistle to the Hebrews reveals to us that we need "solid food" so that we may discern between good and bad (Hebr. 5:14).

But it may be that we succumb to the danger that instead of asking for wisdom in certain situations, we act in accordance to our own wisdom, as is also written about the Israelites: They walked in their own counsels. "If My people would but listen to Me, if Israel would follow My ways..." (Ps. 81:13) Disobedience then leads to the result: "...they do not distinguish between the holy and the common; they teach that there is no difference between the unclean and the clean..." (Ezekiel 22: 26). James warns us that there is also wisdom which is "...earthly, unspiritual, of the devil" (James 3:15), which stems, for instance, from selfishness.

What then are the distinctive marks of divine wisdom? "But the wisdom that comes from heaven is first of all pure, then peace loving, considerate, submissive, full of mercy and good fruit, impartial and sincere" (James 3:17). Many things are spoken of here that serve us well as God-given wisdom. The Scriptures show us additional aspects, almost as in a succession of steps:

To begin with, Paul prays that God "...may give you the Spirit of wisdom and revelation so that you may know Him better" (Eph. 1:17) and "...to fill you with the knowledge of His will through all spiritual wisdom and understanding. And we pray this in order that you may live a life worthy of the LORD and may please Him in every way..." (Col.1:9-10). Then God´s Spirit enables us to express "...spiritual truths in spiritual words" (1 Cor. 2:13). Gifted like this we shall serve others: "...teach and admonish one another with all wisdom..." (Col.

3:16). "Who is wise and understanding among you? Let him show it by his good life, by deeds done in the humility that comes from wisdom" (James 3:13).

2)   The right address

"Now two prostitutes came to the king and stood before him" (3:16).

"...And so they argued before the king" (3:22).

The two women come to the right place with their problem because the king is ultimately responsible for the administration of justice. "Blessed is the man who does not walk in the counsel of the wicked..." (Ps. 1:1)

We believe in the King of Kings. The Creator of the world is "great in counsel, and mighty in work..." (Jer. 32:19; King James Version). And because He has created everything and oversees everything, He is the One to Whom we ought always turn when we need help.

God knows that we cannnot get along by ourselves, so He sent His only Son to us. "For to us a child is born, to us a son is given, and the government will be on His shoulders. And He will be called Wonderful Counselor, Mighty God, Everlasting Father, Prince of Peace" (Isa. 9:6). "The Spirit of the LORD will rest on Him – the Spirit of wisdom and of understanding, the Spirit of counsel and of power, the Spirit of knowledge and of the fear of the LORD" (Isa. 11:2). That is why Paul writes in Col. 2:3 that in Him "...are hidden all the treasures of wisdom and knowledge". He is the Messiah "...who has become for us wisdom from God – that is, our righteousness, holiness and redemption" (1 Cor. 1:30).

It is true that some "...regulations indeed have an appearance of wisdom..." (Col. 2:23) and "...even from your own number men will arise and distort the truth..." (Acts 20:30), but the Spirit of Truth alone will guide us into all truth (John 16:13). If and when we let our LORD alone counsel and guide us and act, we can joyfully join the jubilation: "...Worthy is the Lamb, who was slain, to receive power and wealth and wisdom and strength and honor and glory and praise" (Rev. 5:12).

Week 11

Ezekiel 37:15 – 28

We read in the Parascha (Gen. 44:18 – 47:27) about Joseph and his brothers being reunited after a long period of separation and estrangement. And in Ezekiel 37 we read that Judah and the tribes of Israel are to be led back again under one ruler.
We want to ask ourselves what these wonderful verses concerning Israel´s future mean to us. One thing is for sure: we can only be amazed at the LORD´s guidance of His people Israel.

1) To become one

"...and they will become one in My hand" (v. 19).

After Solomon's reign, the people of Israel were divided into two kingdoms– Israel and Judah, but they shall come together again and are reunited. What about the Christians? Isn't there a frightening split among us? Some years ago it was stated that there were some 500 different denominations and Christian groups in Jerusalem... Attempts to establish unity among Christians often resulted in an ecumenical movement at the expense of clarity and biblical foundation, culminating in the unbelievable statement that Christians and Muslims believed in the same God!

But not only controversy and different theological viewpoints between denominations and churches are concerned. The spiritual struggle is also about unity within a congregation. In

Acts we read about the early church: "All the believers were one in heart and mind" (Acts 4:32). The following statements seem to be a key to that: "They devoted themselves to the apostles´ teaching and to the fellowship, to the breaking of bread and to prayer… and had everything in common" (Acts 2:42+44). Much of this was lost over the years, as we all know. Nevertheless the goal remains the same. Just before being arrested, our LORD Jesus prayed to the Father: "…Holy Father, protect them by the power of Your name –the name You gave Me – so that they may be one as we are one" (John 17:11). And the Apostle Paul directs these words to the Corinthians: "I appeal to you, brothers, in the name of our LORD Jesus Christ, that all of you agree with one another so that there may be no divisions among you and that you may be perfectly united in mind and thought" (1 Cor. 1:10). (In the Jewish New Testament of David H. Stern it says: "that all of you may pursue the same goal".)

2) To be one under the same master

"…There will be one king over all of them…" (v. 22).
"My servant David will be king over them, and they will all have one shepherd…" (v. 24).
In spite of all the differences and styles of worship, one thing remains crucial: "For there is one God and one mediator between God and men, the man Christ Jesus who gave Himself as a ransom for all men…" (1 Tim. 2:5-6). Jesus answers the question concerning the most important law: "…Hear, O Israel, the LORD our God, the LORD is one" (Mk. 12:29). "…you have only one Master and you are all brothers" (Mt. 23:8). Unfortunately it is not self-evident to many Christians that we believe in the "Holy One of Israel". In the context of the question about resurrection, Jesus says: "…have you not read

what God said to you, 'I am the God of Abraham, the God of Isaac and the God of Jacob'? ..." (Mt. 22:31-32).

With regard to unity under one single LORD, it is all the more important to consider what Jesus says: "I have other sheep that are not of this sheep pen. I must bring them also. They too will listen to My voice, and there shall be one flock and one shepherd" (John 10:16). This is therefore unmistakably true: He turned to Israel at the beginning but then additionally turned to the Gentiles. He "...called not only from the Jews but also from the Gentiles" (Rom. 9:24). And then we hear this astonishing statement: "For He Himself is our peace, who has made the two one and has destroyed the barrier, the dividing wall of hostility, by abolishing in His flesh the law with its commandments and regulations. His purpose was to create in Himself one new man out of the two, thus making peace, and in this one body to reconcile both of them to God through the cross, by which He put to death their hostility" (Eph. 2:14-16). Jewish believers and Gentile Christians belong to the same Messianic congregation!

3) Gathered in the Promised Land

"...I will take the Israelites out of the nations where they have gone. I will gather them from all around and bring them back into their own land. I will make them one nation in the land, on the mountains of Israel" (v. 21-22).

It belongs to the countless miracles of God that the Jewish people actually can now return to the very same land which had been promised them about 2000 years before.
What about us Non-Jews? "For here we do not have an enduring city, but we are looking for the city that is to come" (Hebr. 13:14). "And this is what He promised us – even eternal

life" (1 John 2:25). The land we can possess according to God's grace is the heaven where the Almighty One is enthroned. What does Jesus say? "In My Father's house are many rooms…" (John 14:2). And to this promise, the Apostle Peter adds: "But in keeping with His promise we are looking forward to a new heaven and a new earth, the home of righteousness" (2 Peter 3:13).

4) God dwells in the midst

"…and I will put My sanctuary among them forever. My dwelling place will be with them; I will be their God, and they will be My people" (v. 26-27).

God chose Mt. Zion as His special dwelling place. The psalmist says of Jerusalem "…the holy place where the Most High dwells, God is within her…" (Ps. 46:4-5). "Why gaze in envy, O rugged mountains, at the mountain where God chooses to reign, where the LORD Himself will dwell forever?" (Ps. 68:16). "For the LORD has chosen Zion, He has desired it for His dwelling: 'This is My resting place for ever and ever; here I will sit enthroned, for I have desired it" (Ps. 132:13-14).

In his letter to the Corinthians, Paul applies the word from the weekly portion (and from Lev. 26:11-12) in the following way: "…we are the temple of the living God. As God has said: `I will live with them and walk among them, and I will be their God, and they will be My people" (2 Cor. 6:16). Elsewhere, Paul speaks in awe of "…the glorious riches of this mystery, which is Christ in you, the hope of glory" (Col. 1:27).

Week 12

1 Kings 2: 1 – 12

The Torah text for this week (Genesis 47:28 – 50:26) records Jacob blessing his grandsons Ephraim and Manasseh. And what does King David pass on to the next generation? That is what the Haftarah for this week is about.

1) Charge to the next generation

"I am about to go the way of all the earth, he said. So be strong, show yourself a man, and observe what the LORD your God requires: Walk in His ways, and keep His decrees and commands, His laws and requirements, as written in the Law of Moses, so that you may prosper in all you do and wherever you go" (1Kings 2: 2-3).

Here David passes on to his son Solomon what is the most important thing to him, rather what is the most important thing at all, namely the admonishment to be totally obedient to God. (And one chapter later we read that Solomon asks the LORD for a discerning heart so that he can distinguish between right and wrong). Solomon has a shining example in his father. So it is good if someone can say concerning the next generation or his successor what Paul says concerning the young Timothy: "…He will remind you of my way of life…" (1 Corinthians 4:17). The Scripture also provides negative examples, such as the priest Eli. We're told that "Eli´s sons were wicked men…" (1 Sam. 2:12). But instead of severely warning them, calling them to account and punishing them, Eli just says to them: "…Why do you do such things? I hear from all the people about these wicked deeds of yours. No, my sons; it is not a good report that I hear spreading among the LORD's people" (1 Sam. 2:23-24). Here, by contrast, is a good example: "When I was a boy in my father's house, still tender, and an only child of my mother, he taught me and said, 'Lay hold of my words with all your heart; keep my commands and you will live. Get wisdom, get understanding; do not forget my words or swerve from them" (Prov. 4:3-5). Paul addresses Timothy by the words "Guard the good deposit that was entrusted to you – guard it with the help of the Holy Spirit who lives in us" (2 Tim. 1:14).

The Scripture reveals several ways in which we are to guard and implement this deposit in our lives. Here is another of Solomon's proverbs: "Above all else, guard your heart, for it is the wellspring of life. Put away perversity from your mouth, keep corrupt talk far from your lips. Let your eyes look straight ahead, fix your gaze directly before you. Make level paths for your feet and take only ways that are firm. Do not swerve to the right or the left; keep your foot from evil" (Prov. 4:23-27). Paul offers similar advice: "...Keep yourself pure" (1 Tim. 5:22). "...you may fight the good fight, holding on to faith and a good conscience..." (1 Tim. 1:18-19). The aspect of good conscience is taken up again in the following verses: "Do your best to present yourself to God as one approved, a workman who does not need to be ashamed..." (2 Tim. 2:15). We don't have enough space to list the manifold instructions in detail. But here is how Paul sums it up: "The goal of this command is love, which comes from a pure heart and a good conscience and a sincere faith" (1 Tim. 1:5).

While the above mentioned verses mainly concern the relationship of men with God, we also find verses touching on the responsibility of the younger generation to others: "Don't let anyone look down on you because you are young, but set an example for the believers in speech, in life, in love, in faith and in purity" (1 Tim. 4:12). The baton that is handed to young people may also imply the need to continue doing something in the right way that has begun. So, for instance, Paul writes to Titus: "The reason I left you in Crete was that you might straighten out what was left unfinished..." (Titus 1:5).

2) Mastering the past

"Now you yourself know what Joab son of Zeruiah did to me..." (v. 5)
"But show kindness to the sons of Barzillai of Gilead..." (v. 7).
"And remember, you have with you Shimei...who called down bitter curses on me..." (v.8).

Here David tells his son Solomon that he has to take over tasks that are a part of his father´s legacy, so to speak. Some of the tasks are unpleasant.
Although we may not be able to apply the charge given to Solomon in those days to our situation (for instance: *"...do not let his gray head go down to the grave in peace"*, v. 6), we need to ask ourselves how we (especially as Germans) should deal with the legacy of our forefathers. We know about the unspeakable crimes of the Holocaust that were committed or tolerated mainly in the thirties and forties of the 20th century. How do we deal with this? Do we content ourselves with shaking our heads with indignation or accusation of our ancestors? Do we withdraw to the position that we did not take part personally ("mercy of late birth")? How does the Scripture help us find an appropriate behaviour?

To begin with, consider these revealing verses from 2 Sam. 21:1: "During the reign of David, there was a famine for three successive years; so David sought the face of the LORD. The LORD said, ´It is on account of Saul and his blood-stained house; it is because he put the Gibeonites to death'". Note that David is not personally guilty; he is in fact not even related to Saul. But being the legal successor of Saul he is responsible for eliminating the spiritual obstacle that led to the famine. (David atones for the blood of the Gibeonites, and "...after that, God answered prayer in behalf of the land", 2 Sam 21:14).

Notice also what happens when the LORD calls on Israel: "Return, faithless people; I will cure you of backsliding..." (Jer. 3:22). The people answer "Let us lie down in our shame, and let our disgrace cover us. We have sinned against the LORD our God, both we and our fathers; from our youth till this day we have not obeyed the LORD our God" (Jer. 3:25). "O LORD, we acknowledge our wickedness and the guilt of our fathers; we have indeed sinned against you" (Jer. 14:20). They do not just point at the failure of their fathers but as the next generation, they include themselves in the guilt. And we of today have to realize that there is often an aftermath of the former generation´s guilt in our hearts!

We are given a very clear indication by the behaviour of Daniel, the man who gets rescued even out of the lions´ den because he pleases God so much. He prays: "...O LORD, the great and awesome God, who keeps His covenant of love with all who love Him and obey His commands, we have sinned and done wrong. We have been wicked and have rebelled; we have turned away from Your commands and laws" (Dan. 9:4-5). We read a similar prayer of Nehemiah: "...I confess the sin we Israelites, including myself and my father´s house, have committed against You" (Neh. 1:6).

Week 13

Isaiah 27:6 – 28:13 and 29:22-24

The Torah text for this week (Ex. 1:1 – 6:1) is about the appointment of Moses by the LORD who reveals Himself as the God of Abraham, Isaac and Jacob, and it is about the oppression of Israel through the Pharaoh. In the Haftarah we also read of bad times for Israel, but they are put into the context of God´s plan of salvation.

1) Punishment in measure

"Has the LORD struck her (= Israel) as He struck down those who struck her? Has she been killed as those were killed who killed her?" (Isaiah 27:7)
"By warfare and exile You contend with her..."(In the King James Version it says: "In measure, when it shooteth forth, Thou wilt debate with it")."By this, then, will Jacob´s guilt be atoned for..."(27:8-9).
"Woe to that wreath, the pride of Ephraim´s drunkards, to the fading flower, his glorious beauty, set on the head of a fertile valley – to that city, the pride of those laid low by wine! See, the LORD has one who is powerful and strong. Like a hailstorm and a destructive wind, like a driving rain and a flooding downpour, He will throw it forcefully to the ground" (28:1-2).

When thinking of the awful Holocaust it is difficult to understand this concept of "punishment in measure". Therefore we need to diligently consider several aspects of this concept in order to throw light on the subject.

It is certainly true that the LORD is a just and uncompromising God who deals most affectionately with Israel on the one hand and severely punishing them on the other hand. "You have shown Your people desperate times; You have given us wine that makes us stagger" (Psalm 60:3). "You have fed them with the bread of tears; You have made them drink tears by the bowlful.(Ps. 80:5). Why? "But My people would not listen to Me; Israel would not submit to Me. So I gave them over to their stubborn hearts to follow their own devices" (Ps. 81:11-12). And this doesn´t at all apply just to the Jewish people; it is a general divine principle, as it is also made clear in Romans 1:18, 21, 24: "The wrath of God is being revealed from heaven against all the godlessness and wickedness of men...for although they knew God, they neither glorified Him as God nor gave thanks to Him...Therefore God gave them over in the sinful desires of their hearts...". The word "gave them over" is frightening, just as when we read about Judah being taken to Babylon: "It was because of the LORD´s anger that all this happened to Jerusalem and Judah, and in the end He thrust them from His presence" (2 Kings 24:20).

Having chosen Israel, how can God then treat His people so harshly? "I will repay them double for their wickedness and their sin..." (Jeremiah 16:18). Israel "...has received from the LORD´s hand double for all her sins" (Isa. 40:2). Obviously the special punishment is directly related to the fact that Israel has been specially chosen. Similarly we read in the New Testament that from everyone who has been given much, much will be demanded (Luke 12:48).

But – and there are several "buts": To begin with, we learn that we can implore God to be gracious and that He answers prayers: "They forgot the God who saved them...So He said He would destroy them – had not Moses, His chosen one, stood in the breach before Him to keep His wrath from destroying them" (Ps. 106:21-23). Secondly: Not every evil that happened or happens to the Jewish people was or is according to God´s intentions. "...This is what the LORD Almighty says: 'I am very jealous for Jerusalem and Zion, but I am very angry with the nations that feel secure. I was only a little angry, but they added to the calamity" (Zech. 1:14-15). These are words of special significance for the Germans after the Holocaust.

By the way, we should not forget that the LORD in His omnipotence averts harm planned by Israel´s enemies from His people again and again. (We may think of the miraculous rescue during the Yom Kippur war or of how many hostile Palestinian missiles missed their targets or how many planned attacks were thwarted.) And Joseph can even tell his brothers: "You intended to harm me, but God intended it for good..." (Gen. 50:20).

-

Thirdly the Scripture explains to us that concerning Israel the time for punishment is limited – although it may seem long to us. We hear these powerful words: "For a brief moment I abandoned you, but with deep compassion I will bring you back. In a surge of anger I hid My face from you for a moment, but with everlasting kindness I will have compassion on you, says the LORD your Redeemer" (Isa. 54:7-8). Therefore it says: "Speak tenderly to Jerusalem, and proclaim to her that her hard service has been completed, that her sin has been paid for..." (Isa. 40:2). The LORD says with regard to Israel´s redemption: "Awake, awake! Rise up, O Jerusalem, you who have drunk from the hand of the LORD the cup of His wrath, you who have drained to its dregs the goblet... See, I have taken out of your hand the cup that made you stagger; from that cup, the goblet of My wrath, you will never drink again. I will put it into the hands of your tormentors..." (Isa. 51:17+22-23). And there are promises like this one: "Instead of their shame My people will receive a double portion, and instead of disgrace they will rejoice in their inheritance; and so they will inherit a double portion in their land, and everlasting joy will be theirs" (Isa. 61:7).

Fourthly it is important to understand why the LORD gives grace after all the punishment. The LORD says in view of the descendants of David: "If his sons forsake My law and do not follow my statutes, if they violate My decrees and fail to keep My commands, I will punish their sin with the rod, their iniquity with flogging; but I will not take My love from him, nor will I ever betray My faithfulness. I will not violate My covenant or alter what My lips have uttered" (Ps. 89:30-34). Once and for all, the Holy One of Israel committed Himself to faithfully stand by Israel und to lead them until they reach His goal. It is all about His glory! "...It is not for your sake, O house of Israel, that I am going to do these things, but for the sake of My holy name, which you have profaned among the nations where you have gone. I will show the holiness of My great name, which has been profaned among the nations, the name you have profaned among them..." (Ezek. 36:22-23)
Even as we consider all these wonderful promises, we must also hear that the LORD repeatedly speaks of a remnant being mercifully accepted and rescued. Isaiah states: "The Daughter of Zion is left like a shelter in a vineyard, like a hut in a field of melons, like a city under siege. Unless the LORD Almighty had left us some survivors, we would have become like Sodom, we would have been like Gomorrah" (Isa. 1:8-9). About the end times it says: "In that day the remnant of Israel, the survivors of the house of Jacob, will no longer rely on him who struck them down but will truly rely on the LORD, the Holy

One of Israel. A remnant will return, a remnant of Jacob will return to the Mighty God" (Isa. 10:20-21).
Also Paul writes: "So too, at the present time there is a remnant chosen by grace" (Rom. 10:5). "...Israel has experienced a hardening in part until the full number of the Gentiles has come in. And so all Israel will be saved..." (Rom. 11:25-26). Marvelling at God´s paths, Paul exclaims: "Oh, the depth of the riches of the wisdom and knowledge of God! How unsearchable His judgments and His paths beyond tracing out!" (Rom. 11:33).

We, too, can be amazed and can worship the LORD again and again for the grace He has promised us, which we, being from the Gentiles, can experience. Also to us, however, He says: "But small is the gate and narrow the road that leads to life, and only a few find it" (Mt. 7:14). Indeed there is a separation between wheat and chaff (Mt. 3:12). But one thing is for sure: The LORD longs for everyone in His love of salvation!

2)   The Holy One of Jacob

"In that day the LORD Almighty will be a glorious crown, a beautiful wreath for the remnant of His people" (28:5).
"Therefore this is what the LORD, who redeemed Abraham, says to the house of Jacob: 'No longer will Jacob be ashamed; no longer will their faces grow pale. When they see among them their children, the work of My hands, they will keep My name holy; they will acknowledge the holiness of the Holy One of Jacob, and will stand in awe of the God of Israel" (29:22-23).

The Almighty God who revealed Himself to Moses as the God of Abraham, Isaac and Jacob (see Parascha of this week) is called here *"the LORD who redeemed Abraham", "the Holy One of Jacob", "the God of Israel".*

This LORD, in addition to the promise of a prosperous and blessed future – *"...Israel will bud and blossom and fill all the world with fruit" (27:6)* – gives further great promises. But the question to us should be: Do we really sanctify the LORD as the Holy One of Jacob? Do we confess to belong to the God of Israel (Mt. 15:31)? Do we pray: "...Have mercy on us, Son of David"? (Mt. 9:27). Do we celebrate the King of the Jews? (Mt. 27:11)

"Praise be to the LORD, the God of Israel, from everlasting to everlasting. Amen and Amen" (Ps. 41:13).

Week 14

Ezekiel 28:25 – 29:21

The Torah text for this week (Ex. 6:2 – 9:35) essentially shows us by which plagues Egypt is punished because of their oppression of Israel and how the Jewish people are spared those plagues in a supernatural way, even though they were living in the middle of the Egyptians.
Similarly, the Haftarah section confronts Israel´s future with Egypt´s fate. Again we need to discover what the text may mean for our situation.

1)   Living in safety

"This is what the Sovereign LORD says: When I gather the people of Israel from the nations where they have been scattered, I will show Myself holy among them in the sight of the nations. Then they will live in their own land, which I gave My servant Jacob. They will live there in safety and will build houses and plant vineyards..." (Ezekiel 28:25-26).

We know that the LORD kept His promise in a wonderful way, as is recorded in Jer. 16:14-15: "However, the days are coming," declares the LORD, "when men will no longer say, ´As surely as the LORD lives, who brought the Israelites up out of Egypt´, but they will say, ´As surely as the LORD lives, who brought the Israelites up out of the land of the north and out of all the countries where He had banished them´. For I will restore them to the land I gave their forefathers." This promise was shown to be true right before our very eyes by the remarkable waves of return of the Jews during the twentieth century and by the foundation of the State of Israel in 1948. And the promise will be fulfilled further on.

The repatriation into the Promised Land is connected with the promise of protection. "Like birds hovering overhead, the LORD Almighty will shield Jerusalem, He will shield it and deliver it, He will ´pass over´ it and will rescue it" (Isa. 31:5). "He will be the sure foundation for your times, a rich store of salvation and wisdom and knowledge; the fear of the LORD is the key to this treasure" (Isa. 33:6).

We, too, can be glad that the LORD gives safety to His children: "I have set the LORD always before me. Because He is at my right hand, I will not be shaken. Therefore my heart is glad and my tongue rejoices; my body also will rest secure, because You will not abandon me to the grave, nor will You let Your Holy One see decay" (Ps. 16:8-10). "The angel of the LORD encamps around those who fear Him, and He delivers them" (Ps. 34:7). It seems that David cannot praise God enough this safety: "The LORD is my rock, my fortress and my deliverer, my God is my rock, in whom I take refuge. He is my shield and the horn of my salvation, my stronghold" (Ps. 18:2).

What is the basis of our safety? Jesus "…has rescued us from the dominion of darkness…" (Col. 1:13) and intercedes for us with His Father: "My prayer is not that You take them out of the world but that You protect them from the evil one" (John 17:15). How precious is it to have such an intercessor! So we can profess like Paul: "For I am convinced that neither death nor life, neither angels nor demons, neither the present nor the future, nor any powers, neither height nor depth, nor anything else in all creation, will be able to separate us from the love of God that is in Christ Jesus our LORD" (Rom. 8:38-39).

2) Blindness because of high-handedness

"...This is what the Sovereign LORD says: 'I am against you, Pharaoh king of Egypt, you great monster lying among your streams. You say, 'The Nile is mine; I made it for myself'." (29:3)
"...Because you said, 'The Nile is mine; I made it', therefore I am against you and against your streams, and I will make the land of Egypt a ruin and a desolate waste..." (29:9-10).
"It will be the lowest of kingdoms and will never again exalt itself above the other nations. I will make it so weak that it will never again rule over the nations" (29:15).

From the Bible we know other examples of people who boasted and ascribed their success to themselves. For example, consider Simon the sorcerer who "...boasted that he was someone great..." (Acts 8:9). Or think of Nebuchadnezzar who says of himself: "Is not this the great Babylon I have built as the royal residence, by my mighty power and for the glory of my majesty?"(Dan. 4:30). The ruler of Tyre receives divine judgement "...because you think you are wise, as wise as god" (Ezek. 28:6). King Herod lets the people cheer him: "They shouted, 'This is a voice of a god, not of a man'. Immediately, because Herod did not give praise to God, an angel of the LORD struck him down, and he was eaten by worms and died" (Acts 12:22-23).

The Apostle Paul admonishes us that "...in the last days people will be lovers of themselves, ... boastful, proud,... conceited..." (2 Tim. 3:1-4). But it is nonetheless true: "For it is not the one who commends himself who is approved, but the one whom the LORD commends" (2 Cor. 10:18). Again and again we need to realize that we live from God's grace in all matters and that we are richly blessed. " ...What do you have that you did not receive? And if you did receive it, why do you boast as though you did not?" (1 Cor. 4:7). Paul puts it in a nutshell: "... by the grace of God I am what I am..." (1 Cor. 15:10).

3) Pretended aid

"...You have been a staff of reed for the house of Israel. When they grasped you with their hands, you splintered and you tore open their shoulders; when they leaned on you, you broke and their backs were wrenched. Therefore this is what the Sovereign LORD says: I will bring a sword against you..." (29:6-8).
"Egypt will no longer be a source of confidence for the people of Israel..." (29:16).

These words directed towards Egypt in those days is certainly of general significance – as the so called Old Testament isn´t just a history book...
How reliable is the support of those nations considered best to be "friends of Israel" today? How quickly the melodious affirmations fade when it is about avoiding of offences of the Arabic nations, whether in consideration of oil supplies or other own national interests?

Week 15

Jeremiah 46: 13 – 28

The Torah text for this week (Ex. 10:1 – 13:16) reports further on the plagues against the Egyptians and how Israel was exempt from them in an amazing way. "...total darkness covered all Egypt for three days. No one could see anyone else or leave his place for three days. Yet all the Israelites had light in the places where they lived" (Ex. 10:22-23). And we read of the Jewish people being wonderfully rescued from the slavery in Egypt by crossing the Red Sea.
And what do we learn from Jeremiah 46?

1)   The LORD of history

"...about the coming of Nebuchadnezzar king of Babylon to attack Egypt... Pack your belongings for exile, you who live in Egypt, for Memphis will be laid waste and lie in ruins without inhabitant" (vss. 13+19).
"The Daughter of Egypt will be put to shame, handed over to the people of the north... Later, however, Egypt will be inhabited as in times past, declares the LORD" (vss. 24 and 26).

Our LORD decides on the fate of mankind. He treats the nations and His people of Israel according to His wisdom. How often do we read the words "then was fulfilled..."! (For instance concerning the birth of Jesus or in the context of His arrest; see Mt. 1:22 and Mt. 27:9). The history of the world can be divided into specific periods according to the Bible. The Gospel according to Matthew for instance states: "Thus there were fourteen generations in all from Abraham to David, fourteen from David to the exile to Babylon, and fourteen from the exile to the Christ" (Mt. 1:17). The birth of Jesus and His sacrificial death on the cross are the most enormous turning points in history, milestones in God´s plan of salvation, as we read in the account of Golgotha: "At that moment the curtain of the temple was torn in two from top to bottom. The earth shook and the rocks split. The tombs broke open and the bodies of many holy people who had died were raised to life" (Mt. 27:51-52). And let us think of Pentecost/Whitsun. A clearly new epoch was initiated when the Holy Spirit was poured onto people, including even Gentiles. "…So then, God has granted even the Gentiles repentance unto life" (Acts 11:18) and has "…opened the door of faith to the Gentiles" (Acts 14:27).

In this week´s Haftarah we also see especially clearly a theme that runs through all of Scripture: God punishes nations, setting them against each other, and He uses nations and princes as tools for or against His people Israel – always in order to reach His goals.
It is astonishing that the Holy One of Israel "…says of Cyrus, ´He is My shepherd and will accomplish all that I please; he will say of Jerusalem, ´Let it be rebuilt´, and of the temple, ´Let its foundations be laid´ " (Isa. 44:28). Indeed, God even calls him "His anointed" in the following verse!
As a further example, consider Babylon: God´s people are brought there because of their disobedience, which means that Babylon will be used according to God´s plans. The LORD says to Babylon: "I was angry with My people and desecrated My inheritance; I gave them into your hand, and you showed them no mercy… You said, `I will continue forever – the eternal queen!...´" (Isa. 47:6-7). Babylon proudly and complacently elevates herself as God. "Disaster will come upon you, and you will not know how to conjure it away. A calamity will fall upon you that you cannot ward off with a

ransom..." (Isa. 47:11). So a period in favour of Babylon is followed by rejection.

Or consider the Assyrians who are used for a moderate punishment of Israel but complacently and arrogantly pursue their own goals far beyond that role. Therefore they are punished themselves: "Woe to the Assyrian, the rod of My anger, in whose hand is the club of My wrath! I send him against a godless nation, I dispatch him against a people who anger Me, to seize loot and snatch plunder... But this is not what he intends, this is not what he has in mind; his purpose is to destroy.." (Isa. 10:5-7). "When the LORD has finished all His work against Mount Zion and Jerusalem, He will say, ´I will punish the king of Assyria for the wilful pride of his heart and the haughty look in his eyes. For he says: ´By the strength of my hand I have done this, and by my wisdom, because I have understanding. I removed the boundaries of nations..." (Isa. 10:12-13).

Coming back to Egypt, we know that they brutally torment and frighten God´s people in the days of Pharaoh. In Isa.19:17 it´s the other way round: "And the land of Judah will bring terror to the Egyptians; everyone to whom Judah is mentioned will be terrified, because of what the LORD Almighty is planning against them". And then we even read: "So the LORD will make Himself known to the Egyptians, and in that day they will acknowledge the LORD..." (Isa. 19:21). Both is very close together with the Almighty: "The LORD will strike Egypt with a plague; He will strike them and heal them..." (Isa. 19:22).

We learn from many examples that God punishes the peoples because they exalt themselves: "I will punish the world for its evil, the wicked for their sins. I will put an end to the arrogance of the haughty and will humble the pride of the ruthless" (Isa. 13:11). But the God of Abraham, Isaac and Jacob judges the nations especially because of their guilt against Israel: "For the LORD has a day of vengeance, a year of retribution, to uphold Zion's cause" (Isa. 34:8). In one of His sermons about the end times, Jesus speaks about this judgment: "When the Son of Man comes in His glory, and all the angels with Him, He will sit on His throne in heavenly glory. All the nations will be gathered before Him, and He will separate the people one from another as a shepherd separates the sheep from the goats. He will put the sheep on His right and the goats on His left. Then the King will say to those on His right, 'Come, you who are blessed by My Father, take your inheritance...! Then He will say to those on His left, 'Depart from Me, you who are cursed, into the eternal fire...!" (Mt. 25:31-34+41). What is the criterion of decision? "...I tell you the truth, whatever you did for one of the least of these brothers of Mine, you did for Me" (Mt. 25:40). The brothers of Jesus the Jew are of course the Jews.

2) The privileged position of Israel

"Do not fear, O Jacob My servant; do not be dismayed, O Israel. I will surely save you out of a distant place, your descendants from the land of their exile. Jacob will again have peace and security, and no one will make him afraid. Do not fear, O Jacob My servant, for I am with you, declares the LORD. Though I completely destroy all the nations among which I scatter you, I will not completely destroy you. I will discipline you but only with justice; I will not let you go entirely unpunished" (v. 27-28).

God promised Abraham the land of Canaan, a promise that was later extended to Isaac and Jacob as well (see Gen. 17:8 and

Gen. 35:12 for example). The Bible does not name specific borders for any other country except Israel (as in Numb. 34:1-12 or Ezek. 47:13-20). However: "When the Most High gave the nations their inheritance, when He divided all mankind, He set up boundaries for the peoples according to the number of the sons of Israel" (Deut. 32:8). This is an amazing sign of the outstanding importance of Israel! We read how other nations have to give way to the Jewish people: "With Your hand You drove out the nations and planted our fathers, You crushed the peoples and made our fathers flourish" (Ps. 44:2). "He has shown His people the power of His works, giving them the lands of other nations" (Ps. 111:6). Joshua, admonishing his fellows, points at this fact: "You yourselves have seen everything the LORD your God has done to all these nations for your sake; it was the LORD your God who fought for you" (Josh. 23:3). "…I will hand over to you the people who live in the land and you will drive them out before you. Do not make a covenant with them or with their gods" (Ex. 23:31-32). Idolatry must be extinguished. That is the reason for God´s dealing with the nations (see Ps. 105:44-45).

His dealing with Israel is based on the following statement: "…you are a people holy to the LORD your God. Out of all the peoples on the face of the earth the LORD has chosen you to be His treasured possession" (Deut. 14:2). David prays in astonishment: "And who is like Your people Israel – the one nation on earth that God went out to redeem as a people for Himself, and to make a name for Himself, and to perform great and awesome wonders by driving out nations and their gods from before Your people, whom You redeemed from Egypt?" (2 Sam. 7:23). Israel´s uniqueness is further illustrated in that they were given the laws and commandments of God which are our guiding principle still today. "What other nation is so great as to have their gods near them the way the LORD our God is near us whenever we pray to Him? And what other nation is so great as to have such righteous decrees and laws as this body of laws I am setting before you today?" (Deut. 4:7-8).

Alas! We also know about serious disobedience of the chosen people – in this respect Israel has no special position! – and that they therefore were taken captive out of the Promised Land. Yes, the LORD says *"I will not let you go entirely unpunished"* but also *"Jacob will again have peace and security"* and return to the very same land after about 2000 years! This in fact is connected with something amazing and special: "For the LORD has chosen Zion, He has desired it for His dwelling: 'This is My resting place for ever and ever; here I will sit enthroned, for I have desired it" (Ps. 132:13-14).

From today´s point of view one can hardly imagine how the LORD will give quiet, security and peace to Israel. How can that happen? "For the nation or kingdom that will not serve you will perish; it will be utterly ruined" (Isa. 60:12). What a dimension of the special position of God´s first loved and chosen people!

Indeed, much more could be mentioned: This people from which the "bright Morning Star" comes (Rev. 22:16), has the promise of the Almighty God: "As the new heavens and the new earth that I make will endure before Me," declares the LORD, "so will your name and descendants endure" (Isa. 66:22). This is combined with a promise of spiritual cleansing directed to the whole people: "I, even I, am He who blots out your transgressions, for My own sake, and remembers your sins no more" (Isa. 43:25). For His sake, for the sake of His name´s glory!

Week 16

Judges 4:4 – 5:31

The Parascha for this week, Ex. 13:17 – 17:16, deals among other things with Israel´s crossing the Red Sea and the miraculous supply of manna and quails provided by the Lord. The song of Moses praising the rescue is the connection to the Haftarah, where we encounter the song of Deborah.

1) Blessed women

"Deborah, a prophetess,...was leading Israel at that time...She sent for Barak...and said to him, ´The LORD, the God of Israel, commands you: ´Go, take with you ten thousand men of Naphtali and Zebulun and lead the way to Mount Tabor. I will lure Sisera, the commander of Jabin´s army, with his chariots and his troops to the Kishon River and give him into your hands.´ Barak said to her, ´ If you go with me, I will go, but if you don't go with me, I won't go.´ ´Very well´, Deborah said, ´I will go with you. But because of the way you are going about this, the honour will not be yours, for the LORD will hand Sisera over to a woman..." (4:4-9).

Deborah is used by God to pass on a mission of the LORD, to utter a warning as well as a promise, and to ensure that the fearful Barak does in fact go to war. Repeatedly we read about women in the Bible who are used by the LORD in exceptional ways. In addition to Deborah, the prophetesses Huldah and Hannah are also mentioned. When the newly discovered Book of the Law is read before King Josiah after the restoration of the temple, he tears his robes in repentance, wants to act responsively and therefore orders the priest and some leaders to consult the LORD. At this point the prophetess Huldah gets involved. She has to pronounce disaster because of the people's idolatry but at the same time she announces mercy to the king, saying, "because your heart was responsive and you humbled yourself before the LORD..." (2 Kings 22:19). In the context of Jesus being presented as a child in the temple it says about the prophetess Hannah "...she never left the temple but worshiped night and day, fasting and praying. Coming up to them at that very moment, she gave thanks to God and spoke about the child to all who were looking forward to the redemption of Jerusalem" (Luke 2:37-38). This woman was obviously also anointed to a service of intensive prayer, worship and prophecy.

An extraordinary narrative concerns Abigail, the wife of Nabal. "...She was an intelligent and beautiful woman, but her husband, a Calebite, was surly and mean in his dealings" (1 Sam. 25:3). When David asks him to give food for his servants, he coldheartedly refuses in his meanness. Then David, who had previously treated Nabal well, decides to kill every male of his house. In this situation Abigail intervenes, at first without Nabal´s knowledge. She follows David, takes with her plenty of bread, meat, cake and wine and makes it clear to him that he came close to being guilty of bloodshed: "...the LORD has kept you, my master, from bloodshed and from avenging yourself with your own hands..." (1 Sam. 25:26). And she blesses him by the words: "...Let no wrongdoing be found in you as long as you live. Even though someone is pursuing you to take your life, the life of my master will be bound securely in the bundle of the living by the LORD your God. But the lives of your enemies He will hurl away as from the pocket of a sling" (1. Sam. 25:28-29). So she is a wife who not only averts disaster from her household but also gives important spiritual advice and intervenes in intercession.

We can also think of a woman who averts a catastrophe in a much larger framework: Esther. Risking her own life at the royal court, she stands up for her fellow Jews, who were in danger of total extermination. "Then Esther sent this reply to Mordecai: 'Go, gather together all the Jews who are in Susa, and fast for me. Do not eat or drink for three days, night or day. I and my maids will fast as you do. When this is done, I will go to the king, even though it is against the law. And if I perish, I perish" (Esther 4:15-16). To this day, Israel celebrates the feast of Purim in memory of this brave woman and her role in the rescue of her people.

We can think of other examples also: The fearless and clever behaviour of Rahab results in protection of the spies in Jericho (Josh. 2); and Priscilla risks her live for Paul, as he writes in Rom. 16:4. There are also less spectacular actions reported on in the Bible, which the LORD obviously finds important enough to include as examples. Think, for example, about the poor widow who gave just two small copper coins (Mk. 12:41-44), about Tabitha in Joppa "…who was always doing good and helping the poor" (Acts 9:36), or about the "sincere faith" of the grandmother and mother of Timothy and the blessing they were to him (2 Tim. 1:5). And it is a woman, Mary Magdalene, who tells the disciples that she has seen the resurrected Jesus (John 20:18).

The devotion of the woman who pours precious perfume on Jesus' head is commented on by the Messiah: "I tell you the truth, wherever this gospel is preached throughout the world, what she has done will also be told, in memory of her" (Mt. 26:13).

A special status among blessed women is undoubtedly that of Mary, who is granted the privilege of becoming the mother of the Saviour of the world and who humbly accepts the incomprehensible by saying to the angel: "I am the LORD´s servant....May it be to me as you have said..." (Luke 1:38).

As another example, think of Hannah, wife of Elkanah, who gives birth to the prophet Samuel. But remember the touching story that precedes this! Hannah has no children and is therefore disgraced and humiliated. But she implores God and makes a vow: "...O LORD Almighty, if You will only look upon Your servant's misery and remember me, and not forget Your servant but give her a son, then I will give him to the LORD for all the days of his life..." (1 Sam. 1:11). After she bears a child and her disgrace is blotted out, she confirms: "So now I give him to the LORD. For his whole life he will be given over to the LORD..." (1 Sam. 1:28).

Think also of the faithfulness of the Moabite woman Ruth, who is rewarded for it in an extraordinary way. When her Jewish mother-in-law Naomi urges her to stay in Moab, Ruth refuses, saying: "...Where you go I will go, and where you stay I will stay. Your people will be my people and your God my God" (Ruth 1:16). And how does the narrative continue? Ruth marries Boaz, and then it says: "...Boaz the father of Obed, Obed the father of Jesse, and Jesse the father of David" (Ruth 4:21-22) – a line of blessings which continues up to David´s son, Jeshua, as Jesus is called in Hebrew.

Finally the laudatory praise of the housewife in Proverbs 31:10-31 should also be mentioned. It is prayed every Sabbath eve: "A wife of noble character who can find? She is worth far more than rubies." She is praised for her diligence: "She gets up while it is still dark...and her lamp does not go out at night". She cares for her home: "She is like the merchant ships, bringing her food from afar...When it snows, she has no fear for her household…She watches over the affairs of her household…" etc. She is kind to her husband as "she brings him good, not harm, all the days of her life" and "she opens her arms to the poor and extends her hands to the needy". She likes to work and "she can laugh at the days to come". "She speaks with wisdom, and faithful instruction is on her tongue". And remarkably: "She considers a field and buys it". How can that be? There is a decisive condition: "Her husband has full confidence in her".

2) Like the sun

"…But may they who love You be like the sun when it rises in its strength…" (5:31).

There are wonderful statements in Scripture concerning those who love the name of the LORD: They will rejoice in Him (Ps. 5:11), the LORD watches over them (Ps. 145:20) and "…keeps His covenant of love…" with them (Dan. 9:4), and they are promised "…that in all things God works for good of those who love Him…" (Rom. 8:28). Out of love for Him they will keep His commandments, as Jesus says: "Whoever has My commandments and obeys them, he is the one who loves Me. He who loves Me will be loved by My Father, and I too will love him and show Myself to him" (John 14:21). And there are awesome promises from the letter of James: "…to inherit the kingdom He promises those who love Him" (James 2:5) and to "…receive the crown of life that God has promised to those who love Him" (James 1:12).

How pleasing moreover is the comparison how much like the sun are the LORD and those who love Him! It is a metaphor that places the LORD above all: When He stands on a high mountain together with Peter, John and James, and He is transfigured before them, "...His face shone like the sun..." (Mt. 17.2). When John in his vision sees seven golden lampstands, and among the lampstands someone like a son of man, "...His face was like the sun shining in all its brilliance" (Rev. 1:16). Isn't it fascinating that here nearly the same words are used as in our Haftarah text? It accords well what Pauls says about our Creator: "For those God foreknew He also predestined to be conformed to the likeness of His Son..." (Rom. 8:29).

In view of the certainty of our Heavenly Father´s mercy we can and should go on our way rejoicing– like the Ethiopian in Acts 8:27 – similar to what it says about the sun in such pleasing and graphic words: "...the sun, which is like a bridegroom coming forth from his pavilion, like a champion rejoicing to run his course" (Ps. 19:4-5). The sun brings about blessings. In one of his last words, David picks up on this metaphor of the sun, speaking of a man who rules over others: "...When one rules over men in righteousness, when he rules in the fear of God, he is like the light of morning at sunrise on a cloudless morning, like the brightness after rain that brings the grass from the earth" (2 Sam. 23:3-4).

Concerning the Day of Punishment it says that the godless will be burnt up, "but for you who revere My name, the sun of righteousness will rise with healing in its wings..." (Mal. 4:2). "... there will be weeping and gnashing of teeth. Then the righteous will shine like the sun in the kingdom of their Father..." (Mt. 13:42-43).

"But may they who love You be like the sun when it rises in its strength" (5:31).

In conclusion, we should bear in mind: "This is love: not that we loved God, but that He loved us and sent His Son as an atoning sacrifice for our sins" (1 John 4:10).

Week 17

Isaiah 6:1 – 7:6 and 9:6-7

In the center of this week's Torah portion (Ex. 18:1 – 20:26) we read the proclamation of the Ten Commandments on Mount Sinai, asserting the exclusive sovereignty and holiness of the Almighty God. The Israelites receive the guiding principle for the obedience needed to be a holy nation to the glory of the God of Abraham, Isaac and Jacob. The Haftarah is also about the holiness of God and His reign and about appointment to sacred service.

1) Trembling with the holiness of God

"...I saw the LORD seated on a throne, high and exalted, and the train of His robe filled the temple. Above Him were Seraphs...And they were calling to one another: 'Holy, holy, holy is the LORD Almighty, the whole earth is full of His glory'. At the sound of their voices the doorposts and thresholds shook and the temple was filled with smoke. 'Woe to me', I cried, 'I am ruined'..." (6:1-5).

"There is no one holy like the LORD, there is no one besides You..." (1 Sam. 2:2). John in his vision watches four living creatures steadily exclaiming: "...Holy, holy, holy is the LORD God Almighty, who was, and is, and is to come!" (Rev. 4:8). He is the one holding everything in His hands and controlling the fate of the world, "...who is holy and true, who holds the key of David. What He opens no one can shut, and what He shuts no one can open" (Rel. 3:7). He introduces Himself to His people with the words: "I am the LORD, your Holy One, Israel's Creator, your King" (Isa.43:15). About this

"Holy One of Israel" (Ps. 71:22) the psalmist says: "Great is the LORD in Zion; He is exalted over all the nations. Let them praise Your great and awesome name – he is holy" (Ps. 99:2-3).

Indeed, His name is great and awesome. That is why Isaiah trembles at the holiness of the Almighty One and why he is obviously frightened at his own unworthiness. He is aware of being lost without grace. *"...I am ruined! For I am a man of unclean lips,...and my eyes have seen the King, the LORD Almighty" (6:5).* It is unimaginable to him to see the LORD without being punished. There is a similar situation when the Israelites desperately shout at Moses: "...We will die! We are lost, we are all lost! Anyone who even comes near the tabernacle of the LORD will die. Are we all going to die?" (Num. 17:12). That is why the Levites are specially separated "...so that no plague will strike the Israelites when they go near the sanctuary" (Num. 8:19). Let us also keep in mind that God when giving the covenant on Mount Sinai includes the instruction: "...You are to worship at a distance, but Moses alone is to approach the LORD..." (Ex. 24:1-2). It is also interesting that, while the Israelites are crossing the Jordan River, the order is given: "...When you see the ark of the covenant of the LORD your God, and the priests, who are Levites, carrying it, you are to move out from your positions and follow it... But keep distance of about a thousand yards between you and the ark; do not go near it" (Josh. 3:3-4).

The holiness of God is truly awesome. In the last days, when according to the LORD Jesus "...there will be weeping and gnashing of teeth" (Mt. 8:12), it will not be possible to escape from this divine purity and omnipotence. What do we read about the nations? "...They will come trembling out of their dens; they will turn in fear to the LORD our God and will be afraid of You" (Mi 7:17). And the Jews "...will come trembling to the LORD and to His blessings in the last days" (Hos. 3:5).

But reverential awe is due not only in the last days. "The LORD Almighty is the one you are to regard as holy, He is the one you are to fear, He is the one you are to dread" (Isa. 8:13). The LORD says of Levi: "My covenant was with him...; this called for reverence and he revered Me and stood in awe of My name" (Mal. 2:5). And: "...Then the terror of the LORD fell on the people..." (1 Sam. 11:7). The reaction to the resurrection of a young man of Nain is: "They were all filled with awe and praised God..." (Luke 7:16). The New Testament admonishes us: "...live your lives as strangers here in reverent fear" (1 Pt. 1:17). "Therefore, since we are receiving a kingdom that cannot be shaken, let us be thankful, and so worship God acceptably with reverence and awe, for our ´God is a consuming fire´" (Hebr. 12:28-29). "...continue to work out your salvation with fear and trembling" (Phil. 2:12).

This does not mean, however, that we have to live in continual anxiety! It is about awe! "For you did not receive a spirit that makes you a slave again to fear, but you received the Spirit of sonship. And by Him we cry ´Abba, Father´ " (Rom. 8:15). The prophet Nahum writes in a few adjoining verses about the punishing God on the one hand and about His mercy on the other hand: "The LORD is a jealous and avenging God...Who can withstand His indignation? Who can endure His fierce anger?...The LORD is good, a refuge in times of trouble. He cares for those who trust in Him" (Nah. 1:2, 6-7). We can seek refuge in the Almighty God, our Heavenly Father, as a wonderful gift is given us: "Therefore, since we have been justified through faith, we have peace with God through our LORD Jesus Christ, through whom we have gained access by faith unto this grace in which we now stand. And we rejoice in the hope of the glory of God" (Rom. 5:1-2). By this we can understand the seeming conflicting terms astonishingly written side by side in Psalm 2:11: "Serve the LORD with fear and rejoice with trembling".

2) Who is responsible for appointing?

"Then I heard the voice of the LORD saying, 'Whom shall I send? And who will go for us?' And I said, 'Here am I. Send me!" (6:8).

It is clear that the LORD Himself appoints. But why do we read the plural form in the second half of the sentence: "And who will go for *us*?" Is this the form of "pluralis majestatis" which is also used in the secular sector? Or are the Seraphs surrounding the LORD in Isaiah's vision included? I think that here as in other verses of the Bible we find an indication of our God being One, but revealing Himself as Father, Son and Holy Spirit, as a threefold personality in a mysterious way. We know that from the New Testament, of course, but where in the Old Testament can we find further evidence of this doctrine laid down in our creed?

The Spirit of God, the Holy Spirit, is mentioned so often in the Torah and the books of the prophets that there is no need to elaborate. "...the Spirit of God was hovering over the waters" (Gen. 1:2). "Do not cast me from Your presence or take Your Holy Spirit from me" (Ps. 51:11). "And I will put My Spirit in you..." (Ezek. 36:27). "...Not by might nor by power, but by My Spirit, says the LORD Almighty" (Zech. 4:6).

But where in the Old Testament do we find indications of the Son of God?

The first occurrence is in Genesis: "Then God said, 'Let us make man in Our image, in Our likeness...' (Gen. 1:26). Here, too, it is not just the "pluralis majestatis". We learn from the letter to the Colossians that Jesus was involved in the Creation; indeed that He Himself is Creator: "For by Him all things were created: things in heaven and on earth, visible and invisible, ...all things were created by Him and for Him" (Col. 1:16). The Father in Heaven "...in these last days...has spoken to us by His Son, whom He appointed heir of all things, and through whom He made the universe" (Hebr. 1:2). And we shall become more and more similar to this LORD Jesus. "For those God foreknew He also predestined to be conformed to the likeness of His son..." (Rom. 8:29).

When Abraham receives visitors at Mamre, the account begins this way: "The LORD appeared to Abraham...", but then he "...saw three men standing nearby..." (Gen. 18:1-2). This change of singular and plural also occurs several times in verses 8-10.
In the account of Lot facing Sodom and Gomorrah it may seem surprising that the word "LORD" is written twice in the same sentence: "Then the LORD rained down burning sulphur on Sodom and Gomorrah – from the LORD out of the heavens" (Gen. 19:24).
That the Heavenly Father has a Son can be read in Psalm 2:6-7: "I will proclaim the decree of the LORD: He said to Me, 'You are My Son; today I have become Your Father". Acts 13:33 and Hebr. 1:5 confirm that that Jesus Christ is the Son in this verse. God promises David that from his offspring will come the One whose throne will last forever. And He continues: "I will be His Father, and He will be My Son..." (1 Chr. 17:13).

The following verse will cause the scales to fall from the eyes of even the greatest doubters: "...Who has established all the ends of the earth? What is His name, and the name of His son? Tell me, if you know!" (Prov. 30:4).

This only begotten Son of God left the glory He had with His Father. "Shout and be glad, O Daughter of Zion. For I am coming, and I will live among you, declares the LORD..., and you will know that the LORD Almighty has sent Me to you" (Zech. 2:10-11). The LORD of Hosts is the sender and Jesus the Messiah is the one He sends. Also the vision of Daniel is a valuable proof: "As I looked, thrones were set in place, and the Ancient of Days took His seat...Thousands upon thousands attended Him, ten thousand times ten thousand stood before Him...In my vision at night I looked, and there before me was one like a son of man, coming with the clouds of heaven. He approached the Ancient of Days and was led into His presence. He was given authority, glory and sovereign power; all peoples, nations and men of every language worshiped Him. His dominion is an everlasting dominion..." (Dan. 7:9-14).

We return finally to the Haftarah text. It is a pity that Jewish commentaries relate it to Hezekiah, who was still a child at the time. Their commentaries note that the text is in the past, not the future tense, and that it was Hezekiah who led Judah out of its degeneracy through his just, God-pleasing reign. They claim that it was Hezekiah who was the first king after Solomon to re-establish national unity, being seated on David's throne again and serving as the leader of the indestructible holy remnant of Israel. Also in Israel, however, thousands of Jews recognized that the following verses speak of Jeshua, as they call Jesus, and accepted Him as their Saviour:

"For to us a child is born, to us a Son is given, and the government will be on His shoulders. And He will be called Wonderful Counsellor, Mighty God, Everlasting Father, Prince of Peace. Of the increase of His government and peace there will be no end" (Isa. 9:6-7).

Week 18

Jeremiah 34:8 – 22 and 33:25 – 26

The Torah portion for this week (Ex. 21:1 – 24:18) is about dealing justly with servants, about care for the weak and about charity in general. The supplementary text picks this thread up.

1) Responsibility towards the poor and oppressed

"Everyone was to free his Hebrew slaves, both male and female; no one was to hold a fellow Jew in bondage" (34:9).
"Every seventh year each of you must free any fellow Hebrew who has sold himself to you. After he has served you six years, you must let him go free..." (34:14).

It is interesting that the first instruction of the Torah concerning civil life is about the personal rights of those at the lowest social level. The slaves should not be oppressed as the Greeks and Romans did in those times. And fellow Jews who have served as slaves shall be free after six years in order to have a new chance at life. (The same Hebrew word can be translated as either "slave" or "servant".)

Today we have no need to deal with slavery among us. What then might the text say to us?
The Scripture makes very clear just how important the weak, miserable, lonely and oppressed are to the LORD. "Come to Me, all you who are weary and burdened, and I will give you rest" (Mt. 11:28). In one of His speeches about the final judgment the King says: "...I was hungry and you gave Me

nothing to eat, I was thirsty and you gave Me nothing to drink, I was a stranger and you did not invite Me in, I needed clothes and you did not clothe Me, I was sick and in prison and you did not look after Me". When the people to whom these words were addressed reply by saying that they do not know about such situations, He answers: "...I tell you the truth, whatever you did not do for one of the least of these, you did not do for Me" (Mt. 25:42-45).

"Religion that God our Father accepts as pure and faultless is this: to look after orphans and widows in their distress..." (James 1:27). In order not to overlook the widows, the apostles turn the responsibility for them over to seven deacons (Acts 6:1-4). Paul's letters repeatedly deal with the relationship between slaves and their masters (1 Tim.6:1-2; Titus 2:9-10; 1 Pt.2:18-20). Certainly we can appropriately apply these verses to the relationship between leaders and employees. "And masters, ...do not threaten them, since you know that He who is both their Master and yours is in heaven, and there is no favouritism with Him" (Eph. 6:9). The letter to the Colossians also admonishes masters (leaders, managers) to be aware of ultimately being servants of the Heavenly Father themselves. "Masters, provide your slaves with what is right and fair, because you know that you also have a Master in heaven" (Col. 4:1).

This view of the LORD of LORDS provides one principle concerning the treatment of subordinates or weak persons. A second one is seen in Mt. 7:12: "So in everything, do to others what you would have them do to you..." The LORD Jesus touches upon a third principle in the Parable of the Unmerciful Servant: "Shouldn't you have had mercy on your fellow servant just as I had on you?" (Mt. 18:33).

Just as the Jews were to free their fellow Jews (and were not to impose interest on them, according to Lev.25:36), Paul asks us: "Therefore, as we have opportunity, let us do good to all people, especially to those who belong to the family of believers" (Gal. 6:10).

2) Relapse

"So all the officials and people who entered into this covenant agreed that they would free their male and female slaves and no longer hold them in bondage. They agreed, and set them free. But afterward they changed their minds and took back the slaves they had freed and enslaved them again" (34:10-11).
"But now you have turned around and profaned My name..." (34:16).

In this text, the people take back the slaves. Don't we sometimes face the danger of falling back into slavery ourselves? "Don't you know that when you offer yourselves to someone to obey him as slaves, you are slaves to the one whom you obey – whether you are slaves to sin, which leads to death, or to obedience, which leads to righteousness?" (Rom. 6:16).
Jesus makes clear in the Parable of the Sower that some spiritual seed falls along the path. "Some people are like the seed along the path, where the word is sown. As soon as they hear it, Satan comes and takes away the word that was sown in them" (Mk. 4:15). Or we do not even accept the word in gentleness and humbleness. "...Today, if you hear His voice, do not harden your hearts..." (Hebr. 3:7-8). "But because of your stubbornness and your unrepentant heart, you are storing up wrath against yourself for the day of God's wrath..." (Rom. 2:5).

Jesus says: "My sheep listen to My voice; I know them, and they follow Me" (John 10:27). "Whoever has My commands and obeys them, he is the one who loves Me... He who does not love Me will not obey My teaching..." (John 10:21+24).

It is with urgent words that we are warned against relapsing into former sins and against leaving our God. And we also need to pay attention to one another: "See to it, brothers, that none of you has a sinful, unbelieving heart that turns away from the living God. But encourage one another daily, as long as it is called Today, so that none of you may be hardened by sin's deceitfulness" (Hebr. 3:12-13). "It is impossible for those who have once been enlightened, who have tasted the heavenly gift, who have shared in the Holy Spirit, who have tasted the goodness of the word of God and the powers of the coming age, if they fall away, to be brought back to repentance..." (Hebr. 6:4-6). "If they have escaped the corruption of the world by knowing our LORD and Saviour Jesus Christ and are again entangled in it and overcome, they are worse off at the end than they were at the beginning. It would have been better for them not to have known the way of righteousness... Of them the proverbs are true: ´A dog returns to its vomit´, and ´A sow that is washed goes back to her wallowing in the mud" (2 Pt. 2:20-22). When Jesus healed a sick man at the pool Bethesda He said to him: "... See, you are well again. Stop sinning or something worse may happen to you" (John 5:14).

May we remain in Him, "...rooted and built up in Him, strengthened in the faith..." (Col. 2:7)!

Week 19

1 Kings 5: 12 – 6: 13

One of the first verses in the Torah reading for this week (Ex. 25:1 – 27:19) is God's command to Moses: "Then have them make a sanctuary for Me, and I will dwell among them" (Ex. 25:8). And detailed instructions for making and equipment of the tabernacle follow. The Haftarah provides similar instructions concerning the construction of the temple – and it adds two "qualifications": wisdom and obedience.

1) The gift of wisdom

"The LORD gave Solomon wisdom, just as He had promised him" (25:12).

Solomon had prayed for a listening and discerning heart. "God gave Solomon wisdom and very great insight, and a breadth of understanding as measureless as the sand on the seashore" (1 Kings 4:29). And how does Solomon use this wisdom? He builds the temple for his LORD by leading 200,000 workers.

Repeatedly we read in the Bible of people who are endowed with great wisdom. Think, for example, of Stephen, of whom it says: "…they could not stand up against his wisdom or the Spirit by whom he spoke" (Act 6:10). "Blessed is the man who finds wisdom, the man who gains understanding, for she is more profitable than silver and yields better returns than gold" (Prov. 3:13-14). But how can we "find" wisdom? Psalm 111:10 reveals the key: "The fear of the LORD is the beginning of wisdom…". Obviously we have to be trained and live disciplined lives if we are to achieve this wisdom, as "the fear of the LORD teaches a man wisdom..." (Prov. 15:33). Paul orders us: "Be very careful, then, how you live – not as unwise but as wise..." (Eph. 5:15).

We can ask the LORD to give us wisdom. "If any of you lacks wisdom, he should ask God, who gives generously to all without finding fault, and it will be given to him. But when he asks, he must believe and not doubt..." (James 1:5-6). The LORD gives generously to all those who do not trust in their own intelligence and strength but seek Him with their whole heart. "But God chose the foolish things of the world to shame the wise; God chose the weak things of the world to shame the strong... so that no one may boast before Him" (1 Cor. 1:27-29).

What should wisdom bring about in us? The following verses reveal several aspects. Paul prays for the Ephesians that God may give them "...the Spirit of wisdom and revelation, so that you may know Him better" (Eph. 1:17). So it is through wisdom that we should and can come nearer to our LORD and that we can understand more of His nature. This enables us to fill ourselves "...with the knowledge of His will through all spiritual wisdom and understanding..." so that we can "...live a life worthy of the LORD..." (Col. 1:9-10). What belongs to living to God's glory and not to trust in wisdom which "...is earthly, unspiritual, of the devil" (James 3:15)? "...The wisdom that comes from heaven is first of all pure, then peace-loving, considerate, submissive, full of mercy and good fruit, impartial and sincere" (James 3:17).
We should confess our belief in Christ "...in whom are hidden all the treasures of wisdom and knowledge" (Col. 2:3) and "who has become for us wisdom from God – that is, our righteousness, holiness and redemption" (1 Cor. 1:30). Let us proclaim in worship: "...Praise and glory and wisdom and

thanks and honour and power and strength be to our God for ever and ever. Amen!" (Rev. 7:12).

2) The temple

"In the four hundred and eightieth year after the Israelites had come out of Egypt, in the fourth year of Solomon's reign over Israel... he began to build the temple of the LORD" (6:1).
"In building the temple, only blocks dressed at the quarry were used, and no hammer, chisel or any other iron tool was heard at the temple site while it was being built" (6:7).
"The word of the LORD came to Solomon: 'As for this temple you are building, if you follow My decrees, carry out My regulations and keep all My commands and obey them, I will fulfil through you the promise I gave to David your father. And I will live among the Israelites and will not abandon My people Israel" (6:11-13).

As we read of the temple being built in the year 960 B.C. we are almost certainly reminded of the destruction of this magnificent building in 587 B.C. and of the erection of a second temple in 515 B.C. We remember that our LORD Jesus was found there, "... in My Father's house" (Luke 2:49) as a child, and that He taught in the temple (Mk. 14:49). And we certainly have in mind that Jesus prophesied the destruction of that temple (which actually occurred in 70 C.E.) and the rebuilding of it within three days. "But the temple He had spoken of was His body" (John 2:21).

This makes it clear that the term "temple" as used in the Bible does not only refer to physical structures. "However, the Most High does not live in houses made by men. As the prophet says: 'Heaven is My throne, and the earth is My footstool.

What kind of house will you build for Me?´ says the LORD. Or where will My resting place be?" (Acts 7:48-49).

Now what about the question that is often asked whether there will be a third temple someday? The Jews firmly think so, as they regularly pray on the Sabbath: "May it be Your will, HASHEM[5], our God and the God of our forefathers, that the Holy Temple be rebuilt, speedily in our days. Grant us our share in Your Torah, and may we serve You there with reverence, as in days of old and in former years."[6]
Jesus speaks of "the man of lawlessness" who "...will oppose and exalt himself over everything that is called God or is worshiped, so that he sets himself up in God's temple, proclaiming himself to be God" (2 Thess.2:3-4). In the New Jerusalem however, there will be no temple. John writes in Rev. 21:22: "I did not see a temple in the city, because the LORD God Almighty and the Lamb are its temple."

Now let's consider the spiritual meaning of the temple. Paul asks us: "Don't you know that you yourselves are God's temple and that God's Spirit lives in you?" (1 Cor. 3:16). By the words "...you are...God's building" Paul takes up a similar metaphor and stresses: "...no one can lay any foundation other than the one already laid, which is Jesus Christ" (1 Cor. 3:9+11). How this foundation has been laid? By Jesus having given His life for us. From this enormous deed we should understand the awesome responsibility we are confronted with in the following verses: "Do you not know that your body is a temple of the Holy Spirit, who is in you, whom you have received from God? You are not your own, you were bought at

---

[5] HASHEM means "The Name" and is used by Jews in order to avoid the awesome "JHWH".
[6] The Complete Art Scroll Siddur, published by Mesorah Publications Ltd., New York 1994, p.475

a price. Therefore honour God with your body!" (1 Cor. 6:19-20).

We can only do this by distancing ourselves from people or distractions that draw us away from God. Remember how the LORD Jesus drives the money changers and sellers of doves out of the temple by the words: "It is written, He said to them, My house will be called a house of prayer, but you are making it a ´den of robbers´." (Mt. 21:13). "...God's temple is sacred, and you are that temple" (1 Cor. 3:17). "...For what do righteousness and wickedness have in common? Or what fellowship can light have with darkness? ... What agreement is there between the temple of God and idols?..." (2 Cor. 6:14-16).

Let us look again at the word from 1 Kings: Solomon has built the temple by investing great motivation and much effort. That is clearly a sign of his commitment to God but that alone is not sufficient; It has to be combined with obedience. That is why the Holy One of Israel directs these words to Solomon: *"As for the temple you are building, if you follow My decrees..." (6:12)*. Again and again we have to make a deliberate decision to be obedient to our LORD. Then we can claim the wonderful promise: "Him who overcomes I will make a pillar in the temple of My God..." (Rev. 3:12).

But what would the pillars be without a cornerstone? We are "...built on the foundation of the apostles and prophets, with Christ Jesus himself as the chief cornerstone. In Him the whole building is joined together and rises to become a holy temple in the LORD. And in Him you too are being built together to become a dwelling in which God lives by His Spirit" (Eph. 2:20-22). The phrase "You too are being built" refers to the fact that Jews and Christians are made one through the blood of Jeshua.

He is the author and finisher of our faith; we owe everything to Him. It may be an interesting symbol that Solomon, when building the temple, was required to use nothing but stones which were not hammered, i.e., which were formed by the Creator. We belong to the spiritual house only if we are "living stones", made alive and formed by Him who can say of Himself "I am the life". "As you come to Him, the living Stone – rejected by men but chosen by God and precious to Him – you also, like living stones, are being built into a spiritual house to be a holy priesthood..." (1 Pt. 2:4-5).

Week 20

Ezekiel 43: 10 – 27

While the Torah section for this week (Ex. 27:20 – 30:10) gives precise instructions concerning the priestly garments, the altar and the daily offerings in the tabernacle, Ezekiel in an awesome vision describes the temple of the new Jerusalem in detail – an indication of the importance of divine teaching and sanctification.

Accuracy

"...make known to them the design of the temple – its arrangement, its exits and entrances – its whole design and all its regulations and laws. Write these down before them so that they may be faithful to its design and follow all its regulations" (v. 11).

Ezekiel gets a vision of the future temple of Jerusalem. Isn't it amazing how the instructions for the construction of the temple go into so much detail? In the Bible we find no instructions on how to construct church buildings. In fact, church buildings aren't mentioned at all in Scripture! But we find a lot of information about building congregations in a spiritual sense, so that they may be "...the pillar and foundation of the truth" (1 Tim. 3:15). For instance, we read of the distinguishing marks of the first congregation: "They devoted themselves to the apostles´ teaching and to the fellowship, to the breaking of bread and to prayer" (Acts 2:42). We also receive instructions concerning the appointment of leaders and the various tasks of service (1 Tim. 3; Titus 1:5-9; 1 Cor. 12; Eph. 4:11-16) as well as methods of judgement for sin in the congregation (1 Cor. 5).

And the letters to the churches written in the Revelation show us what is especially important to the LORD (Rev. 2+3).

These letters also provide guiding principles for our personal living in faith, as God not only gives regulations to the Jewish people for the construction of the temple but He also tells us that every believer is "God's building" (1 Cor. 3:9), even "God's temple" (1 Cor. 3:16).

The very detailed instructions for building the temple which are received by Ezekiel through a vision should make us prick up our ears regarding how important it is to accurately follow our LORD and His orders. Sometimes we may not understand why our Heavenly Father wants it just as we hear or read. Think, for instance, of the Syrian officer Naaman who has to wash himself in the Jordan River and to do so exactly seven times in order to be healed from leprosy (2 Kings 5). If he had not been obedient we would not read: "...his flesh was restored and became clean like that of a young boy" (2 Kings 5:14). Or think of the man blind from birth on whose eyes Jesus put some mud with saliva. If he had washed his eyes at any place other than the pool of Siloam as he did in obedience to Jesus' instructions, he would not have been healed of his blindness (John 9:1-7). How did the Almighty God enable His people to capture Jericho? By Joshua and the priests and the Israelites following the orders of the LORD exactly with respect to how often, in what formation and in what way they were to surround the town wall (Josh. 6).

When our faithful Shepherd tells us how we can bring down the "walls of the enemy" so to speak, - namely to "...put on the armour of God..." (Eph. 6:13) – then we should get into the habit of doing so accordingly and faithfully.

When Simon Peter, the experienced fisherman, has not caught anything all night, Jesus instructs him to let down the nets again – and at a time when fish are not as likely to get into the net as during the night. The nets begin to break due to the large number of fish. And why? Because Peter does not point to his competence nor trust in his worldly wisdom but instead responds "…Because You say so, I will let down the nets" (Luke 5:5).

What do we rely on? Do we trust in our LORD to be the true "specialist" in our profession, the most competent consultant in our challenges? And do we willingly follow the guidance "from above"? "Commit to the LORD whatever you do, and your plans will succeed" (Prov. 16:3).

Week 21

1 Kings 18: 1-39

The Torah portion for this week (Ex. 30:11 – 34:35) is about sanctification, the tablets of the Law, the golden calf and God´s order of pulling down the altars of idols. The Haftarah is the report on the prophet Elijah opposing the prophets of Baal on Mount Carmel.

1)   Single-mindedness is important

"Elijah went before the people and said, ´How long will you waver between two opinions? If the LORD is God, follow Him; but if Baal is God, follow him.´ But the people said nothing" (v.21).

Followers of Jesus are sometimes said to be single-minded. In view of those verses this can be nothing but a compliment. "For no one can lay any foundation other than the one already laid, which is Jesus Christ" (1 Cor. 3:11).

"On one occasion an expert in the law stood up to test Jesus. ´Teacher, he asked, what must I do to inherit eternal life?´ ´What is written in the law´, He replied. ´How do you read it?´ He answered, ´Love the LORD your God with all your heart and with all your soul and with all your strength and with all your mind´, and, ´Love your neighbour as yourself´. ´You have answered correctly´, Jesus replied. ´Do this and you will live´." (Luke 11:25-28). We know all too well that what matters is doing according to the law. Just to hear and to understand is not sufficient. "When Jesus saw that he had answered wisely,

He said to him, ´You are not far from the kingdom of God..."
(Mk.12:34). Not far – but not yet arrived.

In the synagogues every Sabbath one prays "Shma Yisrael": "Hear, O Israel: The LORD our God, the LORD is one", followed by exactly the verses Jesus quoted in answering the lawyer and then, referring to Deut. 6:6-7: "The commandments that I give you today are to be upon your hearts. Impress them on your children. Talk about them when you sit at home and when you walk along the road, when you lie down and when you get up". The crucial importance of this law becomes very clear here.

Single-mindedness is important. "No one can serve two masters. Either he will hate the one and love the other, or he will be devoted to the one and despise the other..." (Mt. 6:24). Certainly we, too, can expect to be asked the critical question of Elijah if we possibly still *"waver between two opinions"*.
James admonishes us: "...purify your hearts, you double-minded" (James 4:8). David expresses very pithily what really matters: "...give me an undivided heart, that I may fear Your name" (Ps. 86:11; King James Version: "unite my heart").

"For even if there are so-called gods, whether in heaven or on earth (as indeed there are many ´gods´ and many ´lords´), yet for us there is but one God, the Father, from whom all things came and for whom we live; and there is but one LORD, Jesus Christ, through whom all things came and through whom we live" (1 Cor. 8:5-6).

2) Who answers?

"...Then they called on the name of Baal from morning till noon. ´O Baal, answer us!´ they shouted. But there was no

response; no one answered. And they danced around the altar they had made... So they shouted louder and slashed themselves with swords and spears, as was their custom, until their blood flowed. Midday passed, and they continued their frantic prophesying until the time for the evening sacrifice. But there was no response, no one answered, no one paid attention" (vss. 26-29).

What pitiful efforts, and all in vain! It is after all just as described in the Psalm: "The idols of the nations are silver and gold, made by the hands of men. They have mouths, but cannot speak, eyes, but cannot see; they have ears, but cannot hear, nor is there breath in their mouths. Those who make them will be like them, and so will all who trust in them" (Ps. 135:15-18).

What a contrast to the report regarding the contortions of the priests of Baal are God's words spoken to Israel! "Before they call I will answer, while they are still speaking I will hear" (Isa. 65:24). "Does He who implanted the ear not hear?..." (Ps. 94:9).

Sure, sometimes we have to wait for our prayers to be answered, but we know with assurance that our loving Father promises to hear us. "But as for me, I watch in hope for the LORD, I wait for God my Saviour; my God will hear me" (Mi 7:7). "This is the confidence we have in approaching God: that if we ask anything according to His will, He hears us. And if we know that He hears us – whatever we ask – we know that we have what we asked of Him" (1 John 5: 14-15).

3) It is all about the glory of the only God

"...O LORD, God of Abraham, Isaac and Israel, let it be known today that You are God in Israel and that I am Your servant and have done all these things at Your command" (v. 36).
"When all the people saw this, they fell prostrate and cried, 'The LORD – He is God! The LORD – He is God!" (v. 39).

It is the fervent wish of Elijah that the worshippers of idols, God´s enemies, might recognize the Almighty One as the true sovereign. That reminds us of David opposing Goliath by the words: "You come against me with sword and spear and javelin, but I come against you in the name of the LORD Almighty, the God of the armies of Israel, whom you have defied...and the whole world will know that there is a God in Israel" (1 Sam. 17:45-46).

In the Lord´s prayer we pray "hallowed be Your name!" What name actually? What does the LORD say of Himself? He is "...the God of Abraham, the God of Isaac and the God of Jacob... This is My name forever..." (Ex.3:15). It is important for us, too, to worship the LORD as the One who has committed Himself to the people of Israel by the holiness of His name. This Holy One of Israel speaks: "...I will now bring Jacob back from captivity and will have compassion on all the people of Israel, and I will be zealous for My holy name" (Ezek. 39:25). "There is no one like You, O LORD,...And who is like Your people Israel – the one nation on earth whose God went out to redeem a people for Himself, and to make a name for Himself..." (1 Chr. 17:20-21).

"I am the LORD; that is My name! I will not give My glory to another or My praise to idols" (Isa.42:8). Therefore one of the

Ten Commandments is: "You shall not make for yourself an idol in the form of anything in heaven above or on the earth beneath or in the waters below. You shall not bow down to them or worship them; for I, the LORD your God, am a jealous God" (Ex. 20:4-5). All glory is due to the only living God "...whose name is Jealous..." (Ex. 34:14).

Indeed, the name of our God will be connected with glory and praise forever as it says, for instance, in Ps. 48:10: "Like Your name, O God, Your praise reaches to the ends of the earth...". We hear the request in Ps. 96:8: "Ascribe to the LORD the glory due His name..." and yet – does it not happen again and again that we withhold the glory from Him or set aside a part of the glory by appropriating some of it for ourselves, for instance, when telling about our life? The psalmist may have sensed this danger when he expressly declares "Not to us, O LORD, not to us but to Your name be the glory, because of Your love and faithfulness" (Ps. 115:1). Yes, "Glorify the LORD with me, let us exalt His name together" (Ps. 34:3).

Because the name of the LORD is connected with His glory we can and should pray: "Help us, O God our Saviour, for the glory of Your name..." (Ps. 79:9). God makes this connection clear to the Israelites by the following words: "For My own name's sake I delay My wrath; for the sake of My praise I hold it back from you...See, I have refined you, though not as silver; I have tested you in the furnace of affliction. For My own sake, for My own sake, I do this. How can I let Myself be defamed? I will not yield My glory to another" (Isa.48:9-11).We can thankfully join in David's praise: "...He guides me in paths of righteousness for His name's sake" (Ps. 23:3).

When speaking about the divine name and the glory of God we can be nothing but overwhelmed by the wonderful fact that the

Creator of the world came to us in human likeness, that Jesus humbled Himself and became obedient to death on the cross. "Therefore God exalted Him to the highest place and gave Him the name that is above every name, that at the name of Jesus every knee should bow, in heaven and on earth and under the earth, and every tongue confess that Jesus Christ is LORD, to the glory of God the Father" (Phil. 2:9-11).

And how should we intercede for the Jewish people with the Heavenly Father? Here, too, it is all about the name of the LORD. We shall put His name on the Jews: "…This is how to bless the Israelites. Say to them: `The LORD bless you and keep you; the LORD make His face shine upon you and be gracious to you; the LORD turn His face toward you and give you peace.´ So they will put My name on the Israelites, and I will bless them" (Num. 6:23-27).

Week 22

1 Kings 7:13-26

The Torah portion for this week (Ex. 35:1 – 38:20) describes the construction and furnishings of the tabernacle. The Haftarah is about the furnishings of the temple built by Solomon.

"King Solomon sent to Tyre and brought Huram , whose mother was a widow from the tribe of Naphtali and whose father was a man of Tyre and a craftsman in bronze. Huram was highly skilled and experienced in all kinds of bronze work. He came to King Solomon and did all the work assigned to him" (v. 13-14).
"He erected the pillars at the portico of the temple. The pillar to the south he named Jakin and the one to the north Boaz" (v. 21).

1) The pillar as symbol

Pillars are often parts of magnificent buildings, such as the temple of Solomon. But in the Bible the pillar is also repeatedly used as a metaphor.
"…the pillars of the earth are the LORD´s, and He hath set the world upon them" (1 Sam. 2:8; King James Version). Similarly it says in Ps. 75:3: "When the earth and all its people quake, it is I who hold its pillars firm".
"Wisdom has built her house; she has hewn out its seven pillars" (Prov. 9:1). What are the seven pillars? Interpreters point to Isaiah 11, which speaks of a sevenfold spirit with regard to the shoot coming up from the stump of Jesse: "The Spirit of the LORD will rest on Him – the Spirit of wisdom and

of understanding, the Spirit of counsel and of power, the Spirit of knowledge and of the fear of the LORD (Isa.11:2).

The pillar as a symbol of strength and steadiness is found in the report on Jeremiah´s appointment: "Today I have made you a fortified city, an iron pillar and a bronze wall to stand against the whole land – against the kings of Judah, its officials, its priests and the people of the land. They will fight against you but will not overcome you, for I am with you and will rescue you, declares the LORD" (Jer. 1:18-19).

Paul writes that James, Peter and John are "…reputed to be pillars…" (Gal. 2:9), probably pointing to experience, reliability and acceptance.

2) Jakin

The Hebrew word Jakin means "he will found, establish" or "erect, strengthen". Again and again we come across these words in the Bible as they have much to do with the promises and blessings of the LORD.

We think of God´s promise to Noah:"…Everything on earth will perish. But I will establish My covenant with you…" (Gen. 6:17-18). He also made a covenant with Abraham, Isaac and Jacob. And then we read also of Jerusalem: "Yet I will remember the covenant I made with you in the days of your youth, and I will establish an everlasting covenant with you" (Ezek. 16:60).

On the one hand this "establishing" has to do with founding, but on the other hand with pointing out so that the surroundings notice it. The LORD has chosen His people from the whole world in order to be glorified. "He decreed statutes for Jacob and established the law in Israel…" (Ps. 78:5). "The LORD will establish you as His holy people… Then all the peoples on earth will see that You are called by the name of the LORD, and they will fear You" (Deut. 28:9-10).

Another aspect of the term "to establish" concerns restoration. With regard to the end times, the LORD declares: "In that day I will restore David´s fallen tent. I will repair its broken places, restore its ruins, and build it as it used to be, so that they may possess the remnant of Edom and all the nations that bear My name..." (Am. 9:11-12). This restoration does not only concern possession of land, as the following text shows: "This is what the LORD says – the Redeemer and Holy One of Israel – to him who was despised and abhorred by the nation... I will keep you and will make you to be a covenant for the people, to restore the land and to reassign its desolate inheritances, to say to the captives, ´Come out´, and to those in darkness, ´Be free!´..." (Isa. 49:7-9). It is our LORD Jeshua, despised and abhorred, who is appointed to this mission of restoration.

That the good news about how to get from darkness to light applies not only to the Jewish people is seen by God's decision to take "...from the Gentiles a people for Himself...". James makes this clear by taking the verses from Amos as quoted above: "After this I will return and rebuild David´s fallen tent. Its ruins I will rebuild, and I will restore it, that the remnant of men may seek the LORD, and all the Gentiles who bear My name, says the LORD..." (Acts 15:14-17).

Zechariah prophetically proclaims at the birth of John: "Praise be to the LORD, the God of Israel, because He has come and has redeemed His people. He has raised up a horn of salvation for us in the house of His servant David (as He said through His holy prophets of long ago)..." (Luke 1:68-70). The same word "to raise" is used by Jeshua when He speaks about His resurrection: "Destroy this temple, and I will raise it again in three days" (John 2:19).

The Resurrected One is "...such a high priest, who sat down at the right hand of the throne of the Majesty in heaven, and who serves in the sanctuary, the true tabernacle set up by the LORD, not by man" (Hebr. 8:1-2). The Revelation reports on another aspect of this true, perfect tent erected by the Almighty One: "I saw the Holy City, the new Jerusalem, coming down out of heaven from God, prepared as a bride beautifully dressed for her husband. And I heard a loud voice from the throne saying, 'Now the dwelling of God is with men, and He will live with them. They will be His people, and God Himself will be with them and be their God" (Rev. 21:2-3).

So the pillar "Jakin" points to some of the most important aspects of our faith: God´s covenant with Israel, His people being a witness to the world, Israel´s restoration in the country, God´s turning to the Gentiles, Jeshua as the Redeemer, the resurrection of Jeshua, His sitting at the right hand of God, and the new Jerusalem.

3) Boaz

The second pillar at the portico of the temple gets the name "Boaz", meaning "In Him is strength".

The writers of the Psalms confess in manifold ways that in Him alone is our strength: "The LORD is my strength and my shield; my heart trusts in Him, and I am helped. My heart leaps for joy and I will give thanks to Him in song" (Ps. 28:7). "God is our refuge and strength, an ever-present help in trouble" (Ps. 46:1).

"Sing for joy to God our strength; shout aloud to the God of Jacob!" (Ps. 81:1). Yes, David even names the LORD by this term: "...O my strength, come quickly to help me" (Ps.22:19) and "I love You, O Lord, my strength" (Ps. 18:1). Moses confidently confesses: "The LORD is my strength and my song…" (Ex. 15:2) and Isaiah takes these words up:."…The LORD, the LORD is my strength and my song; He has become my salvation" (Isa. 12:2).

These are precious testimonies. It is crucial, however, to let the LORD act so that He can be our strength! "Ascribe ye strength unto God…" (Ps. 68:34; King James Version). How can that happen? David says it well: "My soul clings to You; Your right hand upholds me" (Ps. 63:8). And Paul writes to the Ephesians: "Finally, be strong in the LORD and in His mighty power. Put on the full armour of God so that you can take your stand against the devil´s schemes (Eph. 6:10-11).

"Blessed are those whose strength is in You, who have set their hearts on pilgrimage" (Ps. 84:5). Pilgrimage along the right path requires spiritually clear sight. That is why Paul prays "…that the eyes of your heart may be enlightened in order that you may know … His incomparably great power for us who believe. That power is like the working of His mighty strength" (Eph. 1:18-19). "Then we will no longer be infants, tossed back and forth by the waves, and blown here and there by every wind of teaching and by the cunning and craftiness of men in their deceitful scheming" (Eph. 4:14).

God wants above all for all men to trust in His power and strength. Jeremiah writes in view of the end times: "O LORD, my strength and my fortress, my refuge in time of distress, to You the nations will come from the ends of the earth and say, ´Our fathers possessed nothing but false gods, worthless idols that did them no good. Do men make their own gods? Yes, but they are not gods!´ Therefore I will teach them – this time I will teach them My power and might. Then they will know that My name is the LORD" (Jer. 16:19-21).

"Blessed are those who have learned to acclaim You ... For You are their glory and strength" (Ps. 89: 15+17).

Week 23

1 Kings 7:51 – 8:21

The weekly section (Ex. 38:21 – 40:38) reports on completion and consecration of the tabernacle, the Tent of Meeting, by Moses. Again and again it is stressed that the work was completed "...just as the LORD commanded Moses" (e.g. Ex. 39:32). Then it says: "Then the cloud covered the Tent of Meeting , and the glory of the LORD filled the tabernacle" (Ex. 40:34). The Haftarah is about a similar subject: the consecration of the temple built by Solomon.

1) Consecration of the temple

"Then King Solomon summoned into his presence at Jerusalem the elders of Israel, all the heads of the tribes and the chiefs of the Israelite families, to bring up the ark of the LORD´s covenant from Zion, the City of David" (8:1).
"...sacrificing so many sheep and cattle that they could not be recorded or counted" (8:5).
"There was nothing in the ark except the two stone tablets..." (8:9).
"But the LORD said to my father David. 'Because it was in your heart to built a temple for My Name, you did well to have this in your heart" (8:18).

What do we learn from this report?
What is on our minds? "To build a house for the LORD" – what might this mean to us? Obviously our motivation and our priorities are concerned. "Set your minds on things above, not on earthly things", Paul warns us in Col. 3:2. Our LORD admonishes us: "But seek first His kingdom and His

righteousness..." (Mt. 6:33). Jeshua teaches us to have the right focus in our lives by praying: "...Our Father in heaven, hallowed be Your name, Your kingdom come, Your will be done on earth as it is in heaven" (Mt. 6:9-10). This means that we should allow ourselves to be "...built into a spiritual house..." (1 Pt. 2:5) and to be used to testify "...as those entrusted with the secret things of God" (1 Cor. 4:1). "...but you go and proclaim the kingdom of God" (Luk. 9:60).

For this appointment we need the foundation of God´s word. The psalmist prays: "If Your law had not been my delight, I would have perished in my affliction" (Ps. 119:92). This reminds us of the report concerning the consecration of the temple that *"there was nothing in the ark except the two stone tablets"* with God´s commandments. We are admonished: "Let the word of Christ dwell in you richly..." (Col. 3:16). We can rejoice that the word became flesh in Jesus Christ (John 1:14). We want to look upon Him, the author and perfecter of our faith (Hebr. 12:2), and strive so that it can be said about us – even when we are in distress – "When they looked up, they saw no one except Jesus" (Mt. 17:8).

The Israelites in those days agreed that they wanted to seek and celebrate God´s presence. *"All the men of Israel came together..." (8:2)*. This is not at all self-evident, considering how difficult it is to live in spiritual unity even within a family. How often is unity in a congregation threatened! But how precious is what happened at Pentecost! "When the day of Pentecost came, they were all together in one place....All of them were filled with the Holy Spirit..." (Acts 2:1+4). It is said about the first assembly: "All the believers were one in heart and mind..." (Acts 4:32). Knowing only too well how Satan tries to sow discord again and again, Paul warns us: "...be of one mind.." (2 Cor. 13:11). A spiritual process of growth is necessary "until we all reach unity in faith…" (Eph. 4:13).

During the consecration of the temple the Israelites thankfully brought offerings beyond all measure. What do we give the LORD? "Each man should give what he has decided in his heart to give, not reluctantly or under compulsion, for God loves a cheerful giver" (2 Cor. 9:7). The most important gift to our Redeemer and Saviour is our heart. When a Pharisee asks the LORD Jesus which the greatest commandment in the Law is, He answers: "Love the LORD your God with all your heart and with all your soul and with all your mind" (Mt. 22:37). The consecration of the temple can remind us to dedicate ourselves to the LORD again. "Don´t you know that you yourselves are God´s temple and that God´s Spirit lives in you?" (1 Cor. 3:16).

2) The cloud

"When the priests withdrew from the Holy Place, the cloud filled the temple of the LORD. And the priests could not perform their service because of the cloud, for the glory of the LORD filled His temple" (8:10-11).

Again and again the presence of the LORD and His glory is connected with a cloud. In Deut. 33:26 it says: "There is no one like the God of Jeshurun, who rides on the heavens to help you and on the clouds in His majesty", or in Ps. 68:34: "Ascribe ye strength unto God; His excellency is over Israel, and His strength is in the clouds" (King James Version). When God wants to send manna and quail after the Israelites grumbled "…there was the glory of the LORD appearing in the cloud" (Ex. 16:10). Moses is prepared to receive the tablets of Law by the words: "…I am going to come to you in a dense cloud, so that the people will hear Me speaking with you and will always put their trust in you…" (Ex. 19:9). And we know from Num.9:15 ff. that the LORD leads His people through the desert by a cloud and the appearance of fire. Ezekiel describes his vision of God's glory: "I looked, and I saw a windstorm coming out of the north – an immense cloud with flashing lightning and surrounded by brilliant light…" (Ezek.1:4; see Ezek.10:3-4).

Concerning the transfiguration of Jesus it says: "…a bright cloud enveloped them, and a voice from the cloud said, 'This is My Son, whom I love; with Him I am well pleased. Listen to Him!" (Mt.17:5). Concerning His ascension, we read "…He was taken up before their very eyes, and a cloud hid Him from their sight" (Acts 1:9). And what do we read about the second coming of Jesus? "At that time they will see the Son of Man coming in a cloud with power and great glory" (Luke 21:27). "Look, He is coming with the clouds, and every eye will see Him…" (Rev. 1:7). Hallelujah!

Week 24

Isaiah 43:21 – 44:23

This week´s Torah section (Lev. 1:1 – 5:26) deals with detailed instructions concerning offerings in the Tent of Meeting. Burnt offering, grain offering, fellowship offering, sin offering and guilt offering are described in detail in order to urge Israel to be obedient. The words of Isaiah in the Haftarah are directed to the Jews in a time when they were carried off to Babylon and became negligent towards God. The people are shown how foolish it is to serve idols, and they are reminded of the grace that the only living God has granted them.

1) The initiative

"Yet you have not called upon Me, O Jacob, you have not wearied yourselves for Me, O Israel. You have not brought Me sheep offerings, nor honoured Me with your sacrifices. I have not burdened you with grain offerings nor wearied you with demands for incense... But you have burdened Me with your sins and wearied Me with your offenses. I, even I, am He who blots out your transgressions, for My own sake, and remembers your sins no more" (43:22-25).

What is true with Israel is also true with us: We did not seek God first but He sought us. Jeshua is "...the author and perfecter of our faith..." (Hebr. 12:2). We so easily say: ´I decided for the LORD, I became a convert, I found the way to faith´. It needs to be written into our hearts again: All initiative came and comes from the Almighty God.

He has made us willing to seek Him and to be open towards His word. He surmounted our proud hearts. He first loved us (1 John 4:19). "God demonstrates His own love for us in this: While we were still sinners, Christ died for us" (Rom. 5:8). "You did not choose Me, but I chose you and appointed you to go and bear fruit..." (John 15:16).

"But because of His great love for us, God, who is rich in mercy, made us alive with Christ even when we were dead in transgressions – it is by grace you have been saved" (Eph. 2:4-5). We deserved death, yet we "...are justified freely by His grace through the redemption that came by Christ Jesus" (Rom. 3:24). What a privilege to be entrusted with "...the gospel of God´s grace" (Acts 20:24) and to be able to testify to it! Solomon has a wonderful metaphor for this grace: "..His favour is like dew on the grass" (Prov. 19:12). We cannot influence the dew, it is just there and is a blessing. (By the way, during the dry summer season one gives thanks in synagogues for the dew that refreshes the land.)

Paul is aware of what it means to be set apart from birth (Gal. 1:15) and to be "... predestined according to the plan of Him who works out everything in conformity with the purpose of His will" (Eph. 1:11). The following statement very clearly reminds us again that salvation is nothing we have worked for: God "...has saved us and called us to a holy life - not because of anything we have done but because of His own purpose and grace. This grace was given us in Christ Jesus before the beginning of time, but it has now been revealed through the appearing of our Saviour Christ Jesus..." (2 Tim. 1:9-10).

Israel proclaims the wonderful promise: *"I, even I, am He who blots out your transgressions..." (43:25).* And we can be sure of that: "If we confess our sins, He is faithful and just and will forgive us our sins and purify us from all unrighteousness" (1 John 1:9).

2) The Only One

"This is what the LORD says – Israel´s King and Redeemer, the LORD Almighty: I am the first and I am the last; apart from Me there is no God. Who then is like Me? ... You are My witnesses. Is there any God besides Me? No, there is no other rock; I know not one" (44:6-8).

Those who follow any idols instead of the only true God *"... know nothing, they understand nothing; their eyes are plastered over so the cannot see, and their minds closed so they cannot understand" (44:18).* And it is like this although "...what may be known about God is plain to them, because God has made it plain to them. For since the creation of the world God´s invisible qualities – His eternal power and divine nature - have been clearly seen, being understood from what has been made, so that men are without excuse" (Rom. 1:19-20).

There is only one living God. The LORD Himself emphasizes this again and again so that we might really understand and accept it. "... I am the LORD, and there is no other. I form the light and create darkness, I bring prosperity and create disaster; I, the LORD, do all these things" (Isa. 45:6-7). By these words He presents Himself as the Creator who holds everything in His hands. He is the Almighty One: "See now that I Myself am He! There is no God besides Me. I put to death and I bring to life. I have wounded and I will heal, and no one can deliver out of My hand" (Deut. 32:39). It cannot be said more forcefully than by the frequent repetition of the word "I"!

Just as we hear about the contrast of putting to death and bringing to life, of wounding and healing, a further message is important: "...there is no God apart from Me, a righteous God and a Saviour..." (Isa. 45:21). A righteous king has been announced for Israel by the words: "...This is the name by which He will be called: The LORD Our Righteousness" (Jer. 23:6). We testify the same king in Christ Jesus "...who has become for us wisdom from God – that is, our righteousness, holiness and redemption" (1 Cor. 1:30). "Salvation is found in no one else, for there is no other name under heaven given to men by which we must be saved" (Acts 4:12).

"No, there is no other rock, I know not one", the LORD says of Himself. And we can join David in confessing: "The LORD is my rock..." (Ps. 18:2; see Ps. 31:3) and we can seek refuge with Him: "Be my rock of refuge, to which I can always go; give the command to save me, for You are my rock and my fortress" (Ps. 71:3). As we seek this refuge we can experience Him just as Moses did: "He is the Rock, His works are perfect, and all His ways are just. A faithful God who does no wrong, upright and just is He" (Deut. 32:4). Every Sabbath the prayer for the State of Israel in the synagogues begins with the words "Our Heavenly Father, Rock of Israel and her Redeemer...". While drawing up the founding document for the State of Israel Ben Gurion proclaimed: "With confidence in the Rock of Israel we sign this declaration as witnesses." By the context of the Holy Scripture we know – which is concealed from most Jews for our sake (see Rom. 11:11 and Rom. 11:25) – that Jesus is this Rock who became "a rock of offence" (Rom. 9:33; King James Version) but guided the Israelites already through the desert: "...for they drank from the spiritual rock that accompanied them; and that rock was Christ" (1 Cor. 10:4).

God proclaims *"I am the first and I am the last"*. He is the Eternal One. "Listen to Me, O Jacob, Israel, whom I have called: I am He; I am the first and I am the last. My own hand laid the foundations of the earth, and My right hand spread out the heavens..." (Isa. 48: 12-13). When God announces Israel´s redemption He says: "You are My witnesses, declares the LORD, and my servant whom I have chosen, so that you may know and believe Me and understand that I am He. Before Me no God was formed, nor will there be one after Me. I, even I, am the LORD, and apart from Me there is no saviour" (Isa. 43: 10-11).

The crucified and resurrected Jesus says: "...I am the First and the Last. I am the Living One; I was dead, and behold I am alive for ever and ever! And I hold the keys of death and Hades" (Rev. 1:17-18). "Behold, I am coming soon! My reward is with Me, and I will give to everyone according to what he has done. I am the Alpha and the Omega, the First and the Last, the Beginning and the End" (Rev. 22:12-13).

In this LORD we believe. But let us not forget: He is *"...Israel´s King and Redeemer..." (44:6)!*

Week 25

Jeremiah 7:21 – 8:3 and 9:22-23

In the Torah section for this week (Lev. 6:1 – 8:36), we read about the laws of offerings and how Moses, when ordaining Aaron and his sons ",...did as the LORD commanded him" (Lev. 8:4). The Haftarah makes two main points: (1) that the goal of all outer forms of worship is to lead us through obedience towards a deeper spiritual life and (2) that worship is worthless if combined with unholy conduct.

1) Back or face

"...When I brought your forefathers out of Egypt and spoke to them, I did not just give them commands about burnt offerings and sacrifices, but I gave them this command: Obey Me, and I will be your God and you will be My people. Walk in all the ways I command you, that it may go well with you. But they did not listen or pay attention; instead they followed the stubborn inclinations of their evil hearts. They went backward and not forward" (7:22-24).

This Scripture reflects our lives (and not just the lives of the Jews...!) as a mirror. First of all, we sometimes plug our ears, as described in Zechariah: "...They refused to pay attention; stubbornly they turned their backs and stopped up their ears. They made their hearts as hard as flint and would not listen to the law..." (Zech. 7:11-12). Don't we sometimes belong to those who are "obstinate and stubborn" (Ezek. 2:4)? "I appointed watchmen over you and said, 'Listen to the sound of the trumpet!´ But you said, ´We will not listen´. " (Jer. 6: 17).How sad the Heavenly Father will be if He has to say to me as He once said to Ephraim: "I wrote for them the many things of My law, but they regarded them as something alien" (Hos. 8:12). "…Because of your stubbornness and your unrepentant heart, you are storing up wrath against yourself for the day of God´s wrath…" (Rom. 2:5).

Secondly our failure can be to hear God´s word – maybe even to know it quite well – but by negligence or intention not to act accordingly. "Stop listening to instruction, my son, and you will stray from the words of knowledge" (Prov: 19:27). Don´t we sometimes think that we can get along by ourselves? Hopefully it need not be said about us: "…The evil conceits of their minds know no limits" (Ps. 73:7). If we have turned our backs to the LORD rather than our faces we must literally return.

Thirdly it is dangerous to think that certain pious habits are sufficiently pleasing to God. He says about this: "For I desire mercy, not sacrifice, and acknowledgement of God rather than burnt offerings" (Hos. 6:6). For "…to obey is better than sacrifice, and to heed is better than the fat of rams" (1 Sam. 15:22). What does that mean for us? Maybe one regularly attends services, happily joins in singing, lifts up hands (because others do it like that), and contributes to the collection, but one´s conduct in everyday life does not reflect closeness to God. How grave are the words of the LORD: "For I know how many are your offenses and how great your sins… I hate, I despise your religious feasts, I cannot stand your assemblies… Away with the noise of your songs!..." (Am. 5:12, 21 and 23). What does Paul write? "Therefore, I urge you, brothers, in view of God´s mercy, to offer your bodies as living sacrifices, holy and pleasing to God – this is your spiritual act of worship" (Rom. 12:1).

And a fourth aspect may be briefly mentioned: It can happen that we go our own ways from time to time but nevertheless tacitly expect God´s blessings, or that we even ask the LORD to bless our wrong ways. We cannot turn our faces and backs to Him at the same time! "If anyone turns a deaf ear to the law, even his prayers are detestable" (Prov. 28:9).

2) Boast

"This is what the LORD says: Let not the wise man boast of his wisdom or the strong man boast of his strength or the rich man boast of his riches, but let him who boasts boast about this: that he understands and knows Me, that I am the LORD, who exercises kindness, justice and righteousness on earth, for in these I delight, declares the LORD" (9:23-24).

The Scripture repeatedly shows us how God views boasting. Nebuchadnezzar, for instance, says: "…Is not this the great Babylon I have built as the royal residence, by mighty power and for the glory of my majesty? The words were still on his lips when a voice came from heaven, ´This is what is decreed for you, King Nebuchadnezzar: Your royal authority has been taken from you" (Dan. 4:30-31). God announces to the Assyrian king: "…I will punish the king of Assyria for the wilful pride of his heart and the haughty look in his eyes. For he says, ´By the strength of my hand I have done this, and by my wisdom, because I have understanding…" (Isa.10:12-13). What do we learn from the Proverbs? "Pride goes before destruction, a haughty spirit before a fall" (Prov. 16:18).

Our Creator knows our weaknesses. That's why He says to His people at the time of Moses that it is He who "...gave you manna to eat in the desert, something your fathers had never known, to humble and to test you so that in the end it might go well with you. You may say to yourself, `My power and the strength of my hands have produced this wealth for me´. But remember the Lord your God; for it is He who gives you the ability to produce wealth..." (Deut. 8:16-18). And what about Gideon? Out of ten thousand men prepared for battle against the hostile majority of the Midianites he is allowed to put into action just three hundred "...in order that Israel may not boast against Me that her own strength has saved her" (Judges 7:2).

Again and again we ought to ask ourselves: "...What do you have that you did not receive?..." (1 Cor.4:7). "My soul will boast in the LORD..." (Ps. 34:2).

"...Let him who boasts boast about this: that he understands and knows Me, that I am the LORD..." (9:24). Notice the priorities that Paul establishes in his life: "But whatever was to my profit, I now consider loss for the sake of Christ. What is more, I consider everything a loss compared to the surpassing greatness of knowing Christ Jesus my LORD..." (Phil. 3:7-8).

Week 26

2 Samuel 6:1 – 7:17

The Parascha for this week (Lev. 9:1 – 11:47) focuses on Aaron´s sons Nadab and Abihu, who in a high-handed manner use unauthorized fire for offering and are therefore consumed by fire themselves. The supplementary text from the book of Samuel also describes a tragic event involving disregard for the holiness of divine majesty. But Samuel also relates the great joy of David and the house of Israel as they again bring the ark of the covenant to Jerusalem.

1)   Unrestrained joy

"David and the whole house of Israel were celebrating with all their might before the LORD, with songs and with harps, lyres, tambourines, sistrums and cymbals" (6:5).
"David, wearing linen ephod, danced before the LORD with all his might" (6:14).
"...Michal daughter of Saul watched from a window. And when she saw king David leaping and dancing before the LORD, she despised him in her heart" (6:16).
"David said to Michal, 'It was before the LORD, who chose me rather than your father or anyone from his house when He appointed me ruler over the LORD´s people Israel – I will celebrate before the LORD" (6:21).

Several questions arise from this text:

Do we really rejoice with all our hearts in God´s presence? Certainly! But don´t we in everyday life sometimes quickly pass over the blessings we receive from our good Shepherd?

Sometimes we even forget to thank Him. But is there no difference between thankfulness and joy? In the epistle to the Philippians we hear this call: "Rejoice in the LORD always. I will say it again: Rejoice!" (Phil.4:4).

Is our joy visible? It is precious to have quiet joy but are we also able to audibly and visibly express our enthusiasm about our great God? Peter writes we can be "...filled with an inexpressible and glorious joy..." about Jesus. Then it will forge ahead in jubilation. "O come, let us sing unto the LORD, let us make a joyful noise to the Rock of our salvation" (Ps. 95:1; King James Version). How does that work? "Clap your hands, all your nations, shout to God with cries of joy" (Ps. 47:1). And as in the days of David so, too, today instruments can be used to praise our LORD (see Ps. 150). In the beatitudes Jeshua shouts to His disciples: "Rejoice in that day and leap for joy" (Luke 6:23).

The cause of our rejoicing is so immense that even nature itself will shout for joy, as the Scripture tells us: "...the mountains and hills will burst into song before You, and all the trees of the field will clap their hands" (Isa. 55:12). The LORD says to Israel: "...I have redeemed you. Sing for joy, O heavens, for the LORD has done this; shout aloud, O earth beneath. Burst into song, you mountains, you forests and all your trees, for the LORD has redeemed Jacob, He displays His glory in Israel" (Isa. 44:22-23). Because of this deed of salvation He promises His people: "...Again you will take up your tambourines and go out to dance with the joyful" (Jer. 31:4). Now, is shouting for joy or dancing "too charismatic"? As we have seen there is evidence in the Bible for those expressions of joy. The question in a specific case however is whether we really mean the LORD or whether our style of worship has become somewhat independent and outer forms have become more important than the attitude of our hearts. Similarly as we (without being aware of it) can either routinely recite a prayer, for instance the Lord´s Prayer, or really concentrate on what we are praying, so singing, rejoicing, and dancing can become spiritually half-hearted actions even if they seem to be fervent.

One last question: Do we feel free to shout for joy and to dance? We might be hindered by looking at others around us. We know of David being free from fear of man and committing himself by the words: "I will speak of Thy testimonies also before kings, and will not be ashamed" (Ps. 119:46; King James Version). Are we willing to testify to those around us how much our Redeemer means to us and the reasons we have to be joyful? Jesus says: "If anyone is ashamed of Me and My words, the Son of man will be ashamed of him..." (Luke 9:26).

However, freedom also means not to submit to tacit social pressure and not to join in clapping, lifting up hands or dancing just because others around us are doing so. What is said about David? He danced *"before the LORD"*.

2) Appalling consequence

"They set the ark of God on a new cart ...Uzzah and Ahio, sons of Abinadab, were guiding the new cart with the ark of God on it, and Ahio was walking in front of it" (6:3-4).

"When they came to the threshing floor of Nacon, Uzzah reached out and took hold of the ark of God, because the oxen stumbled. The LORD´s anger burned against Uzzah because of his irreverent act; therefore God struck him down and he died there beside the ark of God" (6:6-7).

There is a turbulent and moving piece of history to this Haftarah: The Philistines take the ark from the Jews and bring it to Ashdod (which belonged to the land of the Philistines at that time), where they put it in the house of their idol Dagon. Thereafter, they also take the ark to other towns of the Philistines. Later on they are severely punished by the LORD with death or tumors. There is just no togetherness of the holy God and men serving idols!

When the Philistines decide to return the ark to Israel they interestingly ask their priests how that should be done and they are told to [?] use a new cart pulled by two cows (1 Sam. 6:1-8). So the ark of the covenant gets to Beth Shemesh. There again something dramatic happens: "...God struck down some of the men of Beth Shemesh, putting seventy of them to death because they had looked into the ark of the LORD..." (1 Sam. 6:19), , which was, of course the place where the tablets of the Testimony were kept and was therefore the place of the encounter of the Holy One of Israel with Moses. "...put in the ark the Testimony, which I will give you. There, above the cover between the two cherubim that are over the ark of the Testimony. I will meet with you and give you all My commands for the Israelites" (Ex. 25:21-22). On Sinai already, when Moses receives the two tablets, God instructs him "... Go down and warn the people so they do not force their way through to see the LORD and many of them perish" (Ex. 19:21).

The people of Beth Shemesh recognize that their punishment is the consequence of offending the Holiness of God, and they shout in fright: "...Who can stand in the presence of the LORD, this holy God?..." (1 Sam. 6:20). Remember also how the children of Israel are instructed while crossing the Jordan: "...When you see the ark of the covenant of the LORD your God, and the priests, who are Levites, carrying it, you are to move out from your positions and follow it... But keep a distance of about a thousand yards between you and the ark, do not go near it" (Josh. 3-4).

How does the narrative of the ark continue? In holy awe the inhabitants of Beth Shemesh bring it to Kirjat Yearim where it remains for twenty years until David decides to bring it to Jerusalem. That is what today´s text is about. Again, as with the Philistines earlier, it says: *"They set the ark of God on a new cart..." (6: 3).* That is the beginning of another disaster. The draught animals break away, the ark is in danger of tipping over, and Uzzah walking beside the cart reaches out and takes hold of the ark. *"The LORD´s anger burned against Uzzah because of his irreverent act; therefore God struck him down and he died there beside the ark of God" (6:7).*

Isn't that strange? After all, Uzzah´s purpose was to avoid misfortune. What is the reason for God´s severe punishment? Two reasons may be relevant here:

First, the LORD had ordered them to make poles for carrying the ark (Ex. 25:14). Similarly it says: "After Aaron and his sons have finished covering the holy furnishings and all the holy articles, and when the camp is ready to move, the Kohathites are to come to do the carrying. But they must not touch the holy things or they will die..." (Num. 4:15). The first offence against the instruction is using a cart for transport instead of letting the Levites carry the ark on their shoulders. But why then are the Philistines not punished, given that they – as we have seen – also used a cart? As pagans they need not observe the same rules.

The second reason for God´s punishment is that Uzzah touches the ark and by this does not show proper awe of the holy ark (6: 6-7). As a result of Uzzah´s death, David is afraid of the

LORD and therefore avoids bringing the ark to the city of David initially but takes it instead to the house of Obed-Edom. Yet when he learns how that house is blessed *"because of the ark of God"* he finally brings it to Jerusalem – this time in fact by carriers. *"When those who were carrying the ark of the LORD had taken six steps, he sacrificed a bull and a fattened calf. David, wearing a linen ephod, danced before the LORD with all his might..." (6:13-14).*

What can be the conclusion for us Christians? Awe of the holiness of the Almighty. "...So worship God acceptably with reverence and awe, for our God is a consuming fire" (Hebr. 12:28-29).

Week 27

2 Kings 4:42 – 5:19

The Torah section of this week (Lev. 12:1 – 15:33) focuses on the instructions on how to deal with leprosy. So it may be helpful to focus on the complementary narrative concerning the healing of Naaman of whom it so tersely says *"...He was a valiant soldier, but he had leprosy"(2 Kings 5:1)*

1) Assistants in blessing

"Now bands from Aram had gone out and had taken captive a young girl from Israel, and she served Naaman´s wife. She said to her mistress, 'If only my master would see the prophet who is in Samaria! He would cure him of his leprosy" (5:2-3).

Interestingly the essential clue as to where to seek healing comes from a girl who was forcibly brought to the household of Naaman. She could have been angry, she could have ignored the situation of her master in disappointment, but instead she has compassion on him and wishes him the best. *"If only my master would..."* She is a Jewish girl. She is a blessing for the Aramean. How much have we, too, been blessed through Jews! Let us remember that most of the authors of the New Testament were Jews. Or we may think of the rich Jewish cultural assets belonging to our western tradition (of which far too many treasures were destroyed by the Nazis) or of the numerous achievements and inventions whose Jewish origins we often do not even realize.

" 'By all means, go,´ the king of Aram replied. 'I will send a letter to the king of Israel..." (5:5)

"The letter he took to the king of Israel read: 'With this letter I am sending my servant Naaman to you so that you may cure him of his leprosy" (5:6).

Notice carefully what may not be so self-evident here: The king allows one of his best officers to be treated in a country with which Aram was hostile at that time. And he gives him a letter of reference. A leper, actually ostracized socially, is given a new chance by his king.

The next person in the chain of blessings is the prophet Elisha. *"...Have the man come to me and he will know that there is a prophet in Israel." (5:8)*
"Elisha sent a messenger to say to him, 'Go, wash yourself seven times in the Jordan, and your flesh will be restored and you will be cleansed" (5:10).

To Elisha it is an affair of heart that the Syrian recognizes the God of Abraham, Isaac and Jacob as the One who is active here. He obviously does not want to come to the fore himself, otherwise he would not have sent a messenger to Naaman. He understands from God what will be necessary for healing and in great certainty of faith proclaims that he expects total healing.

The prescribed therapy seems too simple to the officer, so he turns angrily back. *"Naaman's servants went to him and said, 'My father, if the prophet had told you to do some great thing, would you not have done it? How much more, then, when he tells you, 'Wash and be cleansed!" (5:13)* Upon receiving this counsel, Naaman decides to dip himself in the Jordan seven times. It is not only the great experts and the well-known personalities who bring about blessing in God's kingdom. Here even ordinary servants are used by God to promote the decisive breakthrough.

The Bible is full of further precious examples that can teach us how people are a blessing to each other. For instance, the centurion of Capernaum intervenes for his sick servant (Mt. 8: 5-13). Four men carry a paralytic to Jesus and must even uncover the tiles of the roof in order to get to the LORD. Obviously they are so like-minded that the mat does not overturn in their balancing act. And it is remarkable that the miracle of forgiveness and healing that the paralytic experiences comes about because of the faith of these four men. We do not even know whether the paralytic believes (Luk. 5:17-26). We may also think of the beggar who is crippled from birth and is carried to the gate called Beautiful every day (not just now and then). It is because of the great faithfulness with which the people brought him to the door every day that Peter had the opportunity to heal him. (Acts 3:1-10)] And what a blessing is initiated by the obedience of the centurion Cornelius, setting the course for God´s plan of salvation! (Acts 10).

"Each of us should please his neighbour for his good, to build him up" (Rom. 15:2). "Each of you should look not only to your own interests, but also to the interests of others" (Phil. 2:4). "For we are God´s fellow workers…" (1 Cor. 3:9).

2) Prejudiced determinations

"But Naaman went away angry and said, ´I thought that he would surely come out to me and stand and call on the name of the LORD his God, wave his hand over the spot and cure me of my leprosy" (5:11).

The officer feels insulted that, although he has travelled so far and even has a letter from the king, he is not received in an appropriate ceremony by the well-known prophet personally but just by his courier and just at the front door. He expects healing from the prophet. What about us? During conferences and in some congregations pastoral and healing services are offered by a group of appointed brethren. Does it really not matter to us whom we call on? Sure, there a special gifts and ministries of healing but all help and healing comes ultimately from the LORD!

The Syrian has remarkably concrete ideas as to how the prophet should act. Is it not totally right to expect that the name of the LORD will be proclaimed in that situation? We do not read about Elisha doing so, but we can be confident of his relationship with God and can assume that he proclaimed the name of the Holy One of Israel there in his room. The Bible stresses again and again how important the name of our God is when asking for help (and when praising Him). "Our help is in the name of the LORD, the Maker of heaven and earth" (Ps. 124:8).

Naaman´s expectation of a certain ritual may remind us that also in Christian circles often quite different practices are found, styles of worshipping, preference of a specific sort of songs, postures during prayers, forms of divine service and liturgy. How do we deal with that? Are we inflexible because of our traditions? Do we consider it is possible that the LORD can and will reach us also when we experience services which differ from thsoe of our denomination?

"Are not Abana and Pharpar, the rivers of Damascus, better than any of the waters of Israel? Couldn´t I wash in them and be cleansed? So he turned and went off in rage" (v. 12).

Looking at the Jordan during the time of drought in summer, when it is just a thin little stream, one can easily imagine that the rivers in Syria are more impressive. But is Naaman really led just by superficialities in his reaction? Isn´t it in fact likely that he is unwilling to accept that something good can come from Israel? Perhaps the officer should be healed not only from leprosy but also from his prejudice? How many people of our acquaintance *"turned and went off"* or rebelled when they were spoken to about Israel!

Certainly our great God can heal everywhere, but in His Sovereignty He reserved the right to decide how He wants to do it in each case and where He wants to do it in a special way. Think for instance of the wonderful healing power of the Dead Sea that results from a unique combination of the characteristics of air and water.

3) Exercise of obedience

"So he went down and dipped himself in the Jordan seven times, as the man of God had told him, and his flesh was restored and became clean like that of a young boy" (5:14).

What effort it must have cost this man, who was accustomed to commanding, to do as he himself was commanded! Which inner voices may have been on his mind? "Won´t I make a fool of myself?" "Will I ever be able to tell people at home about this?" "What if it doesn't accomplish anything?" "If there really is healing power in this water then shouldn't it be enough to dip just once or twice?"

Do we also hear such voices in our own lives, making us doubt or hesitate or even refuse to take important steps? Many things we do not understand. Is it for instance really logical to us that the people of Israel have to march around the walls of Jericho once for six days and seven times on the seventh day in order to conquer the city? (Josh. 6) It is an autonomous divine decision.

Again and again our obedience in faith is tested. But we can be well equipped. "The weapons we fight with are not the weapons of the world. On the contrary, they have divine power to demolish strongholds. We demolish arguments and every pretension that sets itself up against the knowledge of God, and we take captive every thought to make it obedient to Christ" (2 Cor. 10:4-5)..

Week 28

2 Kings 7:3–20

As was true last week, the Torah section for this week (Lev. 14:1–15:33) is about instructions concerning leprosy. The prophetic supplementary text describes the amazing story of how four lepers become a blessing for the people of Israel in a time of extreme famine. The report begins by noting that these four men, who have nothing to lose because of the economic catastrophe and because of their leprosy, leave for the camps of the hostile Arameans who are besieging Samaria.

1) God´s creative way of help in battle

"When they reached the edge of the camp, not a man was there, for the LORD had caused the Arameans to hear the sound of chariots and horses and a great army, so that they said to one another, ´Look, the king of Israel has hired the Hittite and Egyptian kings to attack us!´ So they got up and fled in the dusk..." (v. 5 –7)

The Almighty God who created the whole world with all its wondrous diversity, intervenes again and again in world history in a creative way, including ways in which He helps and rescues Israel when they face enemies. A German hymn by Paul Gerhardt says it well: "In every situation You know how to help, You are not lacking means".
Let us look at some examples:

In the report of the Haftarah God causes the Arameans to hear the sound of horses and chariots although there is none. It is the other way round, so to speak, from what the prophet Elisha experiences when Israel is surrounded by Arameans: "... Elisha prayed to the LORD, ´Strike these people with blindness´. So He struck them with blindness, as Elisha had asked" (2 Kings 6:18).

God can both invalidate the laws of nature and put the forces of nature into motion in order to rescue His people. We read about how Joshua is able to put the Amorites to flight and "...the LORD hurled large hailstones down on them from the sky, and more of them died from the hailstones than were killed by the swords of the Israelites... Joshua said to the LORD in the presence of Israel: ´O sun, stand still over Gibeon, O moon, over the valley of Aijalon.´ So the sun stood still, and the moon stopped, till the nation avenged itself on its enemies... There has never been a day like it before or since, a day when the LORD listened to a man. Surely the LORD was fighting for Israel!" (Josh.10:11-14). When Jonathan courageously approaches the guard of the Philistines, the ground shakes and a panic grips the enemies by God (1 Sam. 14:15). God also intervenes in a wonderful way when the three kings of Israel, Judah and Edom go together to war against Moab. The LORD says through Elisha: "...You will see neither wind nor rain, yet this valley will be filled with water..." (2 Kings 3:17). And later it says about the Moabites: "When they got up early in the morning, the sun was shining on the water. To the Moabites across the way, the water looked red – like blood. ´That´s blood!´ they said. ´Those kings must have fought and slaughtered each other. Now to the plunder, Moab!´ But when the Moabites came to the camp of Israel, the Israelites rose up and fought them until they fled..." (2 Kings 3:22-24). And when recalling how God guides, we must not forget to include the note about the division of the Red Sea, by which the Israelites are saved and the Pharaoh and his men are killed (Ex. 14). We also remember how the God of Abraham,

Isaac and Jacob causes the walls of Jericho to collapse when the Israelites have surrounded the town according to His instructions (Josh. 6:20). Indeed, the LORD can also make walls in our lives collapse that we may think are insurmountable.!

Sometimes He who watches over Israel gives victory by confusing the enemies. When Saul fights against the Philistines he "...found the Philistines in total confusion, striking each other with their swords" (1 Sam. 14:20). Gideon also experiences this when competing against the superiority of the Midianites with the mini-troops he has formed according to God´s order: "When the three hundred trumpets sounded, the LORD caused the men throughout the camp to turn to each other with their swords..." (Judges 7:22). We read about confusion of enemies also in Judges 4:15 (King James Version) and Joshua 10:10.

Furthermore it is reported that God who directs men´s hearts frightens Israel´s enemies as He says to Moses regarding the defeat of Sihon, king of the Amorites: "This very day I will begin to put the terror and fear of you on all the nations under heaven. They will hear reports of you and will tremble and be in anguish because of you" (Deut. 2:25). The "reports" of Israel have very much to do with God´s miracles that happened in the past. Therefore it is written in Joshua: "Now when the Amorite kings west of the Jordan and all the Canaanite kings along the coast heard how the LORD had dried up the Jordan before the Israelites until we had crossed over, their hearts melted and they no longer had the courage to face the Israelites" (Joshua 5:1).

The LORD even uses dreams to get the "reports of Israel" to their enemies so that His divine goal is reached. According to

God´s order Gideon and his servant enter the camp of the Midianites for reconnaissance and listen to a soldier telling a dream to another one: "...´A round loaf of barley bread came tumbling into the Midianite camp. It struck the tent with such force that the tent overturned and collapsed.´ His friend responded, ´This can be nothing other than the sword of Gideon son of Joash, the Israelite. God has given the Midianites and the whole camp into his hands" (Judges 7:13-14).

Are occurrences such as these limited to Israel´s past? Not at all. Similar things are also reported from the battles Israel had to fight in 1967 and 1973. In one report, the enemies suddenly saw a big cloud like a hand in heaven which made them flee.

Based on these amazing examples, the message to us can only be to trust that the eternally unchangeable LORD can intervene, and wants to intervene, in our personal situations and struggles in His loving and creative way. "...with God all things are possible" (Mt. 19:26).

2) God cannot be mocked

"...the king sent them after the Aramean army. He commanded the drivers, ´Go and find out what has happened.´ They followed them as far as the Jordan, and they found the whole road strewn with the clothing and equipment the Arameans had thrown away in their head-long flight.... Then the people went out and plundered the camp of the Arameans. So a seah of flour sold for a shekel, and two seahs of barley sold for a shekel, as the LORD had said" (v. 14-16).
"It happened as the man of God had said to the king: ´About this time tomorrow, a seah of flour will sell for a shekel and two seahs of barley for a shekel at the gate of Samaria.´ The

officer had said to the man of God, 'Look, even if the LORD should open the floodgates of the heavens, could this happen?' The man of God had replied, 'You will see it with your own eyes, but you will not eat any of it!' And that is exactly what happened to him, for the people trampled him in the gateway, and he died" (v. 18-20).

The officer, an adviser of the king of Aram, sneeringly rebels against Elisha's prophecy. The standard for him is the current circumstance "...that a donkey's head sold for eighty shekels of silver, and a quarter of a cab of seed pods for five shekels" (2 Kings 6:25; a cab being 0.3 L). If garbage is so extremely expensive how then can Elisha dare to claim those bold ideas... As Elisha has announced in the name of God the officer is punished by death for his scorn.

"Penalties are prepared for mockers...", it says in Proverbs 19:29. The LORD punishes scorn and derision by Gentiles as well as by those who belong to God, namely when His holy name, His divine action or His beloved people of Israel - He binds Himself to them so closely - is concerned.
"And you, son of man, prophesy and say, 'This is what the Sovereign LORD says about the Ammonites and their insults: A sword, a sword, drawn for the slaughter, polished to consume..." (Ezek. 21:28).What insult is spoken of? "...Because you said 'aha!' over My sanctuary when it was desecrated and over the land of Israel when it was laid waste and over the people of Judah when they went into exile" (Ezek. 25:3).
It is the derision of the living God by Goliath that motivates David to act. He carries out God's punishment: "David said to the Philistine, 'You come against me with sword and spear and javelin, but I come against you in the name of the LORD Almighty, the God of the armies of Israel, whom you have

defied....And the whole world will know that there is a God in Israel" (1 Sam. 17:45-46).
Sennacherib, king of Assyria, intimidates the Jewish people by mockery. Isaiah makes the dimension of his behaviour clear to him by order of God, before threatening him with the LORD´s punishment: "Who is it you have insulted and blasphemed? Against whom have you raised your voice and lifted your eyes in pride? Against the Holy One of Israel!" (2 Kings 19:22). "That night the angel of the LORD went out and put to death a hundred and eighty-five thousand men in the Assyrian camp" (2 Kings 19:35). Sennacherib himself gets killed by his sons. What had he said actually? "Who of all the gods of these nations has been able to save his land from me? How then can the LORD deliver Jerusalem from my hand?" (1 Kings 18:35). He not only plays the hero but also equates the idols of the heathens with the living God.

There are situations where the Israelites, too, were guilty of scorn. "The LORD, the God of their fathers, sent word to them through His messengers again and again, because He had pity on His people and on His dwelling place. But they mocked God´s messengers, despised His words and scoffed at His prophets..." (2 Chr. 36:15-16). Concerning the crucifixion of Jesus, we know that He patiently endured scorn and derision by the bystanders, the Pharisees and chief priests and that He even prayed: "...Father, forgive them, for they do not know what they are doing... The people stood watching, and the rulers even sneered at Him. They said, 'He saved others; let Him save Himself if He is the Christ of God, the Chosen One" (Luke 23:34-35). Already in Psalm 22:6-7 it is prophesied that the Messiah will be mocked: "But I am a worm and not a man, scorned by men and despised by the people. All who see Me mock Me..."

Whether we read about people making fun of those who experience the outpouring of the Holy Spirit by saying "they have had too much wine" (Acts 2:13), or about those who scoff at the resurrection of the dead (Acts 17:32) or about mockers who question the return of Jesus in the last days "Where is this ´coming´ He promised?" (2 Pt. 3:4) – it nevertheless remains true: "Blessed is the man who does not walk in the counsel of the wicked or stand in the way of sinners or sit in the seat of mockers..." (Ps. 1:1).

"Do not be deceived: God cannot be mocked..." (Gal. 6:7)

Week 29

Ezekiel 22:1–19

The Parascha (Lev. 16:1 – 18:30) is partly about the Day of Atonement. "This is to be a lasting ordinance for you: Atonement is to be made once a year for all the sins of the Israelites" (Lev. 16:34). Therefore every year in autumn the Day of Atonement is observed.
The prophetic supplementary text for today states a multitude of offences of which Israel was guilty, including idolatry, oppression of the weak, bloodshed, desecration of the Sabbath, slander, immorality.

Every year, between the feast of the Jewish New Year and the Feast of Tabernacles, the Jews observe the prescribed Day of Atonement, trusting in the promise: "…Then, before the LORD, you will be clean from all your sins" (Lev. 16:30). Before the prayers of repentance, they try to resolve any problems in their relationships with one another.

Many Christians tend to label the Jews as legalistic and to point out rather disparagingly that they "did not yet accept Jesus" Let us instead marvel at how detailed the prayers of repentance are as they are specified in the Jewish prayer book![7] We can sense readily how seriously they are taken. Certainly they can help us in our own spiritual lives:

---

[7] The Complete Artscroll Siddur, edited by Rabbi Nosson Sherman, Brooklyn 1994, pages 777-781

Confession of guilt

"Our God and the God of our forefathers, may our prayer come before You, and do not ignore our supplication for we are not so brazen and obstinate as to say before You, HASHEM, our God, and the God of our forefathers, that we are righteous and have not sinned – rather, we and our forefathers have sinned.

We have become guilty, we have betrayed, we have robbed, we have spoken slander. We have caused perversion, we have caused wickedness, we have sinned wilfully, we have extorted, we have accused falsely. We have given evil counsel, we have been deceitful, we have scorned, we have rebelled, we have provoked, we have turned away, we have been perverse, we have acted wantonly, we have persecuted, we have been obstinate. We have been wicked, we have corrupted, we have been abominable, we have strayed. You have let us go astray.

We have turned away from Your commandments and from Your good laws but to no avail. But You are righteous in all that has come upon us, for You have acted truthfully while we have caused wickedness.

What can we say before You, Who dwells on high, and what can we relate to You, Who abides in the highest heavens – for indeed, everything that is hidden and revealed You know. You know the secrets of the universe, and the hiddenmost mysteries of all the living. You probe all innermost chambers and test thoughts and emotions. Nothing is hidden from You and nothing is concealed from Your eyes. And so may it be Your will, HASHEM, our God and the God of our forefathers, that You forgive us all our errors, and You pardon us all our iniquities, and You atone for us all our wilful sins.

For the sins that we have sinned before You[8]
> under duress and willingly,
> through hardness of the heart,
> without knowledge,
> with the utterance of the lips,
> in public or in private,
> through immorality,
> through hard speech,
> with knowledge and with deceit,
> through inner thoughts,
> through wronging a neighbour,
> with insincere confession,
> in a session of vice,
> wilfully and carelessly,
> by showing contempt for parents and teachers,
> by exercising power,
> through desecration of the Name,
> through foolish speech,
> through impure lips,
> with the Evil Inclination,
> against those who know and against those who do

not know.

For them all, O God of forgiveness, forgive us, pardon us, atone for us.

> For the sin that we have sinned before You
> by causing subservience through bribery,
> through denial and false promises,
> through evil talk,
> through scorning,
> in commercial dealings,

---

[8] This is repeated as beginning of the sentence before naming the specific sins

with food and drink,
through interest and extortion,
through haughtiness,
with prying eyes,
with the idle chatter of our lips,
with haughty eyes,
with brazenness

For them all, O God of forgiveness, forgive us, pardon us, atone for us.

For the sin that we have sinned before You
in throwing off Your yoke,
in judgment,
through entrapping a neighbour,
through a begrudging eye,
through light-headedness,
with obstinacy,
with legs that run to do evil,
by gossip-mongering,
through vain oath-taking,
through baseless hatred,
in the matter of extending a hand,
through confusion of heart

For them all, O God of forgiveness, forgive us, pardon us, atone for us.[9]

...those that are revealed to us and those that are not revealed to us. Those that are revealed to us we have already declared before You and confessed them to You; and those that are not revealed to us are revealed and known to You...

---

[9] It follows an enumeration of offences of offerings

You are the Forgiver of Israel and the Pardoner of the tribes of Jeshurun in every generation, and beside You we have no king Who pardons and forgives – only You.

My God, before I was formed I was unworthy, and now that I have been formed, it is as if I had not been formed. I am dust in my life and will surely be so in my death. Behold – before You I am like a vessel filled with shame and humiliation. May it be Your will, HASHEM, my God and the God of my forefathers, that I not sin again. And what I have sinned before You, may You cleanse with Your abundant mercy, but not through suffering or serious illness."

Week 30

Amos 9:7–15

Leviticus 19:1 – 20:27, the section for this week, contains many instructions for a sacred life in Israel. The prophet Amos declares to the Israelites that they fall short of the LORD's high standard and therefore have to be prepared for God´s judgment. But a remnant will be saved, and the LORD will turn the fate of His people.

A remnant

"Surely the eyes of the Sovereign LORD are on the sinful kingdom. I will destroy it from the face of the earth – yet I will not totally destroy the house of Jacob, declares the LORD. For I will give the command, and I will shake the house of Israel among all the nations as grain is shaken in a sieve, and not a pebble will fall to the ground" (v. 8 - 9)

Two somewhat contradictory messages are associated with the term "remnant", which can mean either "only a remnant" or "but a remnant!"
We can see this principle in all of Scripture: Although the LORD would have had reasons enough, He never destroys His chosen people totally but saves a remnant again and again. We can see this already in the account of the Flood "…when God waited patiently in the days of Noah while the ark was being built. In it only a few people, eight in all, were saved through water" (1 Pt. 3:20; see Gen. 7:23). The story about Joseph is another eloquent example. He explains to his brothers: "…God sent me ahead of you to preserve for you a remnant on earth and to save your lives by a great deliverance" (Gen. 45:7).

When Moses gives his fellow countrymen the choice of deciding between blessing or curse, he announces the cost of disobedience: "You who were as numerous as the stars in the sky will be left but few in number..." (Deut. 28:62). Isaiah, too, has to declare: "Though your people, O Israel, be like the sand by the sea, only a remnant will return..." (Isa. 10:22; see also Rom. 9:27). Because Israel assimilates to the idolatry of the nations, they are captured and brought to Assyria: "So the LORD was very angry with Israel and removed them from His presence. Only the tribe of Judah was left" (2 Kings 17:18). In Ezekiel the LORD says: "...I will inflict punishment on you and will scatter all your survivors to the winds" (Ezek. 5:10).

Such a remnant is spoken about in vivid metaphors. When Israel sought refuge with the Egyptians in her own arbitrary way the LORD says"... you will all flee away, till you are left like a flagstaff on a mountaintop, like a banner on a hill" (Isa. 30:17). Elsewhere we read: "The Daughter of Zion is left like a shelter in a vineyard, like a hut in a field of melons..." (Isa. 1:8).

Ezra expresses this very clearly in a prayer of repentance: It is nothing but grace that some of the people are preserved at all: "What has happened to us is a result of our evil deeds and our great guilt, and yet, our God, You have punished us less than our sins have deserved and have given us a remnant like this. Shall we again break Your commands and intermarry with the peoples who commit such detestable practices? Would You not be angry enough with us to destroy us, leaving us no remnant or survivor?" (Ezra 9:13-14).

It is not self-evident why anyone should be spared God's judgment. This is what Amos means when he directs the following words to his fellow Jews: "Hate evil, love good;

maintain justice in the courts. Perhaps the LORD God Almighty will have mercy on the remnant of Joseph" (Amos 5:15). At one point, Ezekiel cries out in fright: "...Ah, Sovereign LORD! Will You completely destroy the remnant of Israel?" (Ezek. 11:13).

No! "...I will spare some, for some of you will escape the sword when you are scattered among the lands and nations. Then in the nations where they have been carried captive, those who escape will remember Me – how I have been grieved by their adulterous hearts..." (Ezek. 6:8-9). A remnant remains, and they have an opportunity for renewal. King Josiah of Judah, when the book of the Law is found, wants to take advantage of this opportunity: "Go and inquire of the LORD for me and for the remnant in Israel and Judah about what is written in this book that has been found..." (2 Chr. 34:21). Again and again, the God of Abraham, Isaac and Jacob gives His beloved people the opportunity to listen to His voice and follow Him. And they hear wonderful promises:

"Listen to Me, O house of Jacob, all you who remain of the house of Israel, you whom I have upheld since you were conceived, and have carried since your birth. Even to your old age and gray hairs I am He, I am He who will sustain you..." (Isa. 46:3-4). It is at the LORD´s blessing that they are liberated from dispersion and oppression. "In that day the LORD will reach out His hand a second time to reclaim the remnant that is left of His people from Assyria, from Lower Egypt, from Upper Egypt, from Cush, from Elam, from Babylonia, from Hamath and from the islands of the sea" (Isa. 11:11; see also Jer. 23:3). With the gathering of the people comes a further promise: "Once more a remnant of the house of Judah will take root below and bear fruit above. For out of Jerusalem will come a remnant, and out of Mount Zion a band of survivors. The zeal of the LORD Almighty will accomplish this" (2 Kings 19:30-31).

We are privileged to be living in a time when we are witnesses of this rooting and bearing fruit in the Promised Land. We can confirm with Paul: "So too, at the present time there is a remnant chosen by grace" (Rom. 11:5). *"They will rebuild the ruined cities and live in them. They will plant vineyards and drink their wine; they will make gardens and eat their fruit. I will plant Israel in their own land, never again to be uprooted from the land I have given them, says the LORD your God" (v. 14-15).*

Those who are left will turn back to the LORD again: "In that day the remnant of Israel, the survivors of the house of Jacob, will no longer rely on him who struck them down but will truly rely on the LORD, the Holy One of Israel. A remnant will return, a remnant of Jacob will return to the Mighty God" (Isa. 10:20-21). There are also amazing statements such as this: "The remnant of Jacob will be in the midst of many peoples like dew from the LORD..." (Mi 5:7). In the end times Israel will be a blessing. Why? "The remnant of Israel will do no wrong; they will speak no lies, nor will deceit be found in their mouths..." (Zeph. 3:13). This is only possible because God will give them a new spirit and a heart of flesh (Ezek. 11:19). And consider this amazing prophecy: "In those days, at that time, declares the LORD, search will be made for Israel´s guilt, but there will be none, and for the sins of Judah, but none will be found, for I will forgive the remnant I spare" (Jer. 50:20). Indeed, "Who is a God like You, who pardons sin and forgives the transgression of the remnant of His inheritance?..." (Mi 7:18). It is because of this cleansing that "those who are left in Zion, who remain in Jerusalem, will be called holy, all who are recorded among the living in Jerusalem" (Isa. 4:3). Once it will happen that the LORD "…will be a glorious crown, a beautiful wreath for the remnant of His people" (Isa. 28:5).

God wants all men to be saved and all men to praise Him. But by the numerous verses mentioned above we realize that because of human failure it is always just a "little flock" (Luk. 12:32) that reaches the goal, "…for many be called, but few chosen" (Mt. 20:16; King James Version). May the LORD grant us mercy to follow Him in obedience and to remain firmly in Him in spite of all temptations! "Small is the gate and narrow the road that leads to life, and only few find it" (Mt. 7:14).

Week 31

Ezekiel 44:15–31

The Parascha for this week (Lev. 21:1–24:23) and the Haftarah focus on life and service of the priests.

1)   The teachers

"But the priests, who are Levites and descendants of Zadok and who faithfully carried out the duties of My sanctuary when the Israelites went astray from Me, are to come near to minister before Me" (v. 15).
"They are to teach My people ..." (v. 23).

All of us need people who are willing to share their knowledge and experiences with us, first of all our parents but also friends, school teachers or superiors. And all of us should serve as good examples to others as far as we are concerned. But in the Bible we see that God appoints specific persons to serve as teachers in a special way.

Yet it is not only about formal lessons or sermons that we are concerned. Consider Bezalel for instance who had knowledge in all sorts of crafts and was given "...the ability to teach others..." by God (Ex. 35:34). And a certain Chenaniah "...gave instruction in singing, because he was skilful" (1 Chr. 15:22, New American Standard Bible).

But of course instruction in the Holy Scriptures is most important. Paul makes this clear by the following words: "Everyone who calls on the name of the LORD will be saved. How, then, can they call on the One they have not believed in?

And how can they believe in the One of whom they have not heard? And how can they hear without someone preaching to them?" (Rom. 10:13-14).

Because they are called to share the Gospel - the truth - the preachers bear a special responsibility. "Not many of you should presume to be teachers, my brothers, because you know that we who teach will be judged more strictly. We all stumble in many ways..." (James 3:1-2). It is a pity that Peter has to warn us that "...there will be false teachers among you. They will secretly introduce destructive heresies, even denying the Sovereign LORD who bought them..." (2 Pt. 2:1). That those seductions are possible at all may have to do with a human weakness, namely that we would like to hear most of all what we find attractive and good for us. "For the time will come when men will not put up with sound doctrine. Instead, to suit their own desires, they will gather around them a great number of teachers to say what their itching ears want to hear. They will turn their ears away from the truth and turn aside to myths" (2 Tim. 4:3-4). We are called to "...obey your leaders and to submit to their authority..." (Hebr. 13:17), but one thing has to precede this: "...Do not believe every spirit, but test the spirits to see whether they are from God..." (1 John 4:1).

The Scripture describes us another danger: "...If you rely on the law and brag about your relationship to God, if you know His will and approve of what is superior because you are instructed by the law; if you are convinced that you are a guide for the blind, a light for those who are in the dark, an instructor for the foolish, a teacher of infants, because you have in the law the embodiment of knowledge and truth – you, then, who teach others, do you not teach yourself?..." (Rom. 2:17–21). A major responsibility of spiritual leaders is not only to teach in accordance with God´s will but also not to stumble in their own behaviour. Therefore Timothy gets the warning: "Watch your life and doctrine closely!..." (1 Tim. 4:16). Several well-known preachers have had to quit their job because their personal conduct was not compatible any more with their preaching. "...Consider the outcome of their way of life..." (Hebr. 13:7). It is interesting that Noah is called "...a preacher of righteousness..." (2 Pt. 2:5) even though he is not usually thought of as a preacher. But it says about him "Noah was a righteous man, blameless among the people of his time, and he walked with God" (Gen. 6:9).

God wants to be the master of all of us. "I will instruct you and teach you in the way you should go..." (Ps. 32:8). As he is our Creator He knows best what is good for us and how we can achieve the goal of our calling. "...Who is a teacher like Him?" (Job 36:22).

2) Distinguishing between the Unholy and the Holy

"They are to teach My people the difference between the holy and the common and show them how to distinguish between the unclean and the clean" (v. 23).

Our LORD is the Holy One, "...the Holy One of Israel..." (Isa.12:6). All glory is due to Him, and so the angels sing "...Holy, holy, holy is the LORD Almighty, the whole earth is full of His glory" (Isa. 6:3). He has chosen and set apart a people – the people Israel – for the sake of His name. "For you are a people holy to the LORD your God. The LORD your God has chosen you out of all the peoples on the face of the earth to be His people, His treasured possession" (Deut. 7:6). Being chosen involves responsibility. "I am the LORD your God; consecrate yourselves and be holy, because I am holy..." (Lev. 11:44).

When we by His mercy experience the LORD and accept Him as our Redeemer, then these words apply to us. "Just as He who called you is holy, so be holy in all you do…" (1. Pt. 1: 15). What does it mean when we pray "hallowed be Your name"? Are we aware of how this impacts our way of life in a very concrete manner?

To distinguish between unholy and holy is crucially important because "…God is light; in Him there is no darkness" (1 John 1:5). The LORD says already to Aaron: "You must distinguish between the holy and the common, between the unclean and the clean, and you must teach the Israelites all the decrees the LORD has given them through Moses" (Lev. 10:10-11). So it is central to the calling of spiritual leaders to point emphatically to the necessity of distinguishing between the unholy and the holy.

But it also says: *"They are …to show them how to distinguish between the unclean and the clean" (v. 23).* "To show" is something you cannot impart to others just by preaching or theory – the personal example "as children of light" is needed (Eph. 5: 8), based on solid food and training as it says in the epistle to the Hebrews: "Solid food is for the mature, who by constant use have trained themselves to distinguish good from evil" (Hebr. 5:14). This solid food, the pure word of God, "…is living and active. Sharper than any double-edged sword, it penetrates even to dividing soul and spirit, joints and marrow; it judges the thoughts and attitudes of the heart" (Hebr. 4:12). So this is the crucial key to distinguishing between unclean and clean, holy and unholy.

Week 32

Jeremiah 32: 6 – 27

The Torah section for this week (Lev. 25:1–26:2) lists the instructions concerning the Sabbath Year (the seventh year) and the so-called Year of Jubilee (the fiftieth year) . Concerning the Year of Jubilee it says: "…Each one of you is to return to his family property and each to his own clan" (Lev. 25:10). The inheritance of the fathers should not pass into the possession of foreigners. The Haftarah describes an example of this principle from the turbulent time when Jeremiah was in jail in Jerusalem because of his prophecy of Babylonian captivity and when Jerusalem was already besieged by the king of Babylon. The prophet gets the order from God to buy a field from family property in the neighbourhood of Jerusalem.

1) Faith and doubts

"Ah, Sovereign LORD, … nothing is too hard for You" (v. 17).
"See how the siege ramps are built up to take the city. Because of the sword, famine and plague, the city will be handed over to the Babylonians who are attacking it… And though the city will be handed over to the Babylonians, You, O Sovereign LORD, say to me, 'Buy the field with silver and have the transaction witnessed" (v. 24-25).
"Then the word of the LORD came to Jeremiah: I am the LORD, the God of all mankind. Is anything too hard for Me?" (v. 26-27)

Notice how closely linked the two are: On the one hand the clear confession to the Almighty God and on the other hand - only a little while later - words meaning 'That cannot be true actually!´ How closely linked belief and doubts often are in our lives also!

Yes, we know that our LORD is the Creator of the whole world and that He can do everything. Yes, we believe that He gave a child to the aged Sarah. "Is anything too hard for the LORD?..." (Gen. 18:14). When reading the words of Jesus that it is easier for a camel to go through the eye of a needle than for a rich man to enter the kingdom of God, we would not ask as the disciples did at that time "Who then can be saved?", but we would subscribe to the answer of Jesus: "With man this is impossible, but with God all things are possible" (see Mt. 19:23-26), wouldn´t we?

Yet don´t we sometimes react like the father of a son with an evil spirit? He turns to the LORD by saying: "...If You can do anything, take pity on us and help us. ´If you can?´ says Jesus. ´Everything is possible for him who believes´. Immediately the boy´s father exclaimed, ´I do believe; help me overcome my unbelief!" (Mk.9:22-24). Or is it foreign to our nature to consider how Peter at first addresses the LORD in strong faith "...tell me to come to You on the water", and then, when he begins to sink because of the storm, cries out "LORD, save me!" (Mt. 14:28+30)? We read also of David: "Why are you downcast, O my soul? Why so disturbed within me? Put your hope in God, for I will yet praise Him, my Saviour and my God" and some verses after that "...Why have You forgotten me?..." (Ps. 42:5+9). Or consider the report on the appearance of the resurrected Jesus: "Then the eleven disciples went to Galilee, to the mountain where Jesus had told them to go. When they saw Him, they worshipped Him, but some doubted" (Mt. 28:16-17). Are we sure that we would not have been among the doubters?

Obviously we need warnings like this: "I want men everywhere to lift up holy hands in prayer, without anger or disputing" (1 Tim. 2:8). "Do everything without complaining or arguing, so that you may become blameless and pure..." (Phil.2:14-15). "...he who doubts is like a wave of the sea, blown and tossed by the wind" (James 1:6).

Let us turn again to our Haftarah text and to Israel to whom God gives such astonishing promises while they are in a threatening situation. Elsewhere the LORD opposes possible sceptics in the following way: "This is what the LORD Almighty says: 'Once again men and women of ripe old age will sit in the streets of Jerusalem, each with cane in hand because of his age. The city streets will be filled with boys and girls playing there.` This is what the LORD Almighty says: 'It may seem marvellous to the remnant of this people at that time, but will it seem marvellous to Me? `declares the LORD Almighty" (Zech. 8:4-6).

"Now faith is being sure of what we hope for and certain of what we do not see" (Hebr. 11:1).

2) Guidance in prayer

The verses 17 – 25 give us insight into Jeremiah´s prayer and provide helpful hints for our prayers.

a) To express who and how the LORD is

"Ah, Sovereign LORD, You have made the heavens and the earth ... You show love ... whose name is the LORD Almighty, great are Your purposes and mighty are Your deeds. Your eyes are open to all the ways of men; You reward everyone according to his conduct and as his deeds deserve" (v. 17–19).

How often do we quickly move on to our requests in prayer instead of first praising our Heavenly Father for His power, mercy and love? We can also learn from Solomon who, when dedicating the temple, begins his intercessory prayer with the words: "O LORD, God of Israel, there is no God like You in heaven above or on earth below – You who keep Your covenant of love with Your servants who continue wholeheartedly in Your way" (1 Kings 8:23; similarly Neh. 1:5 and Dan. 9:4). When Jehoshaphat prays for divine protection at the sight of superior enemies, he begins: "O LORD, God of our fathers, are You not the God who is in heaven? You rule over all the kingdoms of the nations. Power and might are in Your hand, and no one can withstand You" (2 Chr. 20:6).

b) To name concrete experiences with God

"You performed miraculous signs and wonders in Egypt and have continued them to this day, both in Israel and among all mankind… You brought Your people Israel out of Egypt … You gave them this land You had sworn to give their forefathers, a land flowing with milk and honey" (v. 20 – 22).

It is one thing to worship the LORD in His eternal creativity and His love to all mankind. But it is equally important in the presence of the invisible world that I honour Him also for what He did especially for me and my personal surroundings. Solomon does this by saying: "You have kept Your promise to Your servant David my father, with Your mouth You have promised and with Your hand You have fulfilled it – as it is today" (1. Kings 8: 24). Jehoshaphat continues his prayer like this: "O our God, did You not drive out the inhabitants of this land before Your people Israel and give it forever to the descendants of Abraham Your friend?" (2. Chr. 20: 7)

c) To confess sins

"...but they did not obey You or follow Your law; they did not do what You commanded them to do"(v. 23).

Again and again we have to realize that we do not deserve God´s love and that it is an indescribable privilege to be allowed to implore Him at all, because "if we claim to be without sin, we deceive ourselves and the truth is not in us" (1. John 1: 8).

Although he pleases God personally, Daniel nonetheless identifies readily with the sins of his ancestors as he prays "...we have sinned and done wrong. We have been wicked and have rebelled, we have turned away from Your commands and laws. We have not listened to Your servants the prophets..." (Dan. 9: 5 f.). Similarly Nehemiah, before expressing his actual request, comes in an humble and repentant manner to the Holy One of Israel: "Let Your ear be attentive and Your eyes open to hear the prayer Your servant is praying before You ... I confess the sins we Israelites, including myself and my father´s house, have committed against You. We have acted very wickedly toward You" (Neh. 1: 6 f.).

d) To explain the situation and the concern

"See how the siege ramps are built up to take the city. Because of the sword, famine and plague, the city will be handed over to the Babylonians who are attacking it" (v. 24).

In those days the threat to Israel cannot be minimized. And if we are in distress we, too, are invited to clearly state the facts and lament about our misery before the LORD. Of course He knows everything anyway. But the Bible makes it clear that it is good to bring our situation before Him. Hezekiah gives us an eloquent example. When he gets a letter from the king of Assyria threatening and disgracing him, "he spread it out before the LORD... Give ear, O LORD, and ...listen to the words Sennacherib has sent to insult the living God. It is true, O LORD, that the Assyrian kings have laid waste these nations and their lands" (2. Kings 19: 14 – 17). And Jehoshaphat prays: "But now here are men from Ammon, Moab and Mount Seir..." (2. Chr. 20: 10).

When we come to our Heavenly Father in this way we should have in mind His words: *"I am the LORD, the God of all mankind. Is anything too hard for Me?" (v. 27)*. "To Him who is able to do immeasurably more than all we ask or imagine, according to His power that is at work within us, to Him be glory in the church and in Christ Jesus throughout all generations, for ever and ever! Amen" (Eph. 3: 20 f.).

Week 33

Jeremiah 16:19 – 17:14

In the Torah section for this week (Lev. 26:1 – 27:34) the God of Abraham, Isaac and Jacob states what a rich blessing He wants to give His people, but what the consequences are of coming under God´s curse through sin. In a similar way the Haftarah contrasts trusting in the LORD with failure and prophesises that even the nations will one day acknowledge that the one true God has all the power.

1)   The Gentiles´ late acknowledgement

"O LORD, my strength and my fortress, my refuge in time of distress, to You the nations will come from the ends of the earth and say, ´Our fathers possessed nothing but false gods, worthless idols that did them no good. Do men make their own gods? Yes, but they are not gods!´ Therefore I will teach them – this time I will teach them My power and might. Then they will know that My name is the LORD" (16:19-21).

David states "All the gods of the nations are idols...", and he does not leave it like that but exclaims "Ascribe to the LORD, O families of nations, ascribe to the LORD glory and strength!" (Ps. 96:5+7)."Praise the LORD, all you nations, extol Him, all you peoples" (Ps. 117:1). That corresponds with God´s aim. He desires that the whole world submit to Him. This request is also taken up in the Jewish prayer book, the Siddur[10]: "May all inhabitants of the world recognize and understand that You alone are God over all kingdoms of

---

[10] Siddur Shma Kolenu, published with Morascha, Basel/Zurich 1996

earth!" (p. 14) "Therefore we trust in You... that You remove all idols from the earth and totally erase all futile hallucinations; that the world will be erected through the work of the Almighty, that all mortals call upon Your name and all offenders of the earth turn to You" (p. 114). "All peoples that You have created might come and bow before You, LORD, and honour Your name!" (p. 136).

That this aim will be reached is connected very closely with the Jewish people and with the history of Israel. What did the LORD promise to Abram already? "...All peoples on earth will be blessed through you" (Gen. 12:3). The nations might and will recognize the Eternal One by the way He treats Israel. David is aware of this when praying: "May God be gracious to us (!) and bless us and make His face shine upon us, that Your ways may be known on earth, Your salvation among all (!) nations!"[11] (Ps. 67:1-2). Concerning the end of times the LORD turns to Israel with the wonderful promise "... the glory of the LORD rises upon you. See, darkness covers the earth and thick darkness is over the peoples, but the LORD rises upon you and His glory appears over you. Nations will come to your light, and kings to the brightness of your dawn" (Isa. 60:1–3). What God will have done for His people will shine into the world like a torch. "For Zion´s sake I will not keep silent, for Jerusalem´s sake I will not remain quiet, till her righteousness shines out like the dawn, her salvation like a blazing torch. The nations will see your righteousness, and all kings your glory" (Isa. 62:1-2). Because God´s plan of salvation is most closely connected with Jerusalem, there will be a migration of the peoples so to speak: "And many peoples and powerful nations will come to Jerusalem to seek the LORD Almighty and to entreat Him" (Zech. 8:22). "Many nations will come and say, ´Come, let us go up to the mountain of the

---

[11] Exclamation marks added by W.B.

LORD, to the house of the God of Jacob. He will teach us His ways, so that we may walk in His paths..." (Mi 4:2).

The epistle to the Galatians states clearly "...that the blessing given to Abraham might come to the Gentiles through Christ Jesus..." (Gal. 3:14). "...the root of Jesse will stand as a banner for the peoples; the nations will rally to Him" (Isa.11:10). And indeed the Heavenly Father has sent His only Son with a mission for Israel as well as for the Gentiles: "It is too small a thing for You to be My servant to restore the tribes of Jacob and bring back those of Israel I have kept. I will also make You a light for the Gentiles, that You may bring My salvation to the ends of the earth" (Isa. 49:6).

Notice what John can write about this Son of David: "He is the atoning sacrifice for our sins, and not only for ours but also for the sins of the whole world" (1 John 2:2).

2) Drought or source

"This is what the LORD says: 'Cursed is the one who trusts in man, who depends on flesh for his strength and whose heart turns away from the LORD. He will be like a bush in the wastelands; he will not see prosperity when it comes. He will dwell in the parched places of the desert, in a salt land where no one lives" (17:5 -6).
"But blessed is the man who trusts in the LORD, whose confidence is in Him. He will be like a tree planted by the water that sends out its roots by the stream. It does not fear when heat comes; its leaves are always green. It has no worries in a year of drought and never fails to bear fruit" (17:7-8).

"...Those who turn away from You will be written in the dust because they have forsaken the LORD, the spring of living water" (17:13).

When Moses sets before the people the choice between blessing and curse, he specifies the consequences of being disobedient to the God of Abraham, Isaac and Jacob: "The LORD will strike you with wasting disease, with fever and inflammation, with scorching heat and drought, with blight and mildew..." (Deut. 28:22). Again and again we human beings try to manage without God, or we trust in our own understanding. *"Do men make their own gods? Yes, but they are not gods!" (16:20)* It may well be that we have to be led into "wasteland" from time to time in order to think about our way, to see that we "...sowed to please our sinful nature..." (Gal. 6:8) and to repent humbly expecting: *"Heal me, O LORD, and I will be healed; save me and I will be saved..." (17:14).* The fruit of repentance is that we once again establish priority in our lives to the LORD again. If we give special emphasis to our own needs, God´s word as given to us through Haggai admonishes us: "... each of you is busy with his own house. Therefore, because of you the heavens have withheld their dew and the earth its crops. I called for a drought on the fields and the mountains, on the grain, the new wine, the oil and whatever the ground produces, on men and cattle , and on the labour of your hands" (Haggai 1:9–11).
When we go through a time of drought, of spiritual dryness, we should listen to the invitation of our loving Father: "Come, all you who are thirsty, come to the waters!..." (Isa. 55:1). He has promised the people of Israel: "...Water will gush forth in the wilderness and streams in the desert. The burning sand will become a pool, the thirsty ground bubbling springs..." (Isa. 35:6-7). This can already be experienced in a fascinating way in Israel for we know that the LORD promises also streams of

spiritual water to His first loved people: "...Do not be afraid, O Jacob, My servant, Jeshurun, whom I have chosen. For I will pour water on the thirsty land, and streams on the dry ground; I will pour out My Spirit on your offspring and My blessing on your descendants" (Isa. 44:2-3). David confesses in worship: "...With You is the fountain of life..." (Ps. 36:9), and he knows: whose "...delight is in the law of the LORD...He is like a tree planted by streams of water, which yields its fruit in season and whose leaf does not wither. Whatever he does prospers" (Ps. 1:2-3). Our Haftarah text reads similarly - and does not conceal, by the way, that there may be challenges and crises also for those who are blessed by God. But they do not fear *"when heat comes"* and when *"a year of drought"* has to be overcome.

How does our Haftarah text read? *"The heart is deceitful above all things and beyond cure. Who can understand it? I the LORD search the heart and examine the mind, to reward a man according to his conduct, according to what his deeds deserve" (17:9-10).* Once God says to the people of Israel: "My people have committed two sins: They have forsaken Me, the spring of living water, and have dug their own cisterns, broken cisterns that cannot hold water" (Jer. 2:13). We can only ask the author and finisher of our faith again and again for an obedient heart, as "the fear of the LORD is a fountain of life..." (Prov. 14:27). Our Redeemer, Jeshua, says: "Whoever drinks the water I give him will never thirst..." (John 4:14).

"...LORD, give me this water!..." (John 4:15).

Week 34

Hosea 1: 10 – 2: 20

Week by week it is interesting to track down what text is being read as a supplement to the Parascha. Numbers 1:1 – 4:20 provides a report on Israel´s census in the desert. In those days 603.550 men twenty years old or more and additionally 22.000 Levites (a month old or more) are counted. The text in Hosea begins with the promise that God had already given to Abraham (Gen. 22:17): *"Yet the Israelites will be like the sand on the seashore, which cannot be measured or counted..."* (v.10). We see by the following text what further great development can be expected for Israel.

Symbolism of names

The first chapters of the book of Hosea report an enormous change in the fate of the Israelites, about the unfaithfulness in their conduct and about the mercy of the ever loving God who will never give them up. In a very vivid way the disobedience and idolatry of Israel are compared to the actions of an adulterous woman. In fact, the prophet Hosea is ordered to marry a harlot and to have children from her. In this way, he was to experience for himself how painful and disgraceful unfaithfulness is, and then to make it clear to Israel how great and marvellous it is that God does not abandon them but instead turns to them again.

To make the dimensions of divine mercy as clear to us as possible – which is actually beyond our understanding - the LORD not only uses this symbolic action but adds some terms that by their very definition provide new interpretations that should cause us to prick up our ears.

1)   Lo-Ammi

Hosea gets the instruction to call his son "Lo-Ammi", meaning "not my people", "...for you are not My people, and I am not your God" (Hos. 1:9). But the very next verse begins with a "yet!" The sons of Israel will be like the sand on the seashore! *"...In the place where it was said to them, 'You are not My people' they will be called 'sons of the living God' (1:10).* Notice how miraculously God turns to those who deserved the name "Lo-Ammi"! and says, "...I will say to those called 'Not My people' 'You are My people'..." (Hos. 2:23).

But think of what a gift of mercy He extends to us also that we – though totally undeserving - belong to His people through the sacrifice of Jeshua and by personally accepting His work of Redemption! "even us, whom He also called, not only from the Jews but also from the Gentiles. As He says in Hosea, 'I will call them 'My people' who are not My people; and I will call her 'My loved one' who is not My loved one" (Rom. 9: 24-25).

2)   Lo-Ruhamah

According to God's will Hosea is told to call his daughter "Lo-Ruhamah", meaning "no mercy" (Hos. 1:6). This was intended as a highly significant warning to the people to scrutinize their conduct and to return to the right way. And then we read in verse 23: "I will have mercy upon her" (King James Version). The Holy One of Israel cannot but be faithful to His promise of eternal love. This is what He Himself expresses towards Ephraim: "...Though I often speak against him, I still remember him. Therefore My heart yearns for him; I have great compassion for him," declares the LORD (Jer. 31:20). "If you, O LORD, kept a record of sins, O LORD, who could stand? But with You there is forgiveness; therefore You are feared" (Ps. 130:3-4).

The terms Lo-Ammi and Lo-Ruhamah which shall belong to the past according to God´s grace, point also to an important future development in another context: Judah and the tribes of Israel will be united again: *"The people of Judah and the people of Israel will be reunited, and they will appoint one leader ...Say of your brothers, ´My people´ and of your sisters, ´My loved one" (1:11 + 2:1).* We recall the LORD´s symbolic request of Ezekiel to join together two sticks of wood. To this God attaches the promise: "...I will take the Israelites out of the nations where they have gone. I will gather them from all around and bring them back into their own land. I will make them one nation in the land, on the mountains of Israel. There will be one king over all of them and they will never again be two nations or be divided into two kingdoms" (Ezek. 37: 21-22). The only king will be the King of Kings.

3) Jezreel

The LORD commanded Hosea to call his first son Jezreel (Hos. 1:4), indicating God´s judgment. "In that day I will break Israel´s bow in the Valley of Jezreel" (Hos.1: 5). The Valley of Jezreel – located between the Carmel mountains, the Gilboa and the hills of Lower Galil, with the Kishon river and towns as Megiddo and Taanach – is repeatedly a place of hard battles in Israel´s history: There Deborah fights against king Jabin of Hazor (Judges 4 and 5); there the Philistines gather against Israel in the days of David (1 Sam. 29:1); there King Josiah fights against the Egyptian Pharao Neco (2 Kings 23:29); and the last battlefield of mankind will be at Armageddon, near the mountain of Megiddo, according to Rev. 16:16. This Valley of Jezreel, although so heavily involved in bloodshed, suddenly takes on a totally different meaning in the context of God's plan to reunite Judah and Israel: *"The people of Judah and the people of Israel will be reunited ... and will come up out of the land, for great will be the day of Jezreel." (v.1:11).* Why the term Jezreel? The Hebrew word means "God sows". And that's exactly what is said in the verses following our Haftarah text: "In that day I will respond, declares the LORD, 'I will respond to the skies, and they will respond to the earth; and the earth will respond to the grain, the new wine and oil, and they will respond to Jezreel. I will plant her for Myself in the land... " (Hos. 2: 21–23).

This new beginning acquires additional meaning in the following verses: "The days are coming, declares the LORD, when I will plant the house of Israel and the house of Judah with the offspring of men and of animals. Just as I watched over them to uproot and tear down, and to overthrow, destroy and bring disaster, so I will watch over them to build and to plant, declares the LORD" (Jer. 31:27-28).

God also uses this metaphor of plant growth elsewhere with regard to His promise to bring Israel back to the Promised Land. Consider, for instance, His words in Jer. 32:41: "I will rejoice in doing them good and will assuredly plant them in this land with all My heart and soul." Of course the LORD never does anything "half-heartedly", but here He is obviously stressing the intensity of His love. Is it surprising then to read "...the men of Judah are the garden of His delight..." (Isa. 5:7)?

4) Achor

A further symbolic name is "Achor". We come across this term in the report on Achan´s theft. Joshuah takes Achan together with his family and his belongings to the Valley of Achor lest the sin should not weigh on the people of Israel any longer. "...Why have you brought this trouble on us? The LORD will bring trouble on you today" (Josh. 7:25). "Achor" means sorrow or trouble. The name "Achan" is derived from the same stem and can be translated as "the one who saddens". So much concerning the background. But now the term "Achor" is used in a totally different context here in Hosea where an unfaithful wife is the metaphor for Israel: *"Therefore I am now going to allure her; I lead her into the desert and speak tenderly to her. There I will give her back her vineyards, and will make the Valley of Achor a door of hope. There she will sing as in the days of her youth..."* (v. 14-15). The valley of sorrow gets a door of hope!

Entering the door of hope leads to singing. We may think of David´s Psalm: "Blessed are those whose strength is in You, who have their hearts on pilgrimage. As they pass through the valley of Baca, they make it a place of springs..." (Ps. 84:5 -6). (Baca is explained to be a valley of weeping making a well of tears.) The Redeemer Jeshua is sent to proclaim "the year of the LORD´s favour", "...to comfort all who mourn, and provide for those who grieve in Zion –to bestow on them a crown of beauty instead of ashes, the oil of gladness instead of mourning..." (Isa. 61: 2-3).

Interestingly, Isaiah also uses the word "Achor" when he writes, "Sharon will become a pasture for flocks, and the Valley of Achor a resting place for herds, for My people who seek Me" (Isa. 65:10) – that begins in the desert. "*...I will lead* *her into the desert and speak tenderly to her" (v.14).* God knows how He can best reach us: In wasteland, hopelessness, loneliness, misery, when much around us and within us is devastated or bewildered (maybe because of our "wild" conduct), we are more likely to cry to Him. "Out of the depths I cry to You, O LORD; O LORD, hear my voice..." (Ps. 130:1-2). God speaks to Israel: "I cared for you in the desert, in the land of burning heat" (Hos. 13:5). "...The people ... will find favour in the desert..." (Jer. 31:2). But this is preceded by purification. "For You, O God, tested us; You refined us like silver" (Ps. 66:10). Both are near together: "...the kindness and sternness of God..." (Rom. 11:22).

It is through the door of hope that we must enter. Our LORD Jesus says: "I am the gate; whoever enters through Me will be saved..." (John 10: 9).

5) Baal and husband

A final set of terms should also be cited from the Haftarah text: Baal and husband. "At the beginning the LORD says to the unfaithful wife: *"...She is not My wife, and I am not her husband..." (2:2).* And then, after her repentance in the desert, we read: *"In that day, declares the LORD, you will call Me ´my husband´, you will no longer call Me ´my master´ " (2:16).* "My master" is in Hebrew "Baali". This term, devalued through idolatry (2:17), rather expresses false dependence and subordination. When a wife (= Israel) exclaims "my husband" (Hebrew = Ishi), this expresses a personal relationship of love and tenderness. So it is true, then, that the wife (= Israel) has been sent away from the house of her husband (= the land of Israel), but never from His (= God´s) heart.

That is why the Haftarah text ends by the wonderful words: *"I will betroth you to Me forever; I will betroth you in righteousness and justice, in love and compassion. I will betroth you in faithfulness, and you will acknowledge the LORD" (2:19-20).* Can God´s love of His Jewish people be made clear more emphatically than by the metaphor of engagement and by these terms following each other so closely and showing His intentions? In righteousness and in justice and in love and in compassion and in faithfulness and forever!

Week 35

Judges 13: 2 – 25

The Parascha for the week (Numbers 4:21–7:89) includes among others the instructions for "...the Nazirite who vows his offering to the LORD in accordance with his separation..." (Num. 6:21). The Haftarah is about Samson who shall be a Nazirite, a separated one, according to God´s will announced by an angel.

1) **Promise of a son**

"A certain man of Zorah, named Manoah, from the clan of the Danites, had a wife who was sterile and remained childless. The angel of the LORD appeared to her and said, 'You are sterile and childless, but you are going to conceive and have a son" (v.2-3).
"The woman gave birth to a boy and named him Samson..." (v.24).

Repeatedly we read in the Scriptures that God has the birth of a son announced in a very special way. First of all of course we think of the birth of Jesus as announced to Mary by the angel Gabriel: "...Greetings, you who are highly favoured! The LORD is with you." Mary was greatly worried by his words and wondered what kind of greeting this might be. But the angel said to her, "Do not be afraid, Mary, you have found favour with God. You will be with child and give birth to a son, and you are to give him the name Jesus" (Luk. 1:28–31). He is the "Immanuel", as proclaimed in the days of Isaiah (Isa. 7:14).

The birth of John the Baptist was announced in a similarly extraordinary way. The priest Zechariah and his wife Elizabeth, were both well along in years and "...upright in the sight of God, observing all the LORD´s commandments and regulations blamelessly. But they had no children, because Elizabeth was barren..." (Luk. 1:6-7). Once when Zechariah serves as priest the angel Gabriel appears to him and says: "...Do not be afraid, Zechariah, your prayer has been heard. Your wife Elizabeth will bear you a son, and you are to give him the name John... He will be great in the sight of the LORD. He is never to take wine or other fermented drink, and he will be filled with the Holy Spirit even from birth" (Luk. 1:13–15).This message is so contrary to human reason that Zechariah doubts. As a result, Gabriel orders that he is to "...be silent and not able to speak until the day this happens, because you did not believe my words..." (Luk. 1:20).

In the Old Testament we read of Hagar, the Egyptian maid servant of Abraham´s wife. At the instigation of Sarai, Hagar was to bear a child to the 86 year old Abraham. "...When she knew she was pregnant, she began to despise her mistress" (Gen. 16:4). Hagar flees from the humiliation of Sarai. An angel says to her: "...I will so increase your descendants that they will be too numerous to count. The angel of the LORD also said to her, ´You are now with child and you will have a son. You shall name him Ishmael. for the LORD has heard of your misery. He will be a wild donkey of a man ... She gave this name to the LORD who spoke to her, ´You are the God who sees me" (Gen. 16:10–13). Notice that the text says "the LORD who spoke to her" –can it be that the angel is the LORD Himself?

As seen from this perspective, the report on the visit that Abraham receives near the trees of Mamre is interesting, when a son is promised to him and Sarai: "Abraham looked up and saw three men standing nearby. When he saw them, he hurried from the entrance of his tent to meet them and bowed low to the ground. He said, ῾If I have found favour in your eyes, my Lord..." (Gen. 18:2-3). "Where is your wife Sarah?, they asked him. ῾There in the tent´, he said. Then the LORD said, ῾I will surely return to you about this time next year, and Sarah your wife will have a son" (Gen. 18:9-10). Three men – my Lord – they – the LORD. The change in wording suggests that Abraham meets the LORD in His Trinity.

When we encounter an angel we may not always realize that it is, first and foremost, a messenger of God. So "...some people have entertained angels without knowing it" (Hebr. 13: 2). And in the report on the announcement of Samson´s birth we read of a similar uncertainty. It is true that Manoach´s wife – interestingly enough she is never mentioned by name – tells her husband *"A man of God came to me..." (v.6),* but even after Manoach also meets him, we read: *"...Manoach did not realize that is was the angel of the LORD" (v.16).* Therefore he asks the visitor his name. Even when he gets the answer *"Why do you ask my name? It is beyond understanding" (v.18)* the scales do not fall from his eyes. It is only when the angel ascends toward heaven in a flame and does not return that Manoach recognizes the divine appearance and exclaims with fear:*"We are doomed to die! We have seen God! But his wife answered, ῾If the LORD had meant to kill us, He would not have accepted a burnt offering and grain offering from our hands, nor shown us all these things or now told us this" (v.22- 23).* Obviously she is the spiritually more mature person. (Is that perhaps the reason why the angel appeared to her twice in absence of her husband?)

What is special in the story about the angel´s visit to Manoach´s wife is not just the announcement of the end of her infertility but the specific instructions regarding her son Samson. *"Now see to it that you drink no wine or other fermented drink and that you do not eat anything unclean, because you will conceive and give birth to a son. No razor may be used on his head, because the boy is to be a Nazirite, set apart to God from birth, and he will begin the deliverance of Israel from the hands of the Philistines" (v.4-5).* In the Parascha we read the instructions for someone who "...wants to make a special vow, a vow of separation to the LORD as a Nazirite" (Num. 6:2). He or she must abstain from wine and other fermented drink (as we know was also true of John the Baptist, Luk. 1:15) and "during the entire period of his vow of separation no razor may be used on his head..." (Num. 6:5). Therefore Hannah who implores the LORD for a child and receives Samuel according to a prophecy of Eli, the priest, commits herself before God: "...I will give him to the LORD for all the days of his life, and no razor will ever be used on his head" (1 Sam. 1:11). In our Haftarah text it is noteworthy that Manoach´s wife herself must abstain from alcoholic drinks while conceiving the son and bearing the baby. And it is also remarkable that the angel answers Manoach´s question "...what is to be the rule for the boy´s life and work?" (v.12) by ordering again that the mother must not drink any fermented drink nor to eat anything unclean. "...She must do everything I have commanded her" (v.14). Perhaps it is assumed that not only the rule concerning the razor but also the other instructions stated about Nazirites in Num. 6 are known.

2) Angels

In the above context we have already considered a number of things concerning the appearance of angels, but we want to pursue the topic a bit further.

Angels are "ministering spirits" (Hebr. 1:14) sent to fulfil the will of the LORD – though with some exceptions: the devil also has angels (Mt. 25:41), and Peter writes: "...God did not spare angels when they sinned, but sent them to hell putting them into gloomy dungeons to be held for judgment" (2 Pt. 2:4; see Jude 6).

The service of angels we are most familiar with is reflected in our language: ´In that situation I had a guardian angel´. (But do we really think of the angel as an envoy of God?) There are many biblical examples of protection by angels. For instance they shield Lot from violent men in Sodom (Gen. 19:10-11) and guard the people of Israel when crossing the Red Sea (Ex. 14:19). Wonderful promises of God apply to those who have entrusted their lives to the LORD: "For He will command His angels concerning you to guard you in all your ways" (Ps. 91:11).

Besides protection, angels also do service of rescuing and liberation. "The angel of the LORD encamps around those who fear Him, and he delivers them" (Ps. 34:7). When the apostles are arrested it is reported: "But during the night an angel of the LORD opened the doors of the jail and brought them out" (Acts 5:19). God shows His omnipotence miraculously through His angels: Peter, jailed by Herod, sleeps between two soldiers, bound with two chains and guarded by attendants, but an angel "...struck Peter on the side and woke him up. ´Quick, get up!´ he said, and the chains fell off Peter´s wrists. ... They passed the first and second guards and came to the iron gate leading to the city. It opened for them by itself..." (Acts 12:7–10). Nebuchadnezzar throws three Jewish men into the furnace and is shocked to discover: "...Look! I see four men walking around in the fire, unbound and unharmed, and the fourth looks like a son of the gods" (Dan. 3:25). Also in the end times, angels fight for the victory of the LORD of Lords: "And there was war in heaven. Michael and his angels fought against the dragon... The great dragon was hurled down – that ancient serpent called the devil or Satan, who leads the whole world astray. He was hurled to the earth, and his angels with him. Then I heard a loud voice in heaven say: 'Now have come the salvation and the power and the kingdom of our God, and the authority of His Christ..." (Rev. 12:7–10).

There are manifold examples of angels appearing in order to show the way or to appoint someone or to announce something important. Sometimes they appear in a dream as they did to Jacob (Gen. 28:12; Gen. 31:11), to Zechariah (1:8-9) and to Joseph (Mt. 1:20). Moses sees the angel "...in flames of fire from within a bush..." (Ex. 3:2). Zechariah receives an explanation concerning the meaning of his vision of the candlestick and the two olive trees is (Zech. 4:1–6). An angel shows Philip the way to Gaza where he is to meet an important official from Ethiopia (Acts 8:26). To Paul an angel appears during the shipwreck on the way to Rome and says: "...Do not be afraid, Paul. You must stand trial before Caesar; and God has graciously given you the lives of all who sail with you" (Acts 27:24). And from the Christmas narrative we are familiar with the words spoken to the shepherds: "But the angel said to them, 'Do not be afraid, I bring you good news of great joy that will be for all the people. Today in the town of David a Saviour has been born to you; He is Christ the LORD" (Luk. 2:10-11).
But we are probably less aware that Stephen says to the Sanhedrin that they "...have received the law that was put into effect through angels" (Acts 7:53). And the epistle to the Hebrews speaks of "...the message spoken by angels..." (Hebr. 2:2). In Revelation, Jesus speaks to us through an angel: "The revelation of Jesus Christ, which God gave Him to show His servants what might soon take place. He made it known by

sending His angel to His servant John" (Rev. 1:1).And in the last chapter of the Revelation (which mentions angels 67 times) Jesus Himself pronounces: "I, Jesus, have sent My angel to give you this testimony for the churches. I am the Root and the Offspring of David, and the bright Morning Star" (Rev. 22:16).

The task of angels on the one hand is to encourage (for instance Elijah, 1 Kings 19:5 and 2 Kings 1:15, or Gideon, Judges 6:12). On the other hand we read the moving story about the disobedient Balaam: "... and the angel of the LORD stood in the road to oppose him. Balaam was riding on his donkey ... When the donkey saw the angel of the LORD standing in the road with a drawn sword in his hand, she turned off the road ..." (Num. 22:22-23). When reading these words we are very likely to think of the report of the Fall of Man when God drove the man out of the paradise. "...He placed on the east side of the Garden of Eden cherubim and a flaming sword flashing back and forth to guard the way to the tree of life" (Gen. 3:24). We read about God's "destroying angels" (Ps. 78:49) and His angels of judgment (e.g. 1 Chr. 21:12; 2 Kings 19:35). "When the angel stretched out his hand to destroy Jerusalem, the LORD was grieved because of the calamity and said to the angel who was afflicting the people, 'Enough! Withdraw your hand!...' " (2 Sam. 24:16). In the parable of the weeds the LORD explains that "...the harvesters are angels" (Mt. 13:39). The hour of His judgment is announced by an angel (Rev. 14:6-7), and we read of seven angels with seven plagues (Rev. 15).

The LORD is in command of "...thousands upon thousands of angels in joyful assembly" (Hebr. 12:22). Yes, He is the God of hosts. In Gethsemane Jesus says when one of His disciples tries to prevent His capture: "Do you think I cannot call on My Father, and He will at once put at My disposal more than twelve legions of angels?" (Mt. 26:53).

We have considered many examples where single angels were sent to serve. In some cases (as mentioned above concerning Gen.16:7–13 and Gen. 18 for instance, but also in Ex. 3:2–6; Judges 2:1-2) the question remains: who actually is this angel? A messenger of God or the LORD Himself whose name is *"beyond understanding"* (in the wording of our Haftarah text)?

We should ask ourselves: Do we really reckon with angels today? And in our own lives? And if we meet one – will we recognize him as the messenger of God?

Week 36
Zechariah 2:10 – 4:7

The Torah section for this week (Numbers 8:1- 12:16) begins with instructions about the candlestick in the tabernacle, one of the most important symbols in Judaism. The supplementary text describes a night vision of Zechariah about a golden candlestick which is flanked by two olive trees.

1)   The candlestick

"...I see a solid gold lampstand with a bowl at the top and seven lights on it, with seven channels to the lights. Also there are two olive trees by it, one on the right and the other on its left" (4:2-3)
"I asked the angel who talked with me, 'What are these, my lord?' He answered, 'Do you not know what these are?'...This is the word of the LORD to Zerubbabel: 'Not by might nor by power, but by My Spirit', says the LORD Almighty" (4:4-6).

The candlestick with seven lamps, the Menorah, is very important in Judaism. That is why it was included in the coat of arms of the Jewish state. What is its special significance?

The design as prescribed for the tabernacle in Ex. 25:31-40 and Num. 8:1-4 provides some hints: The elaborate decorations of almond flowers and buds are symbols of growth and development. When it says "The buds and branches shall all be of one piece with the lampstand, hammered out of pure gold" (Ex. 25:36), that may point to the glory of the one God. Again and again oil had to be given to the Menorah (Lev. 24:1-4) so that the lamps could be kept burning continually. (Still today we see an "eternal light" – though an electric one – in the synagogues.) In this way the candlestick becomes a sign for spiritual enlightenment, a symbol for the Holy Spirit.

In Isaiah 11:2, where the shoot from the stump of Jesse is announced, the Holy Spirit is described as follows: "The Spirit of the LORD will rest on Him, the Spirit of wisdom and of understanding, the Spirit of counsel and of power, the Spirit of knowledge and of the fear of the LORD". When we look at the shape of the candlestick we discover a remarkable reference to the construction of the sentence quoted above: The three double branches correspond to the three pairs of terms. The shaft in the middle, from which three branches extend to the left and three branches to the right, points to the general expression "Spirit of the LORD". The number "seven" is symbol for perfection.

The priests were responsible for providing freshly-pressed clear kosher oil day by day. Oil, too, is a symbol of the Holy Spirit. The burning light of the lamp reminds of the exclamation: "Come, O house of Jacob, let us walk in the light of the LORD" (Isa. 2:5).
The eternal light stands for the eternal presence of the living God and that He does not change. "...I AM WHO I AM..." (Ex. 3:14). He "...does not change like shifting shadows" (James 1:17).

The candlestick demonstrates also that Israel can, and must, pray for and receive light from above. "For these commands are a lamp, this teaching is a light, and the corrections of discipline are the way to life" (Prov. 6:23). And this is absolutely true for us as well. The Menorah may remind us of our Redeemer who promises us: "...I am the light of the world.

Whoever follows Me will never walk in darkness, but will have the light of life" (John 8:12).

The Menorah also reminds us of Israel's mission to be a blessing to the world and of the promise that the future glory of Zion will be attractive to the whole world. "Arise, shine, for your light has come, and the glory of the LORD rises upon you... Nations will come to your light, and kings to the brightness of your dawn" (Isa. 60:1+3). And what does Jeshua say to His followers? "You are the light of the world..." (Mt. 5:14).

Zechariah sees in his vision the gold candlestick flanked by two olive trees. On the surface they point to the High Priest Joshua and the governor Zerubbabel who played an important part in bringing the Jews back from the Babylonian captivity and in the spiritual renewal of the people. But is it possible that the two olive trees stand also for Israel and the church? In Zech. 4:14 Zechariah gets the answer: "...These are the two who are anointed to serve the LORD of all the earth." (In Hebrew "the anointed" mean "the sons of oil"). In Revelation this metaphor is taken up again: "And I will give power to My two witnesses, and they will prophesy for 1260 days, clothed in sackcloth. These are the two olive trees and the two lampstands that stand before the LORD of the earth" (Rev. 11:3-4).

God gives Zechariah the vision of the candlestick and the two olive trees at a time when the people of Israel are depressed by exile and hostilities. Then a great encouragement comes from the word: *"...Not by might nor by power, but by My Spirit, says the LORD Almighty" (4:6).* Just as Israel will not be rescued from their enemies by an army no matter how strong it is nor by clever politics or firm alliances but by divine instruction and wisdom alone, so we, too, should allow the Holy Spirit to lead us, because "...the one who sows to please the Spirit, from the Spirit will reap eternal life" (Gal. 6:8).

When the LORD intervenes and we let Him act, then also we can say: *"What are you, O mighty mountain?..." (4: 7)*, because "the mountains melt like wax before the LORD..." (Ps. 97:5). What today may loom as a big obstacle causing us worries – the LORD says: "Every valley shall be raised up, every mountain and hill made low; the rough ground shall become level, the rugged places plain" (Isa. 40:4).

2)   The stone

"See, the stone I have set in front of Joshua! There are seven eyes on that one stone, and I will engrave an inscription on it´, says the LORD Almighty, ´and I will remove the sin of this land in a single day" (3:9).

This stone can only be the One we read of already in Gen. 49:24: "...the Shepherd, the Rock of Israel", the promised Immanuel (Isa. 7:14). *"...I am going to bring My servant, the Branch" (3:8)*. When reading carefully we recognize that Zech. 2:11 is also talking about Jeshua: "...I will live among you and you will know that the LORD Almighty (= the Father) has sent Me (= the Son) to you." He is the "stone of help", called "Ebenezer" in 1 Sam. 7:12, and yet "...for both houses of Israel He will be a stone that causes men to stumble and a rock that makes them fall..." (Isa. 8:14; see 1 Pt. 2:8). In Isaiah 28:16 God promises: "...See, I lay a stone in Zion, a tested stone, a precious cornerstone for a sure foundation..." Indeed, "The stone the builders rejected has become the capstone" (Ps. 118:22).

Paul makes it clear to us: You are "... built on the foundation of the apostles and prophets, with Jesus Christ Himself as the chief cornerstone" (Eph. 2:20). And Peter reminds us: "As you come to Him, the living Stone – rejected by men but chosen by God and precious to Him – you also, like living stones, are being built into a spiritual house to be a holy priesthood, offering spiritual sacrifices acceptable to God through Jesus Christ" (1 Pt. 2:4-5).

Week 37

Joshua 2:1 – 24

This section of the Torah (Numbers 13:1 – 15:41) reports that of the twelve spies sent by Moses, only Caleb and Joshua returned with the encouraging and right message: the land "flows with milk and honey". The others spread dreadful news, filling the people with fear. In the chapter of the Haftarah, Joshua now sends spies out, namely to Jericho in preparation for the crossing of the Jordan River.

1) **Blessing in spite of lying?**

"So the king of Jericho sent this message to 'Rahab: 'Bring out the men who came to you and entered your house, because they have come to spy out the whole land'. But the woman had taken the two men and hidden them. She said, 'Yes, the men came to me, but I did not know where they had come from. At dusk, when it was time to close the city gate, the men left. I don't know which way they went. Go after the men quickly. You may catch up with them'. (But she had taken them up to the roof and hidden them under the stalks of flax...") (v.3–6).

Rahab's report is clearly a lie. Can God then tolerate lies and bless a liar in such a remarkable way as we read in the following verses? After all, our God is "the truth" and does not tolerate darkness! The letter of John makes that plain as well: "…God is light; in Him there is no darkness at all. If we claim to have fellowship with Him yet walk in the darkness, we lie …" (1 John 1:5-6).

What about us? When we lie, isn't it true that it is usually because of one of the following conditions (not to say "reasons")? We don't want to admit failure. We want to steer clear of a difficulty or confrontation. We look for a way seeming easier to us. Always it is about ourselves. .

In the case of Rahab it is different (see Hebr. 11:31). And that may be the key to understanding: Rahab resorts to a ruse as she wants to protect the envoys of God's people. Is this not an eloquent example of God's wonderful promise: He will bless those who bless His people (see Gen. 12:3)?

Rahab did not deliberately set out to protect Jews. She was suddenly confronted with the need to provide accommodation for the spies. And there may well be situations today or tomorrow in our lives also where we have to decide spontaneously either to help or to reject. During the reign of the Nazis there were thousands of situations that involved agonizing decisions: to open or to close doors and hearts, to hide and rescue or to extradite. Let us think of the exemplary men and women who in spite of great danger to their own lives at the time of the persecution of the Jews provided Jewish fellow citizens with refuge or the possibility to escape. That was often possible only by dodging laws and regulations, as in the case of the Swede Raoul Wallenberg. Passports were forged, data manipulated and names changed in order to provide even the slightest chance for rescue. The "Avenue of the Righteous" in the memorial site "Yad Vashem" in Jerusalem bears eloquent witness to those rescue operations.

Rahab did not choose the situation; the spies suddenly knock at her door. But when we take the word of Jesus seriously "...Whatever you did for one of the least of these brothers of Mine, you did for Me (Mt: 25:40)," then we will strive to support God's first loved and eternally loved people of Israel. Then we will consider it our holy duty and privilege to do good to individual Jews or to the Jewish state somehow, to support relief organisations, to comfort His people (Isa. 40:1) or …?

2) Unmistakable for the Gentiles

Rahab said to the spies: *"…I know that the LORD has given this land to you and that a great fear of you has fallen on us, so that all who live in this country are melting in fear because of you. We have heard how the LORD dried up the water of the Red Sea for you when you came out of Egypt, and what you did to Sihon and Og, the two kings of the Amorites east of the Jordan, whom you completely destroyed. When we heard of it, our hearts melted and everyone's courage failed because of you, for the LORD your God is God in heaven above and on the earth below" (v.9–11).*

Rahab grew up in a different foreign cultural setting and probably without a religious background. But she has heard about the God of Israel. What specifically has she heard? That God gave the land to the Jews. That He gave them amazing success, which is why the citizens of the country got totally discouraged. That God did the great miracle at the Red Sea. And that the God of Israel is the God who rules over heaven and earth. (Oh, if only all Christians would have internalized all this, for example that we believe in the God of Israel and that it is He who gave the highly contested land to His people and even dedicated it to them by holy oath!)

Rahab knows that the citizens of Jericho are melting in fear because of the powerful actions of God. Similarly we read about the Egyptians in the days of the Pharaoh and of the exodus of the Israelites: "Egypt was glad when they left, because dread of Israel had fallen on them" (Ps. 105:38). And the LORD looked "...at the Egyptian army and threw it into confusion. He made the wheels of their chariots come off so that they had difficulty driving. And the Egyptians said, 'Let's get away from the Israelites! The LORD is fighting for them against Egypt" (Ex.14: 24-25).

When we read about Babylon's ruler of terror, Nebuchadnezzar, we learn something astonishing: When he sees how the three men in the furnace are saved totally unharmed, he calls out: "...Praise be to the God of Shadrach, Meshach and Abednego, who has sent His angel and rescued His servants! ... Therefore I decree that the people of any nation or language who say anything against the God of Shadrach, Meshach and Abednego be cut into pieces and their houses be turned into piles of rubble, for no other god can save in this way" (Dan. 3:28-29). This pagan Nebuchadnezzar recognizes that the God of Israel is also working through Daniel's exceptional interpretation of his dream. "It is my pleasure to tell you about the miraculous signs and wonders that the Most High God has performed for me. How great are His signs, how mighty His wonders! His kingdom is an eternal kingdom, His dominion endures from generation to generation" (Dan. 4:2-3). (It is shocking, however, that this realization and this confession escape the king's view and heart after twelve months. His pride drives the awe away (see Dan. 4:28 – 32).

That the nations might recognize the Almighty One as the one acting on behalf of Israel is brought to the LORD by Jews in their prayers again and again. David for instance prays in Ps. 67:1-2: "May God be gracious to u s and bless u s and make His face shine upon u s , that Your ways may be known on earth, Your salvation among a l l nations."[12]

---

[12] Words spaced out by W.B.

When the temple is consecrated, Solomon intercedes for the foreigners with the words: "...Do whatever the foreigner asks of You, so that all the peoples of the earth may know Your name and fear You, as do Your own people Israel..." (1 Kings 8:43). Hezekiah implores the LORD to rescue him from Sennacherib, king of Assyria, wishing expressly that this may be a testimony to the LORD: "Now, O LORD our God, deliver us from his hand, so that all kingdoms on earth may know that You alone, O LORD, are God" (2 Kings 19:19).

And this missionary concern, so to speak, is brought to the LORD again and again in the synagogues right to the present day -- using these words, for example: "May all inhabitants of the world recognize that You alone are God over all empires of the world"[13]

This is according to God's desire and action. He will act powerfully and mercifully for His beloved people of Israel and "...then the nations will know that I am the LORD, declares the Sovereign LORD, when I show Myself holy through you before their eyes" (Ezek. 36:23).

The God of Abraham, Isaac and Jacob will do it in His wonderful way. But when we belong to those for whom He has done great things, then we should also share it with others "...to the praise of His glorious grace..." (Eph. 1:6).

---

[13] Siddur Schma Kolenu, Basel/Zurich 1996, page 14

Week 38

1 Samuel 11:14 – 12:22

This week's Parascha and Haftarah have one subject in common: rebellion against God's guidance. Numbers 16:1 – 18:32 reports on the grumbling about the leadership of Moses und his brother Aaron. Korach and his followers and afterwards 14.700 Israelites are punished by death. In the Haftarah the prophet Samuel reminds the people that they were repeatedly guilty of desiring a king like the other nations.

1) Rebellion against leadership

"But when you saw that Nahash king of the Ammonites was moving against you, you said to me, 'No, we want a king to rule over us'- even though the LORD your God was your king" (12:12).
"Is it not wheat harvest now? I will call upon the LORD to send thunder and rain. And you will realize what an evil thing you did in the eyes of the LORD when you asked for a king" (12:17).

Several times we read in the Bible that the people of Israel rebel against their leaders. "Miriam and Aaron began to talk against Moses…Has the LORD spoken only through Moses?..." (Num. 12:1-2). In burning anger the LORD punishes Miriam through leprosy. What is the LORD angry about? That in her jealousy she dared speak against the man whom the LORD called "My servant" (Num. 12:8), the leader appointed by God.

In Num. 11:1 it says that the people "...complained about their hardships...". They grumble against their authorities, but actually they are grumbling against God's guidance. When the Israelites long to go back to the pots of meat in Egypt, Moses confronts them with the truth: "Who are we? You are not grumbling against us" (i.e. Moses and Aaron), "but against the LORD" (Ex. 16:8).

Absalom, the son of king David, undermines the authority of his father by coaxing those who look for legal decision: "...Look, your claims are valid and proper, but there is no representative of the king to hear you. And Absalom would add, 'If only I were appointed judge in the land!'...So he stole the hearts of the men of Israel" (2 Sam. 15:3-4, 6). As bad as it is that the son rises against his own father – the sin is above all a rebellion against the anointed one of God of whom the LORD says: "...I took you from the pasture and from following the flock to be ruler over My people Israel" (2 Sam. 7:8).

The God of Abraham, Isaac and Jacob is the LORD of Lords, the LORD of history. That is why Daniel stresses "...that the Most High is sovereign over the kingdoms of men and gives them to anyone He wishes" (Dan. 4:32). Yes, "Praise be to the name of God for ever and ever; wisdom and power are His. He changes times and seasons; He sets up kings and deposes them..." (Dan. 2:20-21).

Paul takes this up in his letter to the Romans and derives from it rules for our behaviour: "Everyone must submit himself to the governing authorities, for there is no authority except that which God has established. The authorities that exist have been established by God. Consequently, he who rebels against the authority is rebelling against what God has instituted, and those who do so will bring judgment on themselves" (Rom. 13:1-2). We know the instruction of Jesus: "...Give to Caesar what is Caesar's, and to God what is God's" (Mt. 22:21). Remember that Paul calls us "...to be subject to rulers and authorities, to be obedient..." (Titus 3: 1). And we read in the letter of Peter "Submit yourselves for the LORD´s sake to every authority instituted among men; whether to the king, as the supreme authority, or to governors, who are sent by him..." (1 Pt. 2:13-14).

The letter to the Ephesians provides us in more detail with an important standard as to how we should behave: "Slaves, obey your earthly masters with respect and fear, and with sincerity of heart, just as you would obey Christ. Obey them not only to win their favour when their eye is on you, but like slaves of Christ, doing the will of God from your heart" (Eph. 6:5-6).

We have seen that rebellion against human leadership is ultimately rebellion against the LORD who has appointed those leaders. Of course we may ask whether the human authority in a specific case is really appointed according to God's will. The God of Israel testifies to His people: "They set up kings without My consent; they choose princes without My approval..." (Hos. 8:4). This is true although Moses warned his people: "When ... you say, 'Let us set a king over us like all the nations around us`, be sure to appoint over you the king the LORD your God chooses..." (Deut. 17:14-15).

Let us come back to our Haftarah text! We read the past history in 1 Sam. 8: The judge Samuel appoints his two sons as judges. They however do not walk in the ways of God. Then the people urge Samuel to appoint a king. One might well think: After the bad experiences with Samuel's sons this wish is justified, even respectable. But it "displeased Samuel" and he speaks with God about it. "And the LORD told him, 'Listen to all that the people are saying to you; it is not you they have rejected, but they have rejected Me as their king" (1 Sam. 8:7; see also – after appointment of Saul – 1 Sam. 10:19). *"... even though the LORD your God was your king" (1 Sam. 12:12).*

If we put someone or something above the *LORD it is "an evil thing"* in the eyes of the LORD*" (12:17)*. He wants to be our king!

In Israel´s history there is a further aspect in the context of our subject: the desire to be like other nations. "…Now appoint a king to lead us, such as all the other nations have" (1 Sam. 8:5). The LORD warns His people explicitly not to say: "We want to be like the nations, like the peoples of the world, who serve wood and stone" (Ezek. 20:32) "…Do not learn the ways of the nations…" (Jer. 10:2). On the one hand, this warning is to protect the Israelites from the danger of following foreign gods (see Josh. 23:6-7; 2 Kings 17:8; Ezek. 11: 12; Ezek. 23:30). On the other hand, the desire to be like the other nations is to disregard being chosen by the Almighty God whose goal it is to be glorified. Israel is "…the one nation on earth that God went out to redeem as a people for Himself, and to make a name for Himself…" (2 Sam. 7:23).

Also we Christians, having experienced the mercy of being chosen, need to heed the warning "…that you must no longer live as the Gentiles do, in the futility of their thinking" (Eph. 4:17). "Do not conform any longer to the pattern of this world…" (Rom. 12:2)."Do you not know that your body is a temple of the Holy Spirit…?" (1 Cor. 6:19).

2) New chance

"If you fear the LORD and serve and obey Him and do not rebel against His commands, and if both you and the king who reigns over you follow the LORD your God – good!"(12:14).
"...You have done all this evil; yet do not turn away from the LORD, but serve the LORD with all your heart. Do not turn away after useless idols. They can do you no good, nor can they rescue you, because they are useless. For the sake of His great name the LORD will not reject His people, because the LORD was pleased to make you His own" (12:20–22).

"You have ... but ..."(12:20). How comforting and how precious it is to hear "it is true, but"! A new beginning is possible. "Because of the LORD´s great love we are not consumed, for His compassions never fail. They are new every morning; great is Your faithfulness" (Lam. 3:22-23). So Israel can hear: "...Return, faithless Israel, declares the LORD, I will frown on you no longer, for I am merciful, declares the LORD, I will not be angry forever. Only acknowledge your guilt..." (Jer. 3:12-13).

Israel realizes that it was wrong to request a king: *"...We have added to all our other sins the evil of asking for a king" (12:19).* They discover that there is a new chance for them if they as well as their king follow the Holy One of Israel. Because He will not abandon His people. What is the reason for that? It is for the sake of His name, as He says in Isaiah 48:9: "For My own name's sake I delay My wrath; for the sake of My praise I hold it back from you, so as not to cut you off."

We believe in this merciful God who reminds us that "if we confess our sins, He is faithful and just and will forgive us our sins and purify us from all unrighteousness" (1 John 1:9).

Unfortunately it can happen again and again that we become guilty. But we can again and again "…approach the throne of grace…" (Hebr. 4:16) with the confidence: "…There is now no condemnation for those who are in Christ Jesus" (Rom. 8:1).

Week 39

Judges 11:1 – 33

This section of the Torah, Numbers 19:1–22:1, reports among other things on Israel´s victory over King Og of Bashan and King Sihon of the Amorites. In the days of the Judges when Jeftah is chosen by the people to lead them, he has to tackle claims brought by the king of another people, the Ammonites, that refer to the war of those days. Jeftah fights against the Ammonites and in case of victory takes a grave vow.

1)   The accuser

The king of Ammon justifies his intentions to wage war with the following words: *"...When Israel came up out of Egypt, they took away my land from the Arnon to the Jabbok, all the way to the Jordan. Now give it back peacefully" (v.13).*

Jeftah has to make it clear (v.14–22) that the king's claim does not correspond to the historical facts, which we also read about in the section of the Torah: "Israel sent messengers to say to Sihon king of the Amorites: ´Let us pass through your country´...But Sihon would not let pass Israel cross his territory. He mustered his entire army and marched out into the desert against Israel. ...Israel, however, put him to the sword and took over his land from the Arnon to the Jabbok, but only as far as the Ammonites, because their border was fortified" (Num. 21:21–24). Deut. 2, too, refers to the same situation. There the LORD says to Israel: "Today you are to pass by the region of Moab at Ar. When you come to the Ammonites, do not harass them or provoke them to war, for I will not give you possession of any land belonging to the Ammonites..." (Deut.

2:18-19). In Deut. 2:37 we find the historical fact: "But in accordance with the command of the LORD our God, you did not encroach on any of the land of the Ammonites, neither along the course of the Jabbok nor that around the towns in the hills."

Let us take a brief look at the current situation of Israel, for which our Haftarah text is astonishingly relevant: a) The historical facts are turned upside down by the enemies, for instance the Jews had "occupied land of the Palestinians" b) It is the God of Abraham, Isaac and Jacob Himself who has enabled Israel to conquer Judea and Samaria and the Golan Heights during the Six Day War, areas they are now expected to give back. *"Now, since the LORD, the God of Israel, has driven the Amorites out before His people Israel, what right have you to take it over?" (v.23).* c) The world applies double standards. This is what also Jeftah has to confront with the Ammonites: *"Will you not take what your god Chemosh gives you? Likewise, whatever the LORD our God has given us, we will possess" (v.24).* d) Claims are suddenly made that have not been made previously, *e.g.*, the "Palestinians" needed a coherent, otherwise not viable land, although they lived in two separate areas without any protest until 1967 in the Gaza Strip (which was under Egyptian control) and the "West Jordan Land" (controlled by Jordan). Similarly Jeftah points out: *"For three hundred years Israel occupied Heshbon, Aroer, the surrounding settlements and all the towns along the Arnon. Why didn't you retake them during that time?" (v. 26).* e) Also in recent years Israel was repeatedly accused of aggression and incitement. As a matter of fact Israel was forced to fight defensive wars. Jeftah then points out: *"I have not wronged you, but you are doing me wrong by waging war against me..." (v. 27).*
That is how relevant the Bible is!

Behind all this distortion and twisting of the truth, behind the attacks against Israel, is – as we well know – God's enemy. "Satan rose up against Israel..." (1 Chron. 21:1). The LORD Jesus tells us: Satan "...is a liar and the father of lies" (John 8:44). This adversary of the Holy One intends to steal God's sown word from us (Mk. 4:15) and also the truth about the beloved people of God, because the LORD has linked the glory of His name to Israel. The devil wants to lull us in his awful way and "...masquerades as an angel of light" (2 Cor. 11:14). Therefore Paul's warning is so important: "Be self-controlled and alert! Your enemy the devil prowls around like a roaring lion looking for someone to devour. Resist him, standing firm in the faith..." (1 Pt. 5:8-9).

What gives us this steadfastness? First of all, that we realize, lay hold of, and confess before the visible and invisible world that "...The reason the Son of God appeared was to destroy the devil's work" (1 John 3:8). The accuser has been defeated! "Therefore, there is now no condemnation for those who are in Christ Jesus" (Rom. 8:1). Paul explains further what makes us steadfast: "Finally, be strong in the LORD and in His mighty power. Put on the full armour of God so that you can take your stand against the devil's schemes" (Eph. 6:10-11; see verses 14-17). Furthermore, we stand steadfast because of the certainty that our Redeemer Himself intercedes for us and gives us strength. "Simon, Simon, Satan has asked to sift you as wheat. But I have prayed for you, Simon, that your faith may not fail..." (Luke 22:31-32). What a privilege to know that the exalted LORD "...is at the right hand of God and is also interceding for us!" (Rom. 8:34). He is Immanu-El, "God with us".

2) The vow

"And Jeftah made a vow to the LORD: 'If you give the Ammonites into my hands, whatever comes out of the door of my house to meet me when I return in triumph from the Ammonites will be the LORD´s, and I will sacrifice it as a burnt offering" (v. 30-31).

In the Bible we find several reports about people who take an oath or commit themselves by swearing. On the one hand there are examples that swearing is a means of confirming a good intention before God. When Ezra wants to make sure that intermarriages in Israel are dissolved he put the people under oath (Ezra 10:5). When Nehemiah wants to make sure that the Jewish men understand that they should be free of debt, he summons them to take an oath (Neh. 5:12). David gives an oath to Saul to be merciful towards Saul's descendants (1 Sam. 24:22).

Sometimes a vow is connected with the occurrence of a specific event: "Then Israel made this vow to the LORD: 'If you will deliver these people into our hands, we will totally destroy their cities" (Num. 21: 2). Or we think of the vow of Hannah who was childless until then: "…O LORD Almighty, if You will only look upon Your servant's misery … and not forget Your servant but give her a son, then I will give him to the LORD for all the days of his life…" (1 Sam. 1:11).
Also the commitment to keep the commandments is documented by a vow: "…all … who are able to understand…bind themselves with a curse and an oath to follow the Law of God…" (Neh. 10:28-29). The description of the renewal of the covenant under the reign of King Asa shows that an oath can also be connected with great joy: "They took an oath to the LORD with loud acclamation, with shouting and

trumpets and horns. All Judah rejoiced about the oath because they had sworn it whole-heartedly. They sought God eagerly, and He was found by them..." (2 Chr. 15:14-15). But here we see also what grave consequences a violation can have: "All who would not seek the LORD, the God of Israel, were to be put to death" (v. 13). It is important to God that vows are fulfilled. In Ps. 50:14 it says: "Sacrifice thank offerings to God, fulfil your vows to the Most High."

How difficult it can sometimes be to act according to an oath is illustrated by the consequences of Israel´s fratricidal war against the tribe of Benjamin. The tribes of Israel swear not to marry their daughters to the men from Benjamin who came back from war. But on the other hand the tribe of Benjamin shall not be wiped out. Judges 21 tells about the great difficulties that are involved in fulfilling that oath.

In our Haftarah text we find a moving example of a careless vow. Jeftah commits himself – in case he were to defeat the enemy - to sacrifice the first person who approaches him at his door. He could not foresee that it will be his own daughter, but he keeps his word (v. 34+39). Similarly thoughtless is Saul's vow when he faces the hostile Philistines: "... Saul had bound the people under an oath, saying, ´Cursed be any man who eats food before evening comes, before I have avenged myself on my enemies..." (1 Sam. 14:24). His son Jonathan, however, does not hear that because he went off spying (which later on leads to the victory), and he eats some honey. Saul is determined to kill him. "But the men said to Saul, ´Should Jonathan die – he who has brought about this great deliverance in Israel? Never! ...So the men rescued Jonathan, and he was not put to death" (v. 45).

The LORD hates false oath (Zech. 8:17). "Cursed is the cheat who has an acceptable male in his flock and vows to give it, but then sacrifices a blemished animal to the LORD..." (Mal. 1:14).

And listen to what the LORD Jesus says: "Again, you have heard that it was said to the people long ago, ´Do not break your oath, but keep the oaths you have made to the LORD´. But I tell you, do not swear at all: either by heaven, for it is God's throne; or by the earth, for it is His footstool; or by Jerusalem, for it is the city of the Great King. And do not swear by your head, for you cannot make even one hair white of black. Simply let your ´Yes´ be ´Yes´, and your ´No´, ´No´; anything beyond this comes from the evil one" (Mt. 5:33–37; see also James 5:12). So Jesus not only opposes a false oath or an unfulfilled vow but shows us that by swearing we presume to assess and determine everything. We raise ourselves to the status of a god, so to speak. A firm Yes or No is adequate to us.

Week 40

Micah 5:6 – 6:8

The Haftarah and the section of the Torah (Numbers 19:1 – 25:9) are connected in content by the names of king Balak and of Balaam. Their story is written in the book of Moses and expressly taken up in Micah 6:5.

1) **Both?**

"The remnant of Jacob will be in the midst of many peoples like dew from the LORD, like showers on the grass, which do not wait for man or linger for mankind. The remnant of Jacob will be among the nations, in the midst of many peoples, like a lion among the beasts of the forest, like a young lion among flocks of sheep, which mauls and mangles as it goes, and no one can rescue. Your hand will be lifted up in triumph over your enemies, and all your foes will be destroyed" (5:7–9).

Israel like dew and yet like a lion! What a contrast! Is it really possible to imagine both together? We need to consult other passages of Scripture to determine whether these two promises that seem to be so incompatible can be confirmed: Israel like dew and like a lion.

To begin, we can note that two characteristics of dew are mentioned in the Bible. Dew can be used to refresh and revive, yet it remains just for a short time. So it says in Hos. 6:4: "…What can I do with you, Judah? Your love is like the morning mist, like the early dew that disappears." Because of their idolatry "…they will be like the morning mist, like the early dew that disappears, like chaff swirling from a threshing floor, like smoke escaping through a window" (Hos. 13:3). That makes it clear: Israel could never be like "dew among many peoples" with its pleasant impact by their own strength or own merits. But fortunately there is also this promise of the LORD: "I will be like the dew to Israel; he will blossom like a lily. Like a cedar of Lebanon he will send down his roots; his young shoots will grow. His splendour will be like an olive tree …" (Hos. 14:5-6).

In Israel one thanks for the dew at the end of the yearly rain period, i.e. beginning on Pessach, because the dried up land is moistened, refreshed and blessed again and again by the dew. Spiritual blessing is granted by God's word as given to Moses, who therefore exclaims: "Listen, O heavens, and I will speak; hear, O earth, the words of my mouth. Let my teaching fall like rain and my words descend like dew, like showers on new grass, like abundant rain on tender plants" (Deut. 32:1-2).

Certainly we have often experienced how God's word strengthened us and refreshed our weary soul. And we can hear the word of Jesus: "Whoever believes in Me, as the Scripture has said, streams of living water will flow from within him" (John 7:38). It is a precious task for us to pass on what we graciously received. As those who are blessed we can be a blessing. Scripture speaks about this concerning Israel also: "Now I will not deal with the remnant of this people as I did in the past, declares the LORD Almighty. The seed will grow well, the vine will yield its fruit, the ground will produce its crops, and the heavens will drop their dew. I will give all these things as an inheritance to the remnant of this people. As you have been an object of cursing among the nations, O Judah and Israel, so will I save you, and you will be a blessing…" (Zech. 8:11– 13). Israel will be a blessing – *"in the midst of many peoples like dew."*

But Scripture also says about the remnant of Israel that they are like a lion *"which mauls and mangles"*. We are reminded of the blessing Jacob says for his son Judah: "...Your hand will be on the neck of your enemies ... You are a lion's cub, O Judah..." (Gen. 49:8-9). Also Balaam – who according to the will of Balak, king of the Moabites, shall curse Israel but by God's guidance cannot but bless them – has in his mind's eye the metaphor of a lion: "The people rise like a lioness; they rouse themselves like a lion..." (Num. 23:24). And further: "...They devour hostile nations and break their bones in pieces; with their arrows they pierce them. Like a lion they crouch and lie down, like a lioness – who dares to rouse them? May those who bless you be blessed and those who curse you be cursed!" (Num. 24:8-9) The Holy One of Israel summons His people as a tool of judgment, as Zech. 9:13 tells us: "I will bend Judah as I bend My bow and fill it with Ephraim. I will rouse your sons, O Zion, against your sons, O Greece, and make you like a warrior's sword."

How is this picture of Israel compatible with the lovely-sounding message about refreshing dew? In both metaphors the point is that Israel shall be used for the goals of the God of Abraham, Isaac and Jacob! And that means in every case: the name of the Almighty God must be glorified!

In Micah 4:13 it says: "Rise and thresh, O Daughter of Zion, for I will give you horns of iron; I will give you hoofs of bronze and you will break to pieces many nations. You will devote their ill-gotten gains to the LORD, their wealth to the LORD of all the earth." What had been desecrated has to be given back to the living God. This is why the Israelites had to wage wars against the heathen and ban them. God leads His people in such a way that He glorifies Himself not only to them but also through them.

2) What is good

"My people, what have I done to you?" (6:3)
"With what shall I come before the LORD?"(6:6)
"He has showed you, O man, what is good. And what does the LORD require of you? To act justly and to love mercy and to walk humbly with your God." (6:8).

The *"case" (Mi 6:1)* between the LORD and the people can be summarized by these three sentences.
God reminds Israel of four of His innumerable blessings (Mi 6:4-5): What else should I have done so that you recognize My love and follow Me? And the people, obviously realizing their disobedience, ask how they can come before the Lord.. They seem to feel that neither burnt offerings or year-old calves nor thousands of rams or ten thousand rivers of oil are appropriate and even sacrificing one's firstborn would not be pleasing to Him.

As an answer to their question, God speaks. *"He has showed you, O man, what is good."* But had the instruction not given repeatedly and in detail to bring burnt offerings and sacrifices? Is this not valid any more? Hardly! The message is this: Without acting justly, without loving mercy, without walking humbly with our God even the biggest offerings are worthless. In Jer. 6: 19 f. we read: "They have not listened to My words and have rejected My law. What do I care about incense from Sheba or sweet calamus from a distant land? Your burnt offerings are not acceptable; your sacrifices do not please Me."

Offerings given in disobedience are rejected by the LORD. That does not exclude offerings following disobedience if we have in mind what Samuel imparts to Saul: "...Does the LORD delight in burnt offerings and sacrifices as much as in obeying the voice of the LORD? To obey is better than sacrifice, and to heed is better than the fat of rams" (1 Sam. 15:22).

So the verses of the Haftarah are not in opposition to the law. Consider also what Paul writes: "So then, the law is holy, and the commandment is holy, righteous and good" (Rom. 7: 12). And our LORD Jesus stresses: "Do not think that I have come to abolish the Law or the Prophets; I have not come to abolish them but to fulfil them" (Mt. 5: 17).

Indeed He showed us what it means *"to love mercy"* – He is in fact mercy and love personified. He not only came to *"act justly"* but He became for us "...our righteousness..." (1 Cor. 1:30). He could say of Himself: "...Learn from Me, for I am gentle and humble in heart..." (Mt. 11:29).

Of course the message about obedience and offerings and about "what is good" applies not only to the people of Israel but also to us today. "...Live as children of light, for the fruit of the light consists in all goodness, righteousness and truth" (Eph. 5:8-9). "...live a life worthy of the calling you have received. Be completely humble and gentle; be patient, bearing with one another in love" (Eph. 4:1-2). These are criteria that apply to "...offering spiritual sacrifices..." (1 Pt. 2:5). We are enabled to do so by the Author and Perfecter of our faith, if we learn *"to walk humbly w i t h our God"* – and that means walking at His side and keeping pace with Him.

Week 41

1 Kings 18:46 – 19:21

The inner connection between the Parascha (Numbers 25:10 – 30:1) and the Haftarah is the subject "zeal for the LORD". In a time when Israel was guilty of sexual immorality and idolatry and when Phinehas obtained atonement through his fearless action, the LORD says: "Phinehas ... has turned my anger away from the Israelites; for he was as zealous as I am for My honour among them..." (Num. 25: 11). In the book of the Kings we read how the Prophet Elijah competes in holy zeal against the priests of Baal on Mount Carmel – and what he has to overcome when Jezebel threatens to kill him.

1)   Finished

"Elijah was afraid and ran for his life ... he himself went a day´s journey into the desert. He came to a broom tree, sat down under it and prayed that he might die. ´I have had enough, LORD´, he said, ´Take my life; I am no better than my ancestors" (19:3-4).
"He replied, ´I have been very zealous for the LORD God Almighty... I am the only one left" (19:10).

Elijah asked for a great miracle for the sake of the Holy One of Israel and God has done so. Elijah has killed 450 idol-worshipping priests in holy wrath. And now he must fear for his life because Jezebel, the wicked wife of the wicked king Ahab, threatens to kill him. He flees and seeks seclusion in the desert. His mental strength is finished.

We read in the Bible about other men who also get to a point in their lives where they think they are no longer able to bear the burden of their spiritual mission. Think, for example, of Moses who is worn down by the ingratitude and incessant grumbling of the people. He comes to the LORD saying: "I cannot carry all these people by myself; the burden is too heavy for me. If this is how You are going to treat me, put me to death right now – if I have found favour in Your eyes..." (Num. 11:14 - 15). Jeremiah, who in his hard mission repeatedly has to announce God´s judgement, fights similar inner conflicts and vents his frustration with the question: "Why did I ever come out of the womb to see trouble and sorrow and to end my days in shame?" (Jer. 20: 18). And surely we are reminded of Job who reaches the limit of what is bearable in his suffering. He cries out: "Oh, that I might have my request, that God would grant what I hope for, that God would be willing to crush me, to let loose His hand and cut me off! Then I would still have this consolation ... that I had not denied the words of the Holy One" (Job 6:8–10).

Back to Elijah. He has been consumed with zeal for the living God. "...O LORD, God of Abraham, Isaac and Israel, let it be known today that You are God in Israel and that I am Your servant and have done all these things at Your command" (1 Kings 18:36). Time and time again we hear about pastors who serve the LORD in a highly motivated and intensive way and then go through a "time in the desert" caused by hostilities or inner conflicts. After striving to get things moving they could almost certainly relate to Elijah's statement: *"I am not better than my ancestors" (19:4)*. There are leaders in congregations who clearly profess the LORD as God of Israel and exert themselves for a lively relation with the people of Israel, but who because they lack support are inclined to share Elijah´s assessment: *"I am the only one left" (19:10)*. The psalmist also laments: "...I have become like a bird alone on a roof" (Ps. 102: 7).

From the report about Elijah we can also learn something about how God deals with various situations in Elijah´s life.

2) In pastoral care

"All at once an angel touched him and said, ´Get up and eat´. He looked around, and there by his head was a cake of bread baked over hot coals, and a jar of water. He ate and drank and then lay down again. The angel of the LORD came back a second time and touched him and said, ´Get up and eat, for the journey is too much for you" (19:5–7).
"The LORD said to him, ´Go back the way you came, and go to the Desert of Damascus... anoint Hazael king over Aram. Also anoint Jehu ... king over Israel and anoint Elisha ... to succeed you as prophet" (19:15-16.).
"Yet I reserve seven thousand in Israel..." (19:18).

The LORD responds to Elijah stepwise with sensitive pastoral care, beginning with an encouraging "get up!" We read a similar account in the book of Joshua when he fears that the enemies might defeat Israel: "... they will surround us and wipe out our name from the earth. What then will You do for Your own great name? The LORD said to Joshua, ´Stand up! What are you doing down on your face?" (Josh. 7:9-10).
But the words spoken to Elijah by the angel are not a brisk "cheer up, no problem!" Instead, they are combined with a gentle touch by order of the merciful God. And the mental encouragement is not the end. The LORD knows quite well that strengthening of the body is also important when we are mentally weak. He provides Elijah with bread and water in a wonderful way. After this first refreshment the angel returns and tells Elijah that he will have to walk a long way. Again

how sensitive that is! Elijah probably would not have been able to cope with this information without the first strengthening. He may instead have been overtaxed.

It is interesting that Elijah, strengthened for forty days and nights, goes specifically to the mountain of the LORD, Mt. Horeb, where Moses was appointed by the LORD to lead the people of Israel (Ex. 3). There God made the covenant with His people. Obviously Elijah is guided by God´s Spirit to visualize, so to speak, the origin of God´s history with Israel. While staying in the cave, Elijah hears the LORD speaking to him. *"What are you doing here, Elijah?"* (19:9). Doesn´t God know? Of course He does! But He probably wants to hear Elijah express his trouble personally once more. (We are reminded of Jesus asking the invalid who has been sick for 38 years: "…Do you want to get well?" (John 5:6) By the way, Elijah, obviously strengthened by the angel, no longer answers that he would prefer to die. It is only after he has expressed his inner condition that he gets the order: "…Go out and stand on the mountain in the presence of the LORD…" (19:11). Get out of the cave where you have withdrawn and wait for the work of God! Our loving Father wants that for us as well: we are not to withdraw into a snail shell or hide in self-pity but we are instead to come to Him with our fears, troubles and sorrows.

At first God tells Elijah only to "stand on the mountain in the presence of the LORD", without further details (and Elijah does not ask "why that?"). Then, as a heavy storm springs up, smashing even rocks, Elijah may well have thought: Now the LORD is going to speak to me. And indeed, sometimes the glory of the LORD appears accompanied by forces of nature, as was true for Ezekiel for instance: "I looked, and I saw a windstorm coming out of the north – an immense cloud with flashing lightning and surrounded by brilliant light. The centre of the fire looked like glowing metal …" (Ezek. 1:4). But

Elijah still has to wait for the voice of the LORD during the earthquake and fire that followed. Being an observant Jew he could have certainly expected the LORD to reveal Himself in the fire, as the Israelites had experienced on Mount Horeb – this very Horeb: "You came near and stood at the foot of the mountain
while it blazed with fire to the very heavens, with black clouds and deep darkness. Then the LORD spoke to you out of the fire..." (Deut. 4:11-12).

"And after the fire came a gentle whisper. When Elijah heard it, he pulled his cloak over his face ...Then a voice said to him..." (19:12-13). As with Elijah, it may often happen to us that our faithful Shepherd does not speak to us in mighty revolutionary ways (although He does great wonders again and again!), but by a verse from the Bible, by advice from a believer, by setting the course nearly unnoticed at first, by a gentle voice, or by the gentle voice of our conscience. "...Not by might nor by power, but by My Spirit, says the LORD Almighty" (Zech. 4:6).

It is amazing that now Elijah is asked once more what he is doing there in the cave. Only after laying out his situation to the LORD again does he get the order to return – namely by the same way that he had come. And the pastoral guidance by the LORD consists not only of getting new appointments – the anointing of two kings- but also of being relieved by the nomination of his successor Elisha whom he shall anoint. To know that he is useful but to be relieved of responsibilities occur close together here.

Only at the very end when Elijah is sustained, he is shown by God that he is not at all *"the only one left"*. *"Yet I have left Me seven thousand in Israel" (19:18; King James Version).*

Human leaders would certainly have recognized the false claim and eliminated it immediately.
What does the LORD Jesus say? "…learn from Me, for I am gentle…" (Mt. 11:29).

Week 42 a[14]

Jeremiah 1:1 – 2:3

In the Parascha (Numbers 30:1 – 32:42) we read about the assignment of Moses concerning the enemies as well as his own people. The appointment of Jeremiah is the focus of the Haftarah.

1) Individual assignment

Jeremiah gets the message from the LORD: *"...I appointed you as a prophet to the nations" (1: 5)*. An immense appointment!

Do only those persons get a special assignment whom the Bible specifically points out – men like Moses, Joshua, David or Paul, for example? There is at least one call all believers have in common: We are "...called into fellowship with His son Jesus Christ our LORD..." (1 Cor. 1:9). This implies a goal which we all share in common: to be transformed into the likeness of Jesus. "Your attitude should be the same as that of Christ Jesus" (Phil. 2:5). This should be discernible to those around us: "So then, men ought to regard us as servants of Christ and as those entrusted with the secret things of God" (1 Cor. 4:1). "...Live as children of light!" (Eph. 5: 8).
But our individual appointments are very different in detail: "...Each one should retain the place in life that the LORD assigned to him and to which God has called him..." (1 Cor.

---

[14] The Parascha section is called „Mattot". When it is combined with the next section "Massei", the text from Jer. 2:4-28 (week "42 b") is read as Haftarah.

7:17). "There are different kinds of service, but the same LORD..." (1 Cor. 12:5; see 1 Cor.12: 28-30).

For each of us, our appointment was determined from the very beginning: *"Before I formed you in the womb I knew you, before you were born I set you apart ..." (1:5).* So Paul writes also: "For those God foreknew He also predestined to be conformed to the likeness of His Son ... And those He predestined, He also called ..." (Rom. 8:29-30). To the Thessalonians Paul writes: "... from beginning God chose you to be saved through the sanctifying work of the Spirit and through belief in the truth. He called you to this through our gospel, that you might share in the glory of our LORD Jesus Christ" (2 Thess. 2:13-14).

2) Inconvenient and difficult and pleasant things

"See, today I appoint you over nations and kingdoms to uproot and tear down, to destroy and overthrow, to build and to plant" (1:10; see v.13–17).

We would like it the easy way; we prefer to choose services that make others happy and contented – or that make ourselves look good ... But what is the call of Jesus to His disciples? "I am sending you out like sheep among wolves..." (Mt. 10:16). And Paul's instruction to Timothy is similar: "...Be prepared in season and out of season; correct, rebuke and encourage- with great patience and careful instruction" (2 Tim. 4:2).
"Go and proclaim in the hearing of Jerusalem: I remember the devotion of your youth, how as a bride you loved Me ..." (2:2).

Again and again we need to hear this gentle reminder from the LORD. Have we "forsaken our first love"? "Remember the height from which you have fallen! Repent and do the things you did at first..." (Rev. 2:5).

3) Getting encouraged, endowed and protected

"Do not be afraid of them, for I am with you and will rescue you, declares the LORD. Then the LORD reached out His hand and touched my mouth and said to me, 'Now, I have put My words in your mouth" (1: 8-9).
"Today I have made you a fortified city, an iron pillar and a bronze wall ... They will fight against you but will not overcome you..." (1:18-19).

"...Do not be afraid; keep on speaking, do not be silent. For I am with you, and no one is going to attack you and harm you..." (Acts 18:9). This *"do not be afraid"*, spoken by the LORD to Paul, certainly applies to us as well when we are on the way on behalf of God.

The LORD is with us (Immanu-El is His name!). That gives us strength and protection. But something else can also encourage us: "Not that we are competent in ourselves to claim anything for ourselves, but our competence comes from God" (2 Cor. 3:5). Our Creator has already prepared in us what we shall serve for: "For we are God´s workmanship, created in Christ Jesus to do good works, which God prepared in advance for us to do" (Eph. 2:10).
We are also equipped to overcome challenges, difficulties and conflicts: "For though we live in the world, we do not wage war as the world does. The weapons we fight with are not weapons of the world. On the contrary, they have divine power to demolish strongholds" (2 Cor. 10:3-4).

4) His word comes true

"The word of the LORD came to me: 'What do you see, Jeremiah?´ 'I see the branch of an almond tree´, I replied. The

LORD said to me, 'You have seen correctly, for I am watching to see that My word is fulfilled" (1:11-12).
(In Hebrew "shaked" = branch of almond tree; "shoked" is the verbal form of "to watch over")

Just as Jeremiah receives God's promise that He keeps His word, so we too can be certain: "For no matter how many promises God has made, they are 'Yes` in Christ. And so through Him the 'Amen' ..." (2 Cor. 1:20). And notice the words with which John begins his message to the church of Laodicea: "...These are the words of the Amen, the faithful and true witness, the ruler of God's creation" (Rev. 3:14).
Again and again we come across the statement in the New Testament "This is a trustworthy saying" (*e.g.,* 1 Tim. 1:15, 3:1 and 4:9; 2 Tim. 2:11; Titus 3:8). "The word became flesh and made His dwelling among us..." (John 1:14).
Praise the LORD!

Week 42 b[15]

Jeremiah 2: 4 - 28

This is one of three "Haftarot of Rebuke" read before the anniversary of the destruction of Jerusalem. (The section of the Torah for this week is Numbers 33:1 – 36:13).

1)   No exception from judgment

"This is what the LORD says: What fault did your fathers find in Me, that they strayed so far from Me? They followed worthless idols and became worthless themselves" (v. 5).
"The priests did not ask, 'Where is the LORD?' Those who deal with the law did not know Me, the leaders rebelled against Me. The prophets prophesied by Baal, following worthless idols" (v. 8).
"...And I will bring charges against your children's children" (v. 9).
"Your wickedness will punish you, your backsliding will rebuke you..." (v. 19).

There is no exception from judgment, neither for the spiritual nor for the political leaders. The ancestors as well as the grandchildren are addressed. "...There is no difference, for all have sinned and fall short of the glory of God", unless they are justified by grace (Rom. 3:22-23). The letter to the Romans shows us that death entered through sin "...and in this way death came to all men, because all sinned" (Rom. 5:12).

---

[15] The Parascha is called „Massei" in Hebrew. In some years it is read together with "Mattot" (see week "42 a").

"Your wickedness will punish you." We cannot escape by pointing our finger at others. "You then, why do you judge your brother? Or why do you look down on your brother? For we will all stand before God´s judgment seat" (Rom. 14:10). Indeed "nothing in all creation is hidden from God´s sight. Everything is uncovered and laid bare before the eyes of Him to whom we must give account" (Hebr. 4:13).

2) Ingratitude as reason for grave transgressions

"They did not ask, 'Where is the LORD, who brought us up out of Egypt and led us through the barren wilderness, through a land of deserts and rifts, a land of drought and darkness, a land where no one travels and no one lives?' I brought you in a fertile land to eat its fruit and rich produce..." (v. 6-7).

How often did it happen to us, too, that the LORD saved us from abyss, led us through periods of darkness, showed us a path in vast desert and provided us with goods in a wonderful way! What about our thankfulness in those cases? We should be "always giving thanks to God the Father for everything, in the name of our LORD Jesus Christ" (Eph. 5:20). "Give thanks in all circumstances, for this is God´s will for you in Christ Jesus" (1 Thess. 5:18).

If we neglect or forget giving thanks it may easily happen that we begin to falter and thereby go astray. "So then ... continue to live in Him, rooted and built up in Him, strengthened in the faith as you were taught, and overflowing with thankfulness" (Col. 2:6-7).

3) Everything or nothing

"...They followed worthless idols and became worthless themselves" (v.5).

"Has a nation ever changed its gods? (Yet they are not gods at all.) But My people have exchanged their Glory for worthless idols" (v.11).
"My people have committed two sins: They have forsaken Me, the spring of living water, and have dug their own cisterns, broken cisterns that cannot hold water" (v. 13) (see v. 26–28).

Israel´s conduct should make us prick up our ears; we, too, need to be admonished that we "...must no longer live as the Gentiles do, in the futility of their thinking. They are darkened in their understanding and separated from the life of God because of the ignorance that is in them due to the hardening of their hearts" (Eph. 4:17-18). When our "...mind is on earthly things" (Phil. 3:19), we easily "...follow deceiving spirits and things taught by demons" (1 Tim. 4:1) and choose our teachers according to what our "...itching ears want to hear" (2 Tim. 4:3). Therefore Paul writes to the Galatians: "I am astonished that you are so quickly deserting the One who called you by the grace of Christ and are turning to a different gospel – which is really no gospel at all" (Gal. 1:6-7).

The consequences are made clear to us in an especially alarming way by the letter to the Hebrews: "Anyone who rejected the law of Moses died without mercy on the testimony of two or three witnesses. How much more severely do you think a man deserves to be punished who has trampled the Son of God under foot, who has treated as an unholy thing the blood of the covenant that sanctified him and who has insulted the Spirit of grace?" (Hebr. 10: 28-29).

Instead of "...walking after vanity" (Jer. 2:5; King James Version), we are offered "all things": "He who did not spare His own Son, but gave Him up for us all – how will He not also, along with Him, graciously give us all things?" (Rom.

8:32). In fact, "…all things are yours … and you are of Christ, and Christ is of God" (1 Cor. 3:21-23).

So it is good for us to come "…to Him who is able to do immeasurably more than all we ask or imagine…" (Eph. 3:20). Our LORD Jesus is the spring of living water, as Jeremiah puts it – "…welling up to eternal life" (John 4:14).

4) Good or bad witness

"…But you came and defiled My land and made My inheritance detestable" (v. 7).
"I had planted you like a choice vine of sound and reliable stock. How then did you turn against Me into corrupt, wild vine?" (v. 21)

Our Creator made us in His image. "His divine power has given us everything we need for life and godliness…" (2 Pt. 1:3), so we can confess with the Psalmist: "I praise You because I am fearfully and wonderfully made; Your works are wonderful, I know that full well" (Ps. 139:14).

As believers we can marvel to hear God's promise to us: "But you are a chosen people, a royal priesthood, a holy nation, a people belonging to God, that you may declare the praises of Him who called you out of darkness into His wonderful light" (1 Pt. 2:9). But there is this vocation "that you may…"! We should be "…a letter from Christ…" (2 Cor. 3:3), we should (as it is written especially concerning overseers and deacons) "…have a good reputation with outsiders…", so that we "…will not fall into disgrace and into the devil´s trap" (1 Tim. 3:7). More often than we may think we are quietly watched by non-Christians. Therefore we should "…live good lives among the pagans … for it is God´s will that by doing good you should silence the ignorant talk of foolish men" (1 Pt. 2:12 + 15).

5) Acknowledgment of guilt

"Have you not brought this on yourselves by forsaking the LORD your God when He led you in the way?" (v.17)
"...Consider then and realize how evil and bitter it is for you when you forsake the LORD your God and have no awe of Me, declares the LORD, the LORD Almighty" (v.19).
"How can you say, 'I am not defiled; I have not run after the Baals'?..." (v. 23)

Are we not inclined to shift the blame to others or to play down our own guilt? Or do we not refuse to recognize our failure as a sin? "But if we judged ourselves, we would not come under judgment" (1 Cor. 11:31). The Holy Spirit wants to reveal to us where we failed. It is good to pray as in Psalm 139:23-24: "Search me, O God, and know my heart; test me and know my anxious thoughts. See if there is any offensive way in me, and lead me in the way everlasting."

James 1:26 reveals a specific danger of deceiving ourselves: "If anyone considers himself religious and yet does not keep a tight rein on his tongue, he deceives himself and his religion is worthless." "If we claim to be without sin, we deceive ourselves and the truth is not in us. If we confess our sins, He is faithful and just and will forgive us our sins and purify us from all unrighteousness" (1 John 1:8-9).

Week 43
Isaiah 1: 1–27

Just as this week's passage from Deut. 1:1 – 3:22 precedes the memorial day of the destruction of Jerusalem, so this third "Haftarah of Rebuke" reminds us of decline and unfaithfulness of Israel, which are the reasons for the destruction.

1)   Run away

"Hear, O heavens! Listen, O earth! For the LORD has spoken: 'I reared children and brought them up, but they have rebelled against Me. The ox knows his master, the donkey his owner's manger, but Israel does not know, My people do not understand.' Ah, sinful nation, a people loaded with guilt, a brood of evildoers, children given to corruption! They have forsaken the LORD; they have spurned the Holy One of Israel and turned their backs on Him" (v. 2 –4). (see v. 21–23)

God's word does not conceal or play down the transgression of men but names it very precisely. We don't want to behave like those pointing at Israel with their fingers and feeling justified in their accusation of the Jews by such texts. No, we want to humbly investigate where we, too, "turned our backs on Him", and we want to be aware anew that we depend totally on the grace of God.

Concerning the subject of "running away", think of the parable of the Lost Son (Luk. 15) who sought his fortune far from the loving father and who ended up with pigs. After all that we have received by God's love, it should be hard to understand why we would turn our backs to Him: "Formerly, when you did not know God, you were slaves to those who by nature are not gods. But now that you know God – or rather are known by God – how is it that you are turning back to those weak and miserable principles? Do you wish to be enslaved by them all over again?" (Gal. 4:8-9). Paul shows us the consequences with remarkable clarity: "...Since they did not think it worthwhile to retain the knowledge of God, He gave them over to a depraved mind, to do what ought not to be done" (Rom: 1:28). The letter to the Hebrews warns us similarly: "See to it, brothers, that none of you has a sinful, unbelieving heart that turns away from the living God. But encourage one another daily, as long as it is called Today ..." (Hebr. 3: 12).

2) Spared

"The Daughter of Zion is left like a shelter in a vineyard, like a hut in a field of melons, like a city under siege. Unless the LORD Almighty had left us some survivors, we would have become like Sodom, we would have been like Gomorrah" (v. 8-9).

It is true that the God of Abraham, Isaac and Jacob has led His eternally chosen people of Israel through extremely hard times, in which they were in danger of being exterminated, but they live nonetheless: "I ask then: Did God reject His people? By no means! ... So at the present time there is a remnant chosen by grace" (Rom. 11:1+5).
Now what about the Gentiles? "...Small is the gate and narrow the road that leads to life, and only a few find it" (Mt. 7:14). "... many be called, but few chosen" (Mt. 20:16; King James Version). What a privilege to belong to them!

Even when the godless world around us seems to be crushing us, our LORD calls to us: "Do not be afraid, little flock, for your Father has been pleased to give you the kingdom" (Luke 12:32).

3) Laid bare

"The multitude of your sacrifices –what are they to Me?, says the LORD... When you come to appear before Me, who has asked this of you, this trampling of My courts? Stop bringing meaningless offerings! Your incense is detestable to Me. New Moons, Sabbaths and convocations – I cannot bear your evil assemblies. .. When you spread out your hands in prayer, I will hide My eyes from you; even if you offer many prayers, I will not listen. Your hands are full of blood" (v. 11–15).

We cannot impose anything upon our Creator. "For we must all appear before the judgment seat of Christ, that each one may receive what is due him for the things done while in the body, whether good or bad" (2 Cor. 5:10). The number of church services attended by us is not crucial. Our heart - that is the point. "Therefore I urge you, brothers, in view of God´s mercy, to offer your bodies as living sacrifices, holy and pleasing to God – this is your spiritual act of worship" (Rom. 12:1). And according to James, a "pure and faultless" service is "... to keep oneself from being polluted by the world" (James 1:27). Sin and solemn assembly cannot stand together before the LORD. Our donations given with stained hands or impure hearts do not bear fruit. "For no one can lay any foundation other than the one already laid, which is Jesus Christ. If any man builds on this foundation using gold, silver, costly stones, wood, hay or straw, his work will be shown for what it is, because the Day will bring it to light. It will be revealed with

fire, and the fire will test the quality of each man's work" (1 Cor. 3:11-13).
God knows our hearts (Acts 15:8), as is clear from God's admonition as written by Isaiah: *"Wash and make yourselves clean. Take your evil deeds out of My sight! Stop doing wrong, learn to do right!..." (v.16-17).*

4) Restored

"Come now, let us reason together, says the LORD, though your sins are like scarlet, they shall be as white as snow; though they are red as crimson, they shall be like wool. If you are willing and obedient, you will eat the best from the land" (v.18-19).
"I will restore your judges as in days of old, your counsellors as at the beginning. Afterward you will be called the City of Righteousness, the Faithful City. Zion will be redeemed with justice, her penitent ones with righteousness" (v.26-27).

What wonderful promises! "If we confess our sins, He is faithful and just and will forgive us our sins and purify us from all unrighteousness" (1 John 1:9). "...The reason the Son of God appeared was to destroy the devil's work" (1 John 3:8).

We cannot but be amazed at how the LORD intercedes for His Zion, which is subject to so much hostility and temptation right to the present moment, and how He makes her the City of Righteousness, to be seen by all. But with regard to our own situation we also know that "God made Him who had no sin to be sin for us, so that in Him we might become the righteousness of God" (2 Cor. 5:21).

Week 44

Isaiah 40: 1–26

While the chapters of Deut. 3:23 – 7:11 focus on the Ten Commandments and the "Shma Jisrael", the prophetic section is the first in a number of "Haftorot of Comfort" following the day of mourning, "Thisha b´Av".

1)   Our relation to God´s people of Israel

"Comfort, comfort My people, says your God. Speak tenderly to Jerusalem..." (v. 1-2)

Comfort is what the Jewish people urgently need again and again after all they have gone through and in all the dangers and hostilities after the foundation of the State and to date. Jerusalem *"...has received from the LORD´s hand double for all her sins" (v.2).* David already had to state in lamentation: *"...I looked for sympathy, but there was none, for comforters, but I found none"* (Ps. 69: 20). The warning to us today is all the more important.

It says in our text regarding the people who have been chosen by our LORD for ever and ever: *"...In the desert prepare the way for the LORD..." (v. 3).* That may also be intended to contribute to the healing of Jewish souls from the incessant wounds by Christians. What we are instructed to do in general, namely to *"...encourage the timid..."* (1 Thess. 5:14), above all concerns the Jewish people as they are so near to the heart of the Holy One of Israel. They are so near to Him that He judges us and the nations according to our relation to Israel. In His end time speech Jesus expresses this in the following way:

"When the Son of Man comes in His glory, and all the angels with Him, He will sit on His throne in heavenly glory. All the nations will be gathered before Him, and He will separate the people one from another as a shepherd separates the sheep from the goats" (Mt. 25:31-32). And in the sequel of this speech the King of the Jews explains: "…Whatever you did to one of the least of these brothers of Mine, you did for Me" (Mt. 25:40). This separation becomes clear in a downright alarming way when God speaks to Zion: "The nation or kingdom that will not serve you will perish; it will be utterly ruined" (Isa. 60:12).

2) Contrasts

The chapter of the Haftarah contains a number of comparisons -- contrasts, really -- that should make us prick up our ears:

a) raised up – made low

"Every valley shall be raised up, every mountain and hill made low; the rough ground shall become level, the rugged places a plain" (v.4).

These words can be interpreted geographically concerning the land of Israel but also spiritually. Think, for example, of what Jesus said: "Whoever exalts himself will be humbled, and whoever humbles himself will be exalted" (Mt. 23:12). This is said by the One about whom we read: "…He humbled Himself and became obedient to death - even death on a cross! Therefore God exalted Him to the highest place and gave Him the name that is above every name …" (Phil 2:8-9).
To us the call in Peter´s letter applies: "Humble yourselves… under God´s mighty hand, that He may lift you up in due time" (1 Pt. 5:6).

b) transient – eternal

"...All men are like grass, and all their glory is like the flowers of the field. The grass withers and the flowers fall, because the breath of the LORD blows on them. Surely the people are grass. The grass withers and the flowers fall, but the word of our God stands forever" (v.6–8).

We need to be reminded of our transience in order to be prepared for Jesus Christ coming back. "Teach us to number our days aright, that we may gain a heart of wisdom" (Ps. 90 :12). "... the rich man will fade away even while he goes about his business. Blessed is the man who perseveres under trial, because when he has stood the test, he will receive the crown of life that God has promised to those who love Him" (James 1:11-12).

But we should also keep in mind that things will not just go on in the same way forever in the world, "...for this world in its present form is passing away" (1 Cor. 7:31). God has a goal, and that has to do with massive changes (see below). But one fact endures: "...In the beginning, O LORD, You laid the foundations of the earth, and the heavens are the work of Your hands. They will perish, but You remain..." (Hebr. 1:10-11). And Jesus says: "Heaven and earth will pass away, but My words will never pass away" (Mt. 24:35). The importance of this eternal word to us as believers is explained by Peter like this: "You have been born again, not of perishable seed, but of imperishable, through the living and enduring word of God" (1 Pt. 1:23).
"The word became flesh..." in our LORD Jesus (John 1:14), who is "...the truth which lives in us and will be with us forever" (2 John 2).

c) almighty – as nothing

"Who has measured the waters in the hollow of his hand, or with the breadth of his hand marked off the heavens? Who has held the dust of the earth in a basket, or weighed the mountains on the scales and the hills in a balance? Who has understood the mind of the LORD, or instructed Him as His counselor?" (v.12-13)
To whom, then, will you compare God? What image will you compare Him to?" (v.18)
"He sits enthroned above the circle of the earth, and its people are like grasshoppers..." (v.22).

The Creator of all life and of the universe spoke and everything came into being! "You are worthy, our LORD and God, to receive glory and honour and power, for You created all things, and by Your will they were created and have their being" (Rev. 4:11). And from the letter to the Colossians we learn about the significance of our LORD Jesus concerning the creation: "He is the image of the invisible God, the firstborn over all creation. For by Him all things were created: things in heaven and on earth, visible and invisible, whether thrones or powers or rulers or authorities; all things were created by Him and for Him. He is before all things, and in Him all things hold together" (Col. 1:15-17).

In the presence of this mighty authority everything else must fade in importance. And so we read: *"Surely the nations are like a drop in a bucket; they are regarded as dust on the scales; He weighs the islands as though they were fine dust ... Before Him all the nations are as nothing; they are regarded by Him as worthless and less than nothing" (v.15+17).*

3) God´s deeds concerning Israel

"You who bring good tidings to Zion, go up on a high mountain. You who bring good tidings to Jerusalem, lift up your voice with a shout, lift it up, do not be afraid; say to the towns of Judah, ´Here is your God!´ See, the Sovereign LORD comes with power, and His arm rules for Him..." (v.9-10).

As we read these verses, we think of our LORD Jesus coming back in great glory and might – in Zion, on the Mount of Olives, in fact (Acts. 1:11). How beautifully is it said in Psalm 50:2: "From Zion, perfect in beauty, God shines forth." "Look, He is coming with the clouds, and every eye will see Him, even those who pierced Him; and all the peoples of the earth will mourn because of Him. So shall it be, amen! ´I am the Alpha and the Omega´, says the LORD God, ´who is and who was, and who is to come, the Almighty" (Rev. 1:7-8). It is from Jerusalem that the returning LORD will exercise His reign.

The coming of the LORD will be accompanied by huge changes in the topography around Jerusalem: *"Every valley shall be raised up, every mountain and hill made low; the rough ground shall become level, the rugged places a plain. And the glory of the LORD will be revealed, and all mankind together will see it..."* (v. 4-5). In Zech.14:4 we read: "... and the Mountain of Olives will be split in two from east to west, forming a great valley, with half of the mountain moving north and half moving south."

Concerning His people God acts in an inconceivable way: "...The deliverer will come from Zion; He will turn godlessness away from Jacob. And this is My covenant with them when I take away their sins" (Rom. 11:26-27). Therefore we read in our text in Isaiah: *"... proclaim to her that her hard service has been completed, that her sin has been paid for..." (v.2).* For to no other nation does God announce something as grand as He announces to Israel: "In those days, at that time, declares the LORD, search will be made for Israel´s guilt, but there will be none, and for the sins of Judah, but none will be found, for I will forgive the remnant I spare" (Jer. 50:20).

Week 45

Isaiah 49:14 - 51:3

The Parascha (Deut. 7:12 – 11:25) calls upon Israel to be thankful, reminds her of the great deeds of God and orders new obedience: "Circumcise your hearts ... and do not be stiff-necked any longer" (Deut. 10:16). The Haftarah serves above all as encouragement and comfort.

1) The right perspective

Two temptations and doubts that are well known to us are found in this text: That the LORD would not see our situation or that He would not be able to help us.
"Zion said, 'The LORD has forsaken me, the LORD has forgotten me'" (49:14).
"...Was My arm too short to ransom you? Do I lack the strength to rescue you?..." (50:2).
It all depends on the way we look at it! What does the text tell us?

a) Remember God´s promises

"Can a mother forget the baby at her breast and have no compassion on the child she has borne? Though she may forget, I will not forget you! See, I have engraved you on the palms of My hands; your walls are ever before Me (49:15-16).
"...Those who hope in Me will not be disappointed" (49:23).
"...Let him who walks in the dark, who has no light, trust in the name of the LORD and rely on his God" (50:10).

The letter to the Hebrews warns us: "Do not throw away your confidence; it will be richly rewarded" (Hebr. 10:35). And Paul adds, "And hope does not disappoint us..." (Rom. 5: 5). We know about the wonderful promise of the LORD: "I have come into the world as a light, so that no one who believes in Me should stay in darkness" (John 12:46). Protection, help and salvation are closely connected with the LORD´s name. Therefore the church in Pergamum is especially commended: "...you remain true to My name. You did not renounce your faith in Me..." (Rev. 2:13). "And everyone who calls on the name of the LORD will be saved" (Acts 2:21). "In Him our hearts rejoice, for we trust in His holy name" (Ps. 33:21).

Just as Zion received the wonderful promise to be sealed, so to speak, by the fact that the God of Abraham, Isaac and Jacob has engraved her on the palms of His hands, so we also have the privilege of hearing: "...God´s solid foundation stands firm, sealed with this inscription: The LORD knows those who are His..." (2 Tim. 2:19).

b) Inquiry about our transgressions

"...Because of your sins you were sold; because of your transgressions your mother was sent away" (50:1).

We must not be "grumblers and faultfinders" (Jude 16) but are instead to follow the call: "Examine yourselves to see whether you are in the faith; test yourselves. Do you not realize that Christ Jesus is in you – unless, of course, you fail the test?" (2 Cor. 13:5).

c) To look at our spiritual sources

"...Look to the rock from which you were cut and to the quarry from which you were hewn; look to Abraham, your father, and

to Sarah, who gave you birth. When I called him he was but one, and I blessed him and made him many" (51:1-2).

As believers we are rooted in the faith of our Jewish fathers: "Understand then, that those who believe are children of Abraham" (Gal. 3:7). "If you belong to Christ, then you are Abraham´s seed, and heirs according to the promise" (Gal. 3:29).

The letter to the Hebrews tells us to "...fix our eyes on Jesus, the author and perfecter of our faith..." (Hebr. 12:2). When reading the word *"rock"* we are reminded of what David confesses: "...You are my rock and my fortress..." (Ps. 31:3) and that Jesus is The Rock. So Paul writes about the wandering people of Israel: "...They drank from the spiritual rock that accompanied them, and that rock was Christ" (1 Cor. 10:4).

2) Amazing changes

We shall be astonished together with Israel how God changes the situation of His people and land so enormously that all of mankind will one day recognize it as His deed. And we can draw several parallels to our own lives.

a) Rescue from enmity

"...those who laid you waste depart from you" (49:17).
"...I will contend with those who contend with you ...Then all mankind will know that I, the LORD, am your Saviour, your Redeemer, the Mighty One of Jacob" (49:25-26).

The Almighty God says to Israel: "Though you search for your enemies, you will not find them. Those who wage war against you will be as nothing at all" (Isa.41:12). At the end of times the Jews will finally not be hated and disgraced any more by the nations: "...He will remove the disgrace of His people from all the earth. The LORD has spoken" (Isa. 25:8).

To the congregation the LORD says: "...In this world you will have trouble. But take heart! I have overcome the world" (John 16:33). Indeed, "Who shall separate us from the love of Christ? Shall trouble or hardship or persecution or famine or nakedness or danger or sword?" (Rom. 8:35).

b) Flourishing and new life

"The LORD will surely comfort Zion and will look with compassion on all her ruins; He will make her deserts like Eden, her wastelands like the garden of the LORD. Joy and gladness will be found in her, thanksgiving and the sound of singing" (51:3).

Even as late as the nineteenth century the land of Israel was described by visitors as hopeless and desolate. Nowadays we can but be amazed by the extensive forests and the blossoming desert. And what about ourselves? Can we also testify that our lives were made new after we deliberately turned to our Saviour Jesus Christ? Can we confess with David: "He lifted me out of the slimy pit, out of the mud and mire ... He put a new song in my mouth, a hymn of praise to our God..." (Ps. 40:2-3)? Don´t we also have reason to exclaim as did Paul: "Praise be to the God and Father of our LORD Jesus Christ, the Father of compassion and the God of all comfort, who comforts us in all our troubles..." (2 Cor. 1:3-4)?

c) Gathering in the land

"Your sons hasten back ... Lift up your eyes and look around, all your sons gather and come to you ... Now you will be too small for your people ... The children born during your bereavement will yet say in your hearing, 'This place is too small for us, give us more space to live in.' Then you will say in your heart, 'Who bore me these?...'" (49:17–21)
"...See, I will beckon to the Gentiles, I will lift up My banner to the peoples; they will bring your sons in their arms and carry your daughters on their shoulders" (49:22).

We have the privilege of living in a time where this gathering in the Promised Land of Israel is happening before our eyes. Since the foundation of the State in 1948 millions of Jews have returned to Israel. And people from other nations have helped them financially or physically.

3) The Redeemer

"The Sovereign LORD has opened my ears, and I have not been rebellious; I have not drawn back. I offered my back to those who beat me, my cheeks to those who pulled out my beard; I did not hide my face from mocking and spitting" (50:5-6).

This verse clearly talks about Jeshua, the Redeemer. John the Baptist says of Him: "The One who comes from heaven is above all. He testifies to what He has seen and heard..." (John 3:31-32). And He himself points out repeatedly how He speaks and acts in complete obedience towards the Heavenly Father: "...He who sent Me is reliable, and what I have heard from Him I tell the world" (John 8:26). "By Myself I can do nothing..." (John 5:30).

We read about the "source of eternal salvation" that "...He learned obedience from what He suffered" (Hebr. 5:8). As was predicted by Isaiah, He endured being beaten, whipped, spit on and mocked. He "...became obedient to death, even death on the cross. Therefore God exalted Him to the highest place and gave Him the name that is above every name, that at the name of Jesus every knee should bow..." (Phil .2:8-10).

So let us bow at the name of our Savior Jesus Christ!

Week 46[16]

Isaiah 54:11 – 55:5

The Haftarah includes not only wonderful promises to God´s people but also the earnest call, "Listen to Me!" In the Parascha (Deut. 11:26 – 16:17) Moses sets before Israel a blessing and a curse, and warns: "See that you do all I command you..." (Deut. 12:32).

1) Established

"O afflicted city, lashed by storms and not comforted, I will build you with stones of turquoise, your foundations with sapphires. I will make your battlements of rubies, your gates of sparkling jewels, and all your walls of precious stones. All your sons will be taught by the LORD, and great will be your children´s peace. In righteousness you will be established. Tyranny will be far from you, you will have nothing to fear..." (54:11-14).
"No weapon forged against you will prevail..." (54:17).

What promises the Almighty God makes to His people and land, which was lashed by storms through thousands of years! Lasting foundations, refinement by most precious stones, heavenly teachings, fearlessness, protection, peace, righteousness – these are presents for Israel.

We are reminded of this description of Jerusalem from the New Testament: "The foundations of the city walls were decorated

---

[16] See exegesis concerning Isaiah 54:1 – 55:5 (week 2)

with every kind of precious stone ... The twelve gates were twelve pearls..." (Rev. 21:19-21).
The LORD gives teachings from heaven to His people of Israel. God had already spoken to Moses: "...I will teach you what to do" (Ex. 4:15). And because they repeatedly did not follow the instructions, He promises a new covenant to Israel: "...I will put My law in their minds and write it in their hearts..." (Jer. 31:33).
When we read that the LORD´s Anointed One was sent "...to preach good news to the poor ... They will be called oaks of righteousness..." (Isa. 61:1-3), then we must again get clear in our minds that this mission is first of all in favour of Israel.

What parallel can be drawn for believers from the nations?
Our LORD wants us to be established and firm also. "He will keep you strong to the end, so that you will be blameless on the day of our LORD Jesus Christ" (1 Cor. 1: 8). This is our hope. "We have this hope as an anchor for the soul, firm and secure. It enters the inner sanctuary behind the curtain, where Jesus, who went before us, has entered on our behalf..."(Hebr. 6:19-20).
Israel hears: *"In righteousness you will be established"*. What about us? We can be sure that we "...are justified freely by His grace through the redemption that came by Christ Jesus" (Rom. 3:24). "God made Him who had no sin to be sin for us, so that in Him we might become the righteousness of God" (2 Cor. 5:21).
And what about the weapons forged against us? We have also been promised, that we can win the struggle – our spiritual struggle – if we are properly equipped: "Pull on the full armour of God so that you can take your stand against the devil´s schemes" (Eph. 6:11).

2) Invited

"Come, all you who are thirsty, come to the waters; and you who have no money, come, buy and eat! Come, buy wine and milk without money and without cost. Why spend money on what is not bread, and your labour on what does not satisfy? Listen, listen to Me, and eat what is good, and your soul will delight in the richest of fare. Give ear and come to Me; hear Me, that your soul may live!..." (55:1–3).

We are also invited by the words of Jesus: "Come to Me, all you who are weary and burdened, and I will give you rest" (Mt. 11:28). "The Spirit and the bride say, ′Come!′ And let him who hears say, ′Come!′ Whoever is thirsty, let him come; and whoever wishes, let him take the free gift of the water of life" (Rev. 22:17).

Hearing the sincere invitation is the first important step: Blessed "...are those who hear the word of God and obey it" (Luke 11:28). To "obey" in this context really means to eat and drink. "...I am the bread of life. He who comes to Me will never go hungry, and he who believes in Me will never be thirsty" (John 6:35).

We are invited to the table of the LORD: "... ′Take and eat; this is My body′. Then He took the cup, gave thanks and offered it to them, saying: ′Drink from it, all of you. This is My blood of the covenant, which I poured out for many for the forgiveness of sins" (Mt. 26:26-28).

3) Inviting

"...I will make an everlasting covenant with you, My faithful love promised to David. See, I have made him a witness to the

peoples, a leader and commander of the peoples. Surely you will summon nations you know not, and nations that do not know you will hasten to you, because of the LORD your God, the Holy One of Israel, for He has endowed you with splendour" (55:3-5).

The whole world will see the glorious change in Israel and will be to a certain extent drawn to it. "And many peoples and powerful nations will come to Jerusalem to seek the LORD Almighty and to entreat Him. This is what the LORD Almighty says, 'In those days ten men from all languages and nations will take firm hold of one Jew by the hem of his robe and say, 'Let us go with you, because we have heard that God is with you" (Zech. 8:22-23)

As Israel will be attractive at global level, those following Jesus should be a reflection of their Saviour by their nature and behaviour. "...Let your light shine before men, that they may see your good deeds and praise your Father in heaven" (Mt. 5:16). Paul admonishes Titus: "In everything set ... an example by doing what is good..." (Titus 2:7).
May we make David´s prayer our own: "May those who hope in You not be disgraced because of me, O LORD, the LORD Almighty; may those who seek You not be put to shame because of me, O God of Israel" (Ps. 69:6).

Week 47

Isaiah 51:12 – 52:12

In this week's passage (Deut. 16:18 – 21:9) Israel is admonished not to bend the law, to abolish the evil, not to follow the detestable idols of the nations, not to fear the enemies, but to trust in the LORD and to listen to the Prophets who have been promised to them. Several of these warnings are taken up in the supplementary text. But first of all this fourth "Haftarah of comfort" is a wonderful encouragement: The LORD will comfort His people, He will rescue Jerusalem, and Israel as well as the nations will recognize Him as Sovereign and Saviour.

1) Who are you?

"...Who are you that you fear mortal men, the sons of men, who are but grass, that you forget the LORD your Maker, who stretched out the heavens and laid the foundations of the earth, that you live in constant terror every day because of the wrath of the oppressor...?" (51:12-13)

Don´t we feel sometimes the same way? We fear the power or behaviour of men and do not think of ourselves as being in His care as children of God. Jesus also has to criticize the disciples when they are in a boat on the stormy sea: "...You of little faith, why are you so afraid?..." (Mt. 8:26). He admonishes us: "Do not be afraid of those who kill the body but cannot kill the soul. Rather, be afraid of the One who can destroy both soul and body in hell" (Mt. 10:28). We need to be on guard against forgetting that "...You did not receive a spirit that makes you a

slave again to fear, but you received the Spirit of sonship. And by him we cry, ´Abba, Father" (Rom. 8:15).
In our section from Isaiah the statements of God are like an answer to the question "who are you?" : *"I am the LORD your God ... I have put My words in your mouth ...You are My people" (51:15-16).*

2)   Awake!

"Awake, awake! Rise up, O Jerusalem, you who have drunk from the hand of the LORD the cup of His wrath, you who have drained to its dregs the goblet that makes men stagger" (51:17).
"Awake. awake, O Zion, clothe yourself with strength. Put on your garments of splendour, O Jerusalem, the holy city..." (52:1).
"Burst into songs of joy together, you ruins of Jerusalem..." (52:9).

It is as if the LORD shouts to His people: ´Do not look at the situation as it was! Go on!´ Yet He does not play down the distress Israel was in: *"...ruin and destruction, famine and sword..." (51:19).* In all that happened to them they did not even experience compassion. But He can promise something to His people that is promised to no other people: He not only averts His wrath from Israel; He even casts the wrath upon the nations that harmed the Jews: *"...See, I have taken out of your hand the cup that made you stagger (King James Version: "the cup of trembling"); from that cup, the goblet of My wrath, you will never drink again. I will put it into the hands of your tormentors, who said to you, ´Fall prostrate that we may walk over you´..."* (51:22-23).

The expression "cup of trembling" leads us to Zechariah: "Behold, I will make Jerusalem a cup of trembling unto all the people round about ... In that day shall the LORD defend the inhabitants of Jerusalem ...And it shall come to pass in that day, that I will seek to destroy all the nations that come against Jerusalem" (Zech. 12:2+8+9; King James Version). That is why Jerusalem can put on her garments of splendour. *"...The uncircumcised and defiled will not enter you again" (52:1).*

"Listen! Your watchmen lift up their voices; together they shout for joy. When the LORD returns to Zion, they will see it with their own eyes" (52:8). Through Isaiah we are ordered to "rejoice with Jerusalem and be glad for her; rejoice greatly with her, all you who mourn over her" (Isa. 66:10). Do we love Jerusalem, the city that our LORD chose as His dwelling place forever? Are we vigilant as watchmen concerning Israel´s development? Do we realize how the Holy One of Israel is fulfilling His promises to Israel today -- by the foundation of the State, by the reunification of Jerusalem, by the process of return, for instance? Do we glorify Him for that and rejoice?

The call "awake!" is also important for our own life. There's a German song that says "Let us look upwards and go forward firmly. We go at the hand of our Master, and our LORD goes with us". In our lives we may have encountered trouble and failure and we may possibly have to bear the consequences of our sins, but "...No one who puts his hand to the plough and looks back is fit for service in the kingdom of God" (Luke 9:62). "...Be patient and stand firm, because the LORD´s coming is near" (James 5:8).

3) Free yourself!

"Shake off your dust!... Free yourself from the chains of your neck... Depart, depart, go out from there! Touch no unclean thing! Come out from it and be pure..." (52:2+11).

In our lives as well the way has to be prepared through separation, change of direction and release, so that one can say: *"...Your God reigns!" (52:7).*
"It is for freedom that Christ has set us free. Stand firm, then, and do not let yourselves be burdened again by a yoke of slavery" (Gal. 5:1). "...Let us purify ourselves from everything that contaminates body and spirit, perfecting holiness out of reverence for God" (2 Cor. 7:1).

4) It is I

Our text begins with God´s words: *"I, even I, am He who comforts you..." (51:12).* There is no change in His loving care. He introduced Himself as "...I am who I am..." (Ex. 3:14).

God is omnipresent, that is what we believe. Nevertheless, it is crucial to be certain in real-life situations: He is here, too. "Who will bring any charge against those whom God has chosen? It is God who justifies. Who is he that condemns? Christ Jesus, who died - more than that, who was raised to life – is at the right hand of God and is also interceding for us" (Rom. 8:33-34). But at all times there was and there still is the danger of pursuing false, supposed gods. "For false Christs and false prophets will appear and perform great signs and miracles..." (Mt. 24:24). That is why our text in Isaiah stresses: "...All day long My name is constantly blasphemed. Therefore

My people will know My name, therefore in that day they will know that it is I who foretold it. Yes, it is I" (52:5-6).

Week 48[17]

Isaiah 54:1 - 10

Deut. 21:10 – 25:19 is the reading from the Torah. There we find a multitude of instructions concerning a charitable and pure life. The text from the prophet Isaiah speaks of the great and never-ending mercy of God (see "Week 2"), which may be the reason it was chosen as the fifth "Haftarah of Comfort". In view of such a merciful LORD we are also encouraged to stretch out to "get more".

"Enlarge the place of your tent, stretch your tent curtains wide, do not hold back.; lengthen your cords, strengthen your stakes. For you will spread out to the right and to the left; your descendants will dispossess nations and settle in their desolate cities" (v. 2-3).

1) Expansion

The modern State of Israel has often been accused of cherishing expansionistic plans of a "Great Israel". (As a matter of fact Israel has withdrawn from specific regions several times, as from Sinai and from the Gaza strip.) But here we are reading about God´s own plans.

We learn something most astonishing from the Song of Moses in Deut. 32:8-9: "When the Most High gave the nations their inheritance, when He divided all mankind, he set up boundaries for the peoples according to the number of the sons of Israel. For the LORD´s portion is His people, Jacob His allotted

---
[17] See exegesis concerning „week 2"

inheritance". What geo-political significance is assigned to Israel by the LORD, whose is the whole world!

In the Bible we encounter no other people on earth besides the Chosen Jewish People, whose boundaries God has specifically determined. It is true that the first promise of land, given to Abram, is still more general: "Lift up your eyes from where you are and look north and south, east and west. All the land that you see I will give to you and your offspring forever" (Gen. 13:14-17). But then it says: "...To your descendants I give this land, from the river of Egypt to the great river, the Euphrates..." (Gen. 15:18). And in Numbers 34:1–12 and in Ezekiel 47:13– 20 the boundaries are named very precisely.

According to the will of God the people of Israel first conquered the southern part of Canaan and later the northern part under the leadership of Joshua. And "when Joshua was old and well advanced in years, the LORD said to him, ´You are very old, and there are still very large areas of land to be taken over" (Josh. 13:1). *"Enlarge the place of your tent!"*

In view of the current area of Israel, we can only be amazed at how far towards the north Israel will extend one day. Of course it is not a matter of space only, but of Israel´s miraculous repatriation into the Promised Land. "...The days are coming, declares the LORD, when men will no longer say, ´As surely as the LORD lives, who brought the Israelites up out of Egypt´, but they will say, ´As surely as the LORD lives, who brought the Israelites up out of the land of the north and out of all the countries where He had banished them´. For I will restore them to the land I gave their forefathers" (Jer. 16:14-15).

2) Spacious place

"Enlarge the place" – do these words in the figurative sense excite us, too? To begin with, let us listen to David´s song of praise: "I will be glad and rejoice in Your love, for You saw my affliction and knew the anguish of my soul. You have not handed me over to the enemy but have set my feet in a spacious place" (Ps. 31:7-8). The LORD knows our distress and oppressions. He does not want to leave us in narrowness and anxiety. On the contrary, we are called "…into the glorious freedom of the children of God" (Rom. 8:21).

When we don´t see a way out, when we are sad about our limitations, then we can know: "…With my God I can scale a wall" (Ps. 18:29). But to take up the metaphor, we really have to scale! Listen to another verse of the Psalms: "…Open wide your mouth, and I will fill it", says the LORD (Ps. 81:10). Here again it is all about the aspect of "wide, large". "…In Christ all the fullness of the Deity lives in bodily form" (Col. 2:9). Do we allow Him to give us from His fullness? Are we really open to what and how He wants to give us? It is our loving Father "…who is able to do immeasurably more than all we ask or imagine…" (Eph. 3:20).

As we are so abundantly blessed, the LORD wants us to also share our blessings. "And God is able to make all grace abound to you, so that in all things at all times, having all that you need, you will abound in every good work" (2 Cor. 9:8). In the spiritual sphere we are allowed to long for "more". And we shall stretch out for more. "Not that I have obtained all this, or have already been made perfect, but I press on …" (Phil 3:12).

Week 49

Isaiah 60:1 - 22

In the weekly section (Deut. 26:1 – 29:8) we read about the promise of the LORD to set Israel "...in praise, fame and honour high above all the nations..." (26:19). The Haftarah is simply and solely a reason for rejoicing over the future glory of Israel.

1)   Israel in glory

"Arise, shine, for your light has come, and the glory of the LORD rises upon you. See, darkness covers the earth and thick darkness is over the peoples, but the LORD rises upon you and His glory appears over you" (v.1-2).
"...And I will adorn My glorious temple" (v.7).
"...And I will glorify the place of My feet" (v.13).
"The sun will no more be your light by day, nor will the brightness of the moon shine on you, for the LORD will be your everlasting light, and your God will be your glory" (v.19).
"Then will all your people be righteous and they will possess the land forever. They are the shoot I have planted, the work of My hands, for the display of My splendour" (v.21).

How often in the twenty-two verses of chapter 60 the word "glory" is found! And what a contrast to the darkness of the nations! Do we remember the situation in Egypt at the times of the ten plagues? "No one could see anyone else or leave his place for three days. Yet all the Israelites had light in the places where they lived" (Ex. 10:23). God puts Israel above all nations of the world. The LORD says: "...I will grant salvation to Zion, My splendour to Israel" (Isa. 46:13).

The eternal God wants to glorify Himself through Israel. That is why He rises over Israel, so powerfully in fact that they receive Him as their eternal light and splendour although they often run away from Him like the other peoples do. It is amazing that in the end all of His people we be declared righteous and saved, and not only a few – or even many – will confess Him as Savior: "You are my lamp, O LORD, the LORD turns my darkness into light" (2 Sam. 22:29). Or: "The LORD is my light and my salvation – whom shall I fear?..." (Ps. 27:1). About future times it says: *"Then will all your people be righteous"*.

What is the place that the LORD will glorify by placing his feet there? Let us think of the temple! David intended "...to build a house as a place of rest for the ark of the covenant of the LORD, for the footstool of our God..." (1 Chr. 28:2). And Ezekiel has the vision of a future temple: "...I looked and saw the glory of the LORD filling the temple of the LORD..." (Ezek. 44:4). In fact Haggai put it this way: "The glory of this present house will be greater than the glory of the former house..." (Haggai 2: 9). May we assume that this "place of His feet" and the "Place of His sanctuary" is also Israel in a wider sense? We read after all: "...The LORD has chosen Zion, He has desired it for His dwelling" (Ps. 132:13). And often we read the expression "house of Israel" in the Scriptures (e.g. Isa. 5:7 and Jer. 33:17).

Let us go a step further: The God of Abraham, Isaac and Jacob puts Israel above the nations for His sake, yet He proclaims: "I will display My glory among the nations..." (Ezek. 39:21). So with a thankful spirit, we realize that we, too, having lived in darkness for a long time, are included in the words spoken in connection with the appearance of the Messiah: "The people walking in darkness have seen a great light; on those living in the land of the shadow of death a light has dawned" (Isa. 9:2). We can stretch out to the one who says of Himself: "...I am the light of the world. Whoever follows Me will never walk in darkness, but will have the light of life" (John 8:12). In this context we can hear His message with astonishment and at the same time as obligation: "You are the light of the world..." (Mt. 5:14).

2) The reaction of the nations

a) They will be attracted by the light of Israel

"Nations will come to your light, and kings to the brightness of your dawn" (v.3).

Nowadays, at a time when Israel is pressed from all sides and is often considered to be the "bogey man" for many undesirable developments in the world, at a time when in Israel corruption and other shortcomings can be found, and when- sadly enough – the Jews are often labelled as "not believing" we can only be amazed when we hear promises such as these spoken to Zion: "The nations will see your righteousness, and all kings your glory..." (Isa. 62:2).
"And many peoples and powerful nations will come to Jerusalem to seek the LORD Almighty and to entreat Him" (Zech. 8:22).
Israel will fulfil an important mission, so to speak: "...In those days ten men from all languages and nations will take firm hold of one Jew by the hem of his robe and say, 'Let us go with you, because we have heard that God is with you" (Zech. 8:23).

b) They bring wealth into the country

"...The wealth on the seas will be brought to you, to you the riches of the nations will come" (v.5)
"Your gates will always stand open, they will never be shut, day or night, so that men may bring you the wealth of the nations..." (v.11).

It was through Moses that the LORD gave the message to His people: "...You will lend to many nations but will borrow from none. The LORD will make you the head, not the tail. If you pay attention to the commands of the LORD your God that I give you this day and carefully follow them, you will always be at the top, never at the bottom" (Deut. 28:12-13). Today we recognize how the world is enriched by Jewish inventions of a surprising variety and how Israel is the world´s leading nation in several fields. But with regard to the end of times it says: "...You will feed on the wealth of nations, and in their riches you will boast" (Isa. 61:6). "I will shake all nations, and the desired of all nations will come, and I will fill this house with glory, says the LORD Almighty" (Haggai 2:7).

c) They help to build up

"Foreigners will rebuild your walls, and their kings will serve you. Though in anger I struck you, in favour I will show you compassion" (v.10).

Foreigners from the nations will serve the people chosen by God. "Aliens will shepherd your flocks, foreigners will work your fields and vineyards" (Isa. 61:5). "Those who are far away will come and help to build the temple of the LORD..." (Zech. 6:15).

May we apply this to those coming to Israel for the sake of Jeshua´s name in order to help in a practical way, to encourage and to comfort the Jews? " The nobles of the nations assemble as the people of the God of Abraham" (Ps. 47:9). David says to the LORD in a psalm: "...Thou hast made me the head of the heathen: a people whom I have not known shall serve me" (Ps. 18:43; King James Version).

d) They will bow before Israel

"The sons of your oppressors will come bowing before you; all who despise you will bow down at your feet and will call you The City of the LORD, Zion of the Holy One of Israel" (v.14).
"Although you have been forsaken and hated, with no one travelling through, I will make you the everlasting pride and the joy of all generations" (v.15).

For thousands of years the situation was like that of which the sons of Korach sang: "You have made us a reproach to our neighbours, the scorn and derision of those around us. You have made us a byword among the nations; the people shake their heads at us" (Ps. 44:13-14). We need but listen to and read the media in these days as proof of that. Whether it be the scorn and threats of an Iranian president, or the abusive language and terror of Hisbullah and Hamas against Israel, or politicians dissociating themselves from Israel and pressuring them to make specific political decisions or Christians across the denominations shaking their heads about the faith and behaviour of the Jews and the situation in Israel – it is still the same as expressed in the psalm.

And then this change! "...He will remove the disgrace of His people from all the earth. The LORD has spoken" (Isa. 25:8).Israel will be rehabilitated among the nations, so to speak. No boycotts, no threats, no condemnation any longer, but shame will turn into admiring appreciation.

Indeed we can only be amazed at the LORD´s promise to Jerusalem: "Then this city will bring Me renown, joy, praise and honour before all nations on earth that hear of all the good things I do for it…" (Jer. 33:9).

Week 50 a[18]

Isaiah 61:10 – 63:9

The Parascha for this week (Deut. 29:9 – 30:20) ends with the words: "Now choose life, so that you and your children may live and that you may love the LORD your God, listen to His voice, and hold fast to Him." Even when we as human beings make the right decision between blessings and curses, the Haftarah (which is also regularly read on the Shabbat preceding the Jewish New Year as a message of great comfort) points out that ultimately everything depends on God´s act of salvation. This is what Jews and Christians have in common.

1) The action is His alone

"...and so He became their Saviour. In all their distress He too was distressed, and the angel of His presence saved them..." (63:8-9).

We confess that Jesus Christ is our Saviour and we know that "Salvation is found in no one else, for there is no other name under heaven given to men by which we must be saved" Acts 4:12). "...No one comes to the Father except through Me", Jesus says (John 14:6).

It is He who was sent "to proclaim the year of God´s favour and the day of vengeance of our God..." (Isa. 61:2). Out text, too, speaks of both favour and vengeance: On one hand *"For the day of vengeance was in My heart..." (63:4)*, on the other hand: *"I will tell of the kindnesses of the LORD, the deeds for which He is to be praised, according to all the LORD has done for us - yes, the many good things He has done for the house of Israel, according to His compassion and many kindnesses" (63:7).*

---

[18] Sometimes the Parascha „Nitzavim" is combined with „VeYalech", Deut. 31:1-30

The LORD's desire for doing good to Israel leaves Him restless. *"For Zion's sake I will not keep silent, for Jerusalem's sake I will not remain quiet, till her righteousness shines out like the dawn, her salvation like a blazing torch" (62:1).*

The Holy One of Israel is the redeemer of His people (Isa. 47:4). And just as He intercedes for the Jewish people, He turns in great wrath and with vengeance against the nations that opposed Israel: *"Who is this coming from Edom, from Bozrah, with his garments stained crimson? ... 'It is I, speaking in righteousness, mighty to save.' Why are Your garments red, like those of one treading the winepress? 'I have trodden the winepress alone; from the nations no one was with Me...I looked, but there was no one to help...I trampled the nations in My anger..." (63:1–6).*
From the Revelation we learn who treads the winepress: "He is dressed in a robe dipped in blood, and His name is the Word of God... He treads the winepress of the fury of the wrath of God Almighty. On His robe and on His thigh He has this name written: KING OF KINGS AND LORD OF LORDS" (Rev. 19:13-16).
He alone is "...the one whom God appointed as judge of the living and the dead" (Acts 10: 42). He alone is taking action.

2)   Nevertheless He involves us

"I have posted watchmen on your walls, O Jerusalem..." (62:6).
"...Prepare the way for the people. Build up, build up the highway! Remove the stones. Raise a banner for the nations" (62:10).
"...Say to the Daughter of Zion, 'See, your Saviour comes!..." *(62:11).*

The Almighty God will reach His goal, this is for sure. Nevertheless He gives us an active part in His rescue process – is that not amazing? Again and again we read about this aspect in the Scriptures.
The LORD acts in sovereignty and with might and yet expects our "cooperation". For example consider what Moses says regarding taking possession of the Promised Land by Israel: "Then the LORD

will drive out all these nations before you, and you will dispossess nations larger and stronger than you" (Deut. 11:23).

So we can only be surprised to learn that God gives us the following responsibility: *"...You who call on the LORD, give yourselves no rest, and give Him no rest till He establishes Jerusalem and makes her the praise of the earth" (62:6-7).* Are we really allowed to storm the Almighty One with our prayers? Yes, He wants us to pray for the sake of Jerusalem's future – although it is absolutely certain that He could reach His goal without us. It is good to make the prayer of David our own when interceding for Jerusalem: "For the sake of my brothers and friends I will say, 'Peace be within you'. For the sake of the house of the LORD our God, I will seek your prosperity" (Ps. 122:8-9). Given that our spiritual roots are in Judaism, the Jews are our brethren for whom we should pray. A second motivation for intercession is the fact that our LORD chose Jerusalem as His dwelling place.

Since we are called to be watchmen, it is our responsibility to watch carefully the development in and around Israel. Knowing that our LORD is the LORD of all history, who writes history with His people of Israel, we cannot close our eyes to political developments .

"Prepare the way for the people", how can that happen? Obviously it is all about helping to remove barriers. How many painful wounds inflicted by Christians have not yet been healed in Jewish souls! How do we keep our Jewish brethren - through false theology, spiritual arrogance and Christian custom (Christmas trees, icons etc.) - from recognizing the God we believe in? "Speak tenderly to Jerusalem..." the LORD exclaims through Isaiah (40: 2).

"Build up the highway! Remove the stones" may also mean that we are anxious to remove barriers from our own hearts. Do we still harbor reservations about the Jewish people? About what do we feel annoyance? We should ask ourselves if and in what situations we have ever parroted thoughtless, false, or venomous words about the Jews. This can only be shown by the Holy Spirit. Repentance and "enlightened eyes of or hearts" (Eph. 1: 18) result in being willing to

stand up for Israel against others. Then we ought not to leave without comment the wrong, distorting reports of the media, the derisive remarks or reviling jokes told in our presence. Then we need to take a stand for the truth – based on biblically sound love of Israel and for the sake of the Holy One of Israel.

Week 50 b[19]
Shabbat Shuva

Hosea 14:2 -10[20]; Joel 2:15 – 27; Micah 7:18 - 20

At the end of his life Moses hears these words of the LORD, as recorded in the Parascha (Deut. 31:1-30): "…These people will soon prostitute themselves to the foreign gods of the land they are entering … For I know how rebellious and stiff-necked you are…" (vss. 16 and 27). On Shabbat Shuva, the Shabbat of Return, we come across verses that call repeatedly for repentance but also offer marvellous promises of gifts of God´s grace.

1) To be uncompromising

"Return, O Israel, to the LORD your God. Your sins have been your downfall! Take words with you and return to the LORD…" (Hosea 14:1-2).

In Israel, preparation for Yom Kippur, the Day of Atonement, involves intensive inquiry of conscience and quiet. Again and again we, too, need to check our spiritual lives and to orientate ourselves to the LORD again. Jesus exclaimed: "…Repent, for the kingdom of heaven is near!" (Mt. 4:17). We have to be thankful that we still live in a time of grace. "Or do you show

---

[19] Sometimes the Haftarah is being read as supplementary text to the Parascha "Ve Yalech", sometimes to the Parascha "Haasinu" (Deut. 32:1-52), see "week 51"

[20] See exegesis concerning Hosea 12:13 – 14:10, „week 7"

contempt for the riches of His kindness, tolerance and patience, not realizing that God's kindness leads you towards repentance?" (Rom. 2:4). "Let us then approach the throne of grace with confidence, so that we may receive mercy and find grace to help us in our time of need" (Hebr. 4:16).

Our text gives us some hints of what causes God's disapproval: Relying on human help (*"Assyria cannot save us"*), aiming too high (*"we will not mount war-horses"*), and glorifying our own deeds (*"we will never again say 'our gods' to what our own hands have made"*, Hos. 14:3).

The LORD Himself wants to lead us. When we "mount horses" and go off our own, we do not submit to His plan. "As it is, you boast and brag. All such boasting is evil" (James 4:16). How humble is it what David prays: "My heart is not proud, O LORD, my eyes are not haughty; I do not concern myself with great matters or things too wonderful for me" (Ps. 131:1).

How easily it can happen that we are proud of our own "achievements"! Paul must remind us: "…What do you have that you did not receive?…" (1 Cor. 4:7). After healing a man crippled from birth, Peter and John for the sake of God's glory have to repudiate emphatically all admiration directed to them: "…Why do you stare at us as if by our own power or godliness we had made this man walk?" (Acts 3:12).

Repeatedly we are warned not to be conceited regarding our own strength or intelligence. "If anyone thinks he is something when he is nothing, he deceives himself" (Gal. 6:3). "…Let him who boasts boast in the LORD" (1 Cor. 1:31). When we try to bring something about on our own, or when we rely on human help instead of God's help, we deprive our Heavenly Father of the honour due to Him. And in so doing, we put something or someone above the One entitled to the first place. We know that the Bible speaks of idolatry in this context as belonging to "the works of the flesh" (Gal: 5:19; King James Version), which prevents us from inheriting the kingdom of God – as Paul tells us with urgency (1 Cor. 6:9). To be relieved from the slavery of idolatry is therefore part of returning to the LORD. In our text in Hosea 14:8 we read: *"O Ephraim, what more have I to do with idols?..."*

"Even now, declares the LORD, return to Me with all your heart, with fasting and weeping and mourning. Rend your heart and not your garments. Return to the LORD your God..." (Joel 2:12-13)

Here it is all about a total, true and sincere, not half-hearted return to God. "Trust in the LORD with all your heart and lean not on your own understanding" (Prov. 3:5). How does Jesus answer the Pharisees when asked about the greatest commandment? He refers back to the "Shma Jisrael" in Deut. 6:4: "...Love the LORD your God with all your heart and with all your soul and with all your mind" (Mt. 22:37). David expresses his strong desire to succeed in this, by these words: "...Give me an undivided heart that I may fear Your name" (Ps. 86:11). This is a crucial point, because we know that "no one can serve two masters..." (Mt. 6:24).

Even fasting – a form of all around intensive prayer so to speak – may remain a superficial and sanctimonious practice. But we find detailed instruction in the Scriptures how it should be done. "Is not this the kind of fasting I have chosen: to loose the chains of injustice and untie the cords of the yoke, to set the oppressed free and break every yoke? Is it not to share your food with the hungry and to provide the poor wanderer with shelter – when you see the naked, to clothe him, and not to turn away from your own flesh and blood?" (Isa. 58:6-7).

"Let the priests, who minister before the LORD, weep between the temple porch and the altar. Let them say: 'Spare Your people, O LORD..." (Joel 2:17).

It is good to have spiritual leaders who intercede for us and pray for mercy on our behalf. And when we claim that Jeshua "...has made us to be a kingdom and priests to serve His God and Father..." (Rev. 1:6), then it belongs to our priestly tasks not only to pray for our people but also for Israel, that the LORD´s merciful eyes may be on His people.

2)   Promises of the LORD

"...YOU do not stay angry forever but delight to show mercy" (Mi 7:18).
"...YOU will tread our sins underfoot and hurl all our iniquities into the depths of the sea"(Mi 7:19).
"I will heal their waywardness and love them freely..." (Hos. 14:4).

We can get too accustomed to confessing that our God is a merciful God. But here we learn again to pay attention: He even delights in showing mercy! Of His own free will and His own accord He does indeed forgive and heal. What a loving Father!

In the Haftarah verses it is of course also important to look at God´s concrete promises in the context to Israel. Concerning His beloved Jewish people we read:

"You will be true to Jacob, and show mercy to Abraham, as You pledged on oath to our fathers in days long ago" (Mi 7:20).
"...Never again I will make you an object of scorn to the nations" (Joel 2:19).
I will be like the dew to Israel; he will blossom like a lily ... his young shoots will grow..." (Hos. 14:5-6).
"I will repay you for the years the locusts have eaten – the great locust and the young locust, the other locusts and the locust swarm – My great army that I sent among you" (Joel 2:25).
"...Never again will My people be shamed" (Joel 2:26).

God will ensure that there will be rehabilitation of the Jewish people among the international community after all the centuries of disgrace and persecution. (See Isa. 25:8 and 60:14).

He not only gathers His people in the Promised Land after they have been dispersed for centuries, but He also intends for this land to blossom anew – and He wants it to expand as well. And He assures Israel of quiet and security (see Isa. 41:12).

The reaction in our prayers can only be *"...that we may offer the fruit of our lips" (Hos. 14:2).*
"... let us continually offer to God a sacrifice of praise – the fruit of lips that confess His name" (Hebr. 13:15).

Week 51

2 Samuel 22:1 - 51

In the center of the Parascha "Haasinu" (Deut. 32:1–52) is the "Song of Moses", which he wrote shortly before his death with the background of the disobedience of the people in mind. In it, he describes and praises God´s faithfulness and His wonderful deeds for Israel. David also wrote a detailed psalm of thanks (Ps. 18) shortly before his death. This was chosen as Haftarah (2 Sam. 22). There the LORD is praised in a wide range of terms: *"Rock, fortress, deliverer, shield, horn of salvation, stronghold, refuge, saviour, support, lamp"*

1) Equipment for the battle

"With your help I can advance against a troop, with my God I can scale a wall" (v.30)
"He trains my hands for battle; my arms can bend a bow of bronze" (v.35)
"You armed me with strength for battle; You made my adversaries bow at my feet" (v.40).

David´s life, like ours, is not without battle. Again and again David has to fight against enemy troops and hostile men. As Christians we also face a spiritual battle as we encounter troubles, trials and temptations (2 Cor. 6:4; James 1:2) or perhaps we are rejected and hated because of our faith (John 15:18; 1 Pt. 2:19). We have to withstand many tests, with the intention that our faith shall be proved and get stronger. "Blessed is the man who perseveres under trial, because when he has stood the test, he will receive the crown of life…"

(James 1:12). We often come across the terms "perseverance" and "to overcome" in the Bible; in Revelation these terms are often connected with precious promises (Rev. 2:7+11+17+26; Rev. 3:5+12+21).

It is a "struggle against sin" (Hebr. 12:4), so "...let us run with perseverance the race marked out for us. Let us fix our eyes on Jesus, the author and perfecter of our faith..." (Hebr. 12:1-2). As we think about Jesus who in spite of all temptations and hostility remained without sin and totally defeated the enemy, these words from Paul can encourage us: "Fight the good fight of the faith!..." (1 Tim. 6:12). We can fight in the name of our Redeemer, like David says: "All the nations surrounded me, but in the name of the LORD I cut them off. They surrounded me on every side, but in the name of the LORD I cut them off" (Ps. 118:10-11). David prays also: "Praise be to the LORD my Rock, who trains my hand for war, my fingers for battle" (Ps. 144:1).

Now, how are we as "soldiers of Christ Jesus" (2 Tim. 2:3) equipped for the spiritual battle? First of all we need to realize that it is a battle in the spiritual realm – even when we are dealing with people we have really problems with. When malice or spitefulness is hurled at us, someone is being used by God´s enemy in order to shake our trust in God. "For our struggle is not against flesh and blood, but against the rulers, against the authorities, against the powers of this dark world and against the spiritual forces of evil in the heavenly realms" (Eph. 6:12). It is therefore especially crucial to be well equipped. "For though we live in the world, we do not wage war as the world does. The weapons we fight with are not the weapons of the world. On the contrary, they have divine power to demolish strongholds" (2 Cor. 10:3-4).

What are these weapons to "...take stand against the devil´s schemes"? (Eph. 6:11). Paul admonishes us: "...put on the full armour of God!" which he describes as follows: "Stand firm then, with the belt of truth buckled around your waist, with the breastplate of righteousness in place, and with your feet fitted with the readiness that comes from the gospel of peace. In addition to all this, take up the shield of faith, with which you can extinguish all the flaming arrows of the evil one. Take the helmet of salvation and the sword of the Spirit, which is the true word of God" (Eph. 6:13–17).

2) Led into freedom

"In my distress I called to the LORD... my cry came to His ears" (v.7).
"He reached down from on high and took hold of me; He drew me out of deep waters" (v.17).
"He brought me out into a spacious place; He rescued me because He delighted in me" (v.20).
"You broaden the path beneath me..." (v.37).
"...from violent men You rescued me" (v.49).

David professes what we, too, can experience time and again: When we call out to the Almighty God He helps us out of our fears, oppressions and inhibitions. We have the privilege of coming to Him with our prayer: "The troubles of my heart have multiplied; free me from my anguish" (Ps. 25:17). Then we can experience what David expresses so well: "We have escaped like a bird out of the fowler´s snare; the snare has been broken, and we have escaped" (Ps. 124:7).

God´s enemy - this *"violent man"* – wants to torment us through fear and to force us into his slavery. But to those who have decisively entrusted themselves to the living God, Paul can say: "...You did not receive a spirit that makes you a slave again for fear, but you received the Spirit of sonship. And by him we cry: ´Abba, Father´ " (Rom. 8:15). The Son of God has granted us through His sacrificial death not to be "slaves to sin" (Rom. 6:20) any more. He took upon Himself all our iniquities and defeated hell, death and devil. Hallelujah! He had indeed completed the mission He had been appointed for: "... to proclaim freedom for the captives and release from darkness for the prisoners..." (Isa. 61:1). Jeshua Himself says us: "So if the Son sets you free, you will be free indeed" (John 8:36), as He is the truth, and "...the truth will set you free" (John 8:32; see also 2 Cor. 3:17). Yes, we are called "...into the glorious freedom of the children of God" (Rom. 8:21).

We can be free of sorrows, fear of men and anxiety about the future, and we can be confident: "There is now no condemnation for those who are in Christ Jesus" (Rom. 8:1). Our Redeemer Immanuel has come "...that by His death He might destroy him who holds the power of death – that is, the devil – and free those who all their lives were held in slavery by their fear of death" (Hebr. 2:14-15).

3) Righteousness of God

"The LORD has dealt with me according to my righteousness; according to the cleanness of my hands He has rewarded me" (v.21).
The LORD has rewarded me according to my righteousness, according to my cleanness in His sight" (v.25).

How shall we apply these verses to our lives? Is it possible for us to claim that we were obedient to the LORD all the time? (By the way, the same David prays in another situation: "My guilt has overwhelmed me like a burden too heavy to bear", Ps. 38:4). After all we read the serious warning: "If we claim to be without sin, we deceive ourselves and the truth is not in us" (1 John 1:8). Of course we should make every effort to ensure that our lives please God and that we have pure hearts and hands. But we need the mercy and forgiveness of Jesus again and again. "I know that nothing good lives in me, that is, in my sinful nature. For I have the desire to do what is good, but I cannot carry it out" (Rom. 7:18).

Praise God: Jesus Christ has become the righteousness that is valid before the Holy One, He has become "our righteousness" (1 Cor. 1:30)! "God made Him who had no sin to be sin for us, so that in Him we might become the righteousness of God" (2 Cor. 5:21).

When we belong to Jesus, the Heavenly Father sees us as having been cleansed through the blood of Jeshua. He sees the righteousness His Son bought for a price. In His sight we are pure. It is in this sense that we could say like David: *"The LORD has rewarded me according to my righteousness, according to my cleanness in His sight."*

Week 52

Joshua 1:1 - 18

In the final chapters of the Torah (Deut. 33:1 – 34:12) we read how Moses blesses the twelve tribes of Israel and – as their legacy, so to speak – proclaims once more: "There is no one like the God of Jeshurun... The eternal God is your refuge... Blessed are you, O Israel! Who is like you, a people saved by the LORD?..." (33:26–29). And about the successor of Moses, the passage says: "Now Joshua son of Nun was filled with the spirit of wisdom because Moses had laid his hands on him..." (34:9).

1) Mission

"...Now then, you and all these people, get ready to cross the Jordan River into the land I am about to give to them – to the Israelites" (v.2).

Joshua receives the order from God to lead the people of Israel after the death of Moses. It is therefore necessary for him to set out personally. It is not enough for a leader to show the way to others. Even a very good explanation would not be sufficient. He himself has to set out. We may never have to lead a people of some hundred thousand men, but we may be called to lead a company, a small group, a congregation, a family, or a marriage. Are we aware of the calling to practice our leadership in such a way that the goal of the LORD can be achieved?

Again and again we read in the Scriptures about divine appointments: Jesus says to the fishermen Simon Peter and Andrew: "Come, follow Me, and I will make you fishers of men!" (Mt. 4:19). "At once" they follow His call! Matthew the tax collector is called to follow Jesus -- although he is regarded as unworthy by men! (Mt. 9:9).Peter is sent to the Gentiles in Caesarea – although at the beginning he does not understand the meaning of that mission (Acts 10:9-23). Jeremiah is appointed – although he is young (Jer. 1:1-6).

Joshua and the people had to cross the Jordan River in those days, so it was necessary for them to overcome an obstacle. When God is calling, limits and limitations shall not play any part. It is important to leave things behind (like the nets the fishermen were accustomed to), to break with old habits (like the tax collector), to let oneself in for something unknown (like Peter), to throw overboard objections and doubts (like Jeremiah) or or ...

2) Admonition

"Be strong and courageous... Be strong and very courageous. Be careful to obey all the law My servant Moses gave you... Then you will be prosperous and successful" (v.6–8).

Do we also have to be strong in order to reach the goal? It is not a question of our own strength, as the LORD says: "...My power is made perfect in weakness..." (2 Cor. 12:9). Our Heavenly Father is willing to work in us and through us. That is why Paul intercedes for the Ephesians, praying that God "...may strengthen you with power through His Spirit in your inner being" (Eph. 3:16). When we read in 1 Cor. 16:13 "...be men of courage, be strong!", we need to recognize that this is preceded by the words "be on your guard; stand firm in the faith". But how can we be strengthened in faith? As one example, we read the following concerning Abraham: "He was strong in faith, giving glory to God" (Rom. 4:20, New James

Version). We find further instructions in the letter of Paul to the Ephesians: "Finally, be strong in the LORD and in His mighty power. Put on the full armour of God ...", which he then goes on to describe (Eph. 6:10–17).

Joshua is admonished *"to obey all the law"* given to him through Moses. Does this also apply to us? Many people nowadays make light of this question, equating law with unspiritual legalism and take the easy way out by saying that it is enough to live in the time of grace. But how can we ignore these words of Jesus? "Do not think that I have come to abolish the Law or the Prophets; I have not come to abolish them but to fulfill them. I tell you the truth, until heaven and earth disappear, not the smallest letter, not the least stroke of a pen will by any means disappear from the Law until everything is accomplished. Anyone who breaks one of the least of these commandments and teaches others to do the same will be called least in the kingdom of heaven" (Mt. 5:17–19). "All Scripture is God-breathed and is useful for teaching, rebuking, correcting and training in righteousness, so that the man of God may be thoroughly equipped for every good work" (2 Tim. 3:16-17), or, according to the King James Version, "...that the man of God may be perfect". This concerns reaching the goal, as Joshua is told *"Then you will be prosperous and successful"*. The expression "all Scripture" includes of course the Torah. Having in mind that the appropriate translation of the term "Torah" is "teaching, instruction" rather than "law", we see that we need the Torah.

3) Encouragement

"I will give you every place where you set your foot, as I promised Moses" (v.3)

"...Do not be terrified; do not be discouraged, for the LORD your God will be with you wherever you go" (v.9).

For Joshua, God's instructions do not stop with the burden of a hard mission and with admonishment; God goes on to give him great, almost inconceivable, encouragement at the same time.
Verse 3 speaks into the special situation of the people of Israel – that much is certain. But it may also remind us how important it is for us to walk in the footsteps of Jesus. As we consider verse 9, we may think of the wonderful promise of Jesus: "...Surely I am with you always, to the very end of the age" (Mt. 28:20). In the LORD´s prayer our Saviour intercedes for us with the Father with these words: "Father, I want those You have given Me to be with Me where I am..." (John 17:24). We can therefore be amazed by the encouragement of Paul's words: "Don´t you know that you yourselves are God´s temple and that God´s Spirit lives in you?" (1 Cor. 3:16).

4) Supply

"...Get your supplies ready. Three days from now you will cross the Jordan here to go in and take possession of the land the LORD your God is giving you for your own" (v.11).

The people of Israel needed food in order to get new strength and to survive on the long way towards their destination. We, in turn, need spiritual food if we are to win the spiritual battle and reach the goal. We remember the parable of Jesus: "At that time the kingdom of heaven will be like ten virgins who took their lamps and went out to meet the bridegroom. Five of them were foolish and five were wise. The foolish ones took their lamps but did not take any oil with them. The wise, however, took oil in jars along with their lamps" (Mt. 25:1–4). Then the bridegroom came and "...the virgins who were ready went in with him to the wedding banquet. And the door was shut" (Mt. 25:10). We know that the oil is a symbol of the Holy Spirit. "May ... the fellowship of the Holy Spirit be with you all" (2 Cor. 13:13), Paul prays and warns us: Do not put out the Spirit´s fire" (1 Thess. 5:19), but "...keep your spiritual fervour..." (Rom. 12:11).

5) Place of destination

"Your territory will extend from the desert to Lebanon, and from the great river, the Euphrates – all the Hittite country – to the Great Sea on the west" (v.4).

Joshua´s mission is about taking possession of the Promised Land. We don´t read about any other people in the Bible to which God assigned a clearly outlined geographic area. However: "When the Most High gave the nations their inheritance, when He divided all mankind, He set up boundaries for the peoples according to the number of the sons of Israel" (Deut. 32:8). On the other hand the boundaries of the Promised Land are concretely defined: *"Your territory will extend from ... to..."*.

What is our "territory"? It is good if we know that God has placed us where we are. And it is important to realize : "...Here we do not have an enduring city, but we are looking for the city that is to come" (Hebr. 13:14). When we have laid our earthly life totally into the hands of our Saviour Jesus Christ, we can trust: "...The gift of God is eternal life in Christ Jesus our LORD" (Rom. 6:23). "Now we know that if the earthly tent we live in is destroyed, we have a building from God, an eternal house in heaven, not built by human hands" (2 Cor. 5:1).

6) Back up

"Then they answered Joshua: 'Whatever you have commanded us we will do... Only may the LORD your God be with you as He was with Moses" (v.16-17).

Joshua is backed by the people, not only through the promise to follow him, but above all through blessings. What was the situation when Moses fought against Amalek? As long as he held up his hands towards heaven, the Israelites had the upper hand, but whenever he lowered his hands, the enemies were winning. When Moses grew tired "...Aaron and Hur held his hands up..." (Ex. 17:10–12). This is a beautiful metaphor for intercession in unity.

We too are called to intercede for others and especially for our leaders. "I urge, then, first of all, that requests, prayers, intercession and thanksgiving be made for everyone – for kings and all those in authority, that we may live peaceful and quiet lives in all godliness and holiness" (1 Tim. 2:1-2).

As disciples of Jesus we are "a royal priesthood" (1 Pt. 2:9) and one of the major duties of priests is to intercede for the people. The Scriptures point out with urgency that it is one of our special tasks to intercede for Israel and the Jewish people, whose roots we are allowed to share (see for instance Ps. 122:6-9; Isa. 62:6-7). "...This is how you are to bless the Israelites. Say to them: 'The LORD bless you and keep you; the LORD make His face shine upon you and be gracious to you, the LORD turn His face toward you and give you peace.' So they will put My name on the Israelites, and I will bless them" (Num. 6:23–27).

Rosh Hashanah

1 Samuel 1:1 – 2:10

On the Jewish New Year's Day, we read in the Torah – in chapters 21 and 22 of Genesis – that despite her great age, Sarah is granted the promised son Isaac. And we learn in addition that Abraham is prepared to sacrifice his son to the LORD on Mount Moriah. The Supplementary text for New Year's Day likewise tells of a woman, Hannah, to whom a son is granted after a long period of childlessness and who acts self-sacrificially by consecrating him to life-time service of God. It is significant symbolism to read about new life at the beginning of a new year.

1) **God answers prayers.**

"In bitterness of soul Hannah wept much and prayed to the LORD. And she made a vow, saying, O LORD Almighty, if you will ... not forget your servant but give her a son, then I will give him to the LORD for all the days of his life" (1:10 f.).
"Elkanah lay with Hannah his wife, and the LORD remembered her. So in the course of time Hannah conceived and gave birth to a son. She named him Samuel" (1:19 f.).

God answers prayers. This is an important message, very appropriate to the beginning of a new year. We know this very well, of course, and each of us has experienced this personally already. Yet it is good to be reminded of this truth again and again, particularly since there are times when this great certainty is in danger of getting lost.

Just as the loving Father listens to the sobbing and yearning of Hannah, so in the days of Egyptian slavery he does not let the outcry of the enslaved Israelites go unanswered. "And their cry for help because of their slavery went up to God. God heard their groaning and He remembered His covenant with Abraham, with Isaac and with Jacob. So God looked on the Israelites and was concerned about them" (Ex. 2:23–25). David has a similar experience: "The cords of the grave coiled around me; the snares of death confronted me. In my distress I called to the LORD; I called out to my God. From His temple He heard my voice; my cry came to His ears" (2 Sam. 22:6 f.). Many of us may have experienced this personally: "I called on Your name, O LORD, from the depths of the pit. You heard my plea" (Lam. 3:55 f; see Ps. 34:4 and Ps. 120:1).

David calls God specifically "You who hear prayer..." (Ps. 65:2). And yet: don´t we sometimes find that God does not answer our prayers – or seems not to answer? Don´t we have our problems concerning this subject now and then? It starts with God granting our requests and we don´t realize it (and therefore don´t give thanks to Him)! Maybe our prayer has been quite some time ago, and we don´t connect a later positive change with our prior prayer. Secondly it may be that we hope for an immediate act of the LORD, but His blessing in this special matter is granted only later. After all, our loving Father knows at what time anything is best for us; sometimes He wants to test us to see whether we remain steadfastly committed to Him even while waiting. Thirdly we may expect God to answer our prayer in a specific way. Indeed, we may lay specific expectations before him and then be astonished if He does not answer. Fourthly it may happen that we ask Him for something which seems desirable to us and that, although God gives us something even more important instead, we are disappointed initially.

Finally it may be that we sometimes ask for something that we should know from Scripture is against the will of God. That is similar to the response of the people of Israel when they find the King of Kings is not sufficient for them: "... you will cry out for relief from the king you have chosen, and the LORD will not answer you in that day" (1 Sam. 8:18). It is for our admonition that James writes: "When you ask, you do not receive, because you ask with wrong motives, that you may spend what you get on your pleasures" (James 4:3).

However, our problems may start even earlier: "Then they will call to Me but I will not answer; they will look for Me but will not find Me. Since they hated knowledge and did not choose to fear the LORD, since they would not accept My advice and spurned My rebuke ..." (Prov. 1:28–30). Anyone who lives without fear of God and is far from Him cannot expect that the LORD will answer prayers under this condition. Likewise it is written: "... you who hate good and love evil, ... they will cry out to the LORD, but He will not answer them. At that time He will hide His face from them because of the evil they have done" (Mi 3:2–4).

But praise the LORD: There is a chance to repent! We can confess the filth of our life to the Saviour Jesus Christ and be sure that He does not reject an earnest prayer of repentance. "If we confess our sins, He is faithful and just and will forgive us our sins and purify us from all unrighteousness" (1 John 1:9). Let us also read what God says to Josiah, the king of Judah: "Because your heart was responsive and you humbled yourself before the LORD when you heard what I have spoken against this place and its people,... I have heard you, declares the LORD" (2 Kings 22:19; similar: 2 Chron. 33:12 f. to Manasseh of Judah). "The LORD is far from the wicked but He hears the prayer of the righteous" (Prov. 15:29).

Indeed, "The prayer of a righteous man is powerful and effective" (James 5:16).

2) The Almighty and Omniscient One

"For the LORD is a God who knows, and by Him deeds are weighed" (2:3).
"The LORD brings death and makes alive; He brings down to the grave and raises up. The LORD sends poverty and wealth; He humbles and He exalts" (2:6 f.).
"For the foundations of the earth are the LORD´s; upon them He has set the world" (2:8).
"The LORD will judge the ends of the earth" (2:10).

The praise of Hannah is nothing short of an adoring confession of the greatness of God. And these verses from the first chapter of the Haftarah are very appropriate at the beginning of a new year because they are an important orientation for inner direction in a new period of time.

God is the Omniscient One. He surveys the whole universe. His perspective includes – beyond our imagination – everything that was, that is and that will be. He knows about the situation of His Israel and of the congregation of Jesus. The circumstances of the world politics are transparent before Him. He is acquainted with each of His creatures. "From heaven the LORD looks down and sees all mankind" (Ps. 33:13). Our challenges, troubles, fears, doubts, questions, hopes, plans and limitations are not unknown to Him. "The LORD knows those who are His" (2 Tim. 2:19). He knows about our needs: "My God will meet all your needs according to His glorious riches in Christ Jesus" (Phil. 4:19). "He who did not spare His own son, but gave Him up for us all – how will He not also, along with Him, graciously give us all things?" (Rom. 8:32)

But our LORD knows our failures as well. "From heaven the LORD looks down and sees all mankind; from his dwelling place He watches all who live on earth – He who forms the hearts of all, who considers everything they do" (Ps. 33:14 ff.). "For we must all appear before the judgment seat of Christ, that each one may receive what is due him for the things done while in the body, whether good or bad" (2 Cor. 5:10). As far as we are concerned: will it be "gold, silver, costly stones, wood, hay or straw"? "The fire will test the quality of each man´s work. If what he has built survives, he will receive his reward. If it is burned up, he will suffer loss; he himself will be saved, but only as one escaping through the flames" (1 Cor. 3:12–15).

If we have accepted the Son of God, the promised Immanuel, into our lives as our personal LORD, then we can know: "There is now no condemnation for those who are in Christ Jesus" (Rom.8:1). In Jeshua we have an intercessor with the Father in Heaven. So when we read *"The LORD will judge the ends of the earth",* we need not be afraid. Indeed, when we reflect on the flagrant injustice in the world, it is comforting to know that it is God who will speak the final word. "And the heavens proclaim His righteousness, for God Himself is judge" (Ps. 50:6). Also with regard to the innumerable and unjustified blame placed on Israel, it is good – and at the same time admonishing – to hear: "In those days and at that time, when I restore the fortunes of Judah and Jerusalem, I will gather all nations and bring them down to the valley of Jehoshaphat. There I will enter into judgment against them concerning My inheritance, My people Israel, for they scattered My people among the nations and divided up My land" (Joel 3:1 f.).

As with Israel, we recognize that *"He humbles and He exalts"*. The Holy One of Israel speaks to Zion: "For the nation or kingdom that will not serve you will perish; it will be utterly ruined. ... The sons of your oppressors will come bowing before you; all who despise you will bow down at your feet" (Isa. 60:12 and 14). As a basic principle the LORD says: "I will put an end to the arrogance of the haughty and will humble the pride of the ruthless" (Isa. 13:11).

We are admonished as well as encouraged by the words of James: "Humble yourselves before the LORD, and He will lift you up" (James 4:10).

Yom Kippur

Isaiah 57:14 - 58:14

Yom Kippur, the Day of Atonement, is considered to be the holiest holiday in Israel. On that day, Jewish people make every effort to set themselves right with God and to seek reconciliation with others. It is a day of total quiet –including the quiet of little or no traffic -- and fasting.

1) The dwelling place of God

"For this is what the High and Lofty One says – He who lives forever, whose name is holy: `I live in a high and holy place , but also with him who is contrite and lowly in spirit, to revive the spirit of the lowly and to revive the heart of the contrite" (57:15)

What tension within these verses! The grand Almighty Creator of the world is not inaccessibly far away; isn´t that incomprehensible?
It is true: He dwells in the heights. "Who is like the LORD our God, the One who sits enthroned on high?" (Ps. 113:5). Isaiah prays: "Look down from heaven and see from Your lofty throne , holy and glorious" (Isa. 63:15). And our LORD Jesus Himself teaches us to pray: "Our Father in heaven..." (Mt. 6:9).

On the other hand listen to the command that God gives to Moses: "Then have them make a sanctuary for Me, and I will dwell among them" (Ex. 25:8). He even gives exact instructions how to build the "tent of meeting" which was to include the Ark of the Covenant. When the Israelites are in

Canaan they get the following order concerning their service and sacrifices: "You are to seek the place the LORD your God will choose from among all your tribes to put His name there for His dwelling. To that place you must go" (Deut. 12:5). God who is enthroned in heaven draws near to mankind. But why does He determine a specific meeting place, given that He is omnipresent? Maybe it is to make it easier for the people to imagine that God is present? Does attention get more focused on God when the people set out for a certain location? Is the assembly at one and the same place meant to be good for unity?

The question of King Solomon is quite understandable: "But will God really dwell on earth? The heavens, even the highest heaven, cannot contain you" (2 Kings 8:27). Nevertheless the Holy One of Israel is pleased to have a temple erected for Him. The history is remarkable, however: David explains his desire to build a house for the LORD with these words: "Here I am, living in a palace of cedar, while the Ark of God remains in a tent" (2 Sam. 7:2). Then Nathan, the Prophet, gives him this message: "The LORD declares to you that the LORD Himself will establish a house for y o u "(emphasized by W.B.) God promises an everlasting kingdom in Jerusalem and specifies that it will be David´s son (Solomon) who will build the temple in Jerusalem (2 Sam. 7:11–16). Solomon consecrates the temple to the LORD and receives this precious promise: "I have consecrated this temple, which you have built, by putting My name there forever. My eyes and My heart will always be there" (1 Kings 9:3).

The God of Abraham, Isaac and Jacob has turned His heart towards Jerusalem in a special way: "For the LORD has chosen Zion, He has desired it for His dwelling: ´This is My resting place for ever and ever; here I will sit enthroned , for I have desired it" (Ps. 132:13 f; see Ps. 68:16 and Ps. 76:2). Jerusalem is "the holy place where the Most High dwells" (Ps. 46:4).

Nowhere in Scripture do we read that God cancelled His promise to dwell in Jerusalem. On the other hand we know that we can reach our LORD through our prayers any time and everywhere. What a privilege! He is omnipresent. What an incomprehensible promise we receive in faith: Jesus Christ came to dwell in us! When we decided to live our lives with Him then the reminder of Paul applies to us: "Don´t you know that you yourselves are God´s temple and that God´s Spirit lives in you? ... God´s temple is sacred, and you are that temple" (1 Cor,. 3:16 f.). Perhaps this is an appropriate time to remember this verse from the Haftarah: *"I live in a holy place"*.

But now we also read in the text of our Haftarah that the LORD dwells with those who are *"contrite and lowly in spirit"*. The One dwelling in the highest heaven bows down to those who are degraded, pitiable, humiliated and humble. That He is especially near to them reveals His nature: "...The LORD is full of compassion and mercy" (James 5:11). Just when we are shattered, when we feel "stuck", when we are aware of our inabilities, our impossibilities and our failures, our loving Father wants to be near to us and to lift us up. "A bruised reed He will not break, and a smouldering wick He will not snuff out" (Isa. 42:3). He speaks to Israel, who is so tormented: "As a mother comforts her child, so will I comfort you" (Isa. 66:13). And to us He is also "...the Father of compassion and the God of all comfort" (2 Cor. 1:3).

2) Piety check

On Yom Kippur you can experience in Israel the desire of the Jews to put their lives right before God. The Haftarah reminds them that outer forms of piety are not sufficient for a purification and new beginning. This should be a warning for us as well. How often may it have been that we attended a service but did not draw any lessons from the sermon, that we left the church as we had entered it, as it were? How often may we have prayed for right guidance without first seeking forgiveness for going astray? *"For day after day they seek Me out; they seem eager to know My ways, as if they were a nation that does what is right and has not forsaken the commands of its God. They ask Me for just decisions and seem eager for God to come near them"* (Isa. 58:2).

Maybe we have asked the question before: `Why does God not answer? After all, I have done such and such…and I also …´ The people of Israel in those days have a similar question concerning their fasting: *"Why have we fasted, they say, and You have not seen it? Why have we humbled ourselves, and You have not noticed?"* (Isa. 58:3) Fasting is a special means of prayer, as it were. But just as we can get through a prayer – the LORD´s Prayer, for instance – without paying true inner attention to it, so a time of fasting can also run the risk of being superficial, in spite of our best intentions. Then it will not be accompanied by decisions for renewed obedience in the spiritual dimension. The Haftarah identifies specific barriers that make it difficult for our *"voice to be heard on high"* (58:4). *"On the day of your fasting you do as you please…"* (58:3). The LORD speaks of quarrels, violence, defamation, oppression, chains of injustice, omitted aid and denied comfort. This enumeration may be a check-list for our own behaviour.

What precious incentive for correction the Lord gives us!
"Then your light will break forth like the dawn, and your healing will quickly appear; then your righteousness will go before you, and the glory of the LORD will be your rear guard. Then you will call, and the LORD will answer" (58:8 f.) *"You will be like a well-watered garden, like a spring whose waters never fail"* (58:11).

Sukkot[21]

1 Kings 8:54 – 66

That the eighth day – i.e., the day after the seven days of the Feast of Tabernacles -- is celebrated, goes back to Leviticus 23:36: "For seven days present offerings made to the LORD by fire, and on the eighth day hold a sacred assembly and present an offering made to the LORD by fire. It is the closing assembly; do no regular work." While in the Diaspora this "Shmini Azeret" (= the eighth of the feast) is followed by "Simchat Torah" (= the feast of joy about the Torah) on the next day, in Israel both feasts are celebrated on the same day.
The text of the Haftarah follows the earnest prayer of Solomon spoken on the occasion of the consecration of the temple.

1) Nothing has failed

"He stood and blessed the whole assembly of Israel in a loud voice, saying: 'Praise be to the LORD, who has given rest to His people Israel just as He promised. Not one word has failed of all the good promises He gave through His servant Moses" (v. 55 f.)

We read very similar words in the book of Joshua: "The LORD gave them rest on every side, just as He had sworn to their forefathers... Not one of all the LORD´s good promises to the house of Israel failed; every one was fulfilled" (Josh. 21:44 f.; see Josh. 23:14). It is also written about Samuel: "The LORD was with Samuel as he grew up, and He let none of His words fall to the ground" (1 Sam. 3:19). Balaam, guided by the Holy

---

[21] The Haftarah is read on the eighth day of Sukkot.

Spirit, utters: "God is not a man, that He should lie, nor a son of man, that He should change His mind. Does He speak and then not act? Does He promise and not fulfil?" (Numb. 23:19)

How double-minded we human beings are! We promise something with the best of intentions but then do not keep our promise. We hold out a prospect of something casually and just forget about it. We say something and secretly we mean something totally different. But with the Almighty God there is no gap between intention and saying and deed! "And God said; ´Let there be light´, and there was light" (Gen. 1:3). At almost the end of his life – after all of his experiences with God - Moses sings of the LORD using these wonderful words: "He is the rock, His works are perfect, and all His ways are just. A faithful God who does no wrong, upright and just is He" (Deut. 32:4).

Moses can even shout to the people the mighty words: "Know therefore that the LORD your God is God; He is the faithful God, keeping His covenant of love to a thousand generations of those who love Him and keep His commands" (Deut. 7:9). His covenant of peace will not be removed (Is. 54: 10). That is why Paul, in the context of Israel as God´s chosen people, can point out: "God´s gifts and His call are irrevocable" (Rom. 11:29). And to us the following applies: "God, who has called you into fellowship with His Son Jesus Christ our LORD, is faithful" (1 Cor. 1:9). We can be certain that our Saviour is "a merciful and faithful high priest in service to God" (Hebr. 2:17). Again and again we need His intercession and can trust in Him.: "If we are faithless, He will remain faithful, for He cannot disown Himself" (2 Tim. 2:13).

This is the very basis of our faith, as "God´s solid foundation stands firm" (2 Tim. 2:19). "For no one can lay any foundation other than the one already laid, which is Jesus Christ" (1 Cor. 3:11). Let us keep in mind the words of the Haftarah: *"Not one word has failed"* of God´s promises. It is written about Jeshua: "No matter how many promises God has made, they are ´Yes´ in Christ. And so through Him the ´Amen´..." (2 Cor. 1:20). Therefore: "Let us hold unswervingly to the hope we profess, for He who promised is faithful" (Hebr. 10:23).

2) The right prayer for justice

"And may these words of mine, which I have prayed before the LORD, be near to the LORD our God day and night, that He may uphold the cause of His servant and the cause of His people Israel according to each day´s need, so that all the peoples of the earth may know that the LORD is God and that there is no other" (v. 59 f.).

Again and again the Jewish people have been fought against and have been hard-pressed, displaced, and accused. Again and again injustice befell them. Solomon prays for justice for Israel and David likewise implores the LORD: "Awake, and rise to my defense! Contend for me, my God and LORD. Vindicate me in Your righteousness, O LORD my God" (Ps. 35:23 f.). Let us act in accordance with Ps. 37:5: "Commit your way to the LORD; trust in Him and He will do this: He will make your righteousness shine like the dawn, the justice of your cause like the noonday sun." God says about Himself: "I am the LORD, who exercises kindness, justice and righteousness on earth, for in these I delight" (Jer. 9:23). And especially for the hard-pressed souls of the Israelis this message may be like balm: "He upholds the cause of the oppressed..." (Ps. 146:7).

But injustice and oppression that happen to someone can also be God´s punishment. Therefore Micah prays: "Because I have sinned against Him, I will bear the LORD´s wrath, until He pleads my case and establishes my right" (Mi 7:9). So perhaps we have to get over waiting periods.

Now, how are we to think about the justice that Solomon is praying for – and that Israel is still longing for today? It definitely will occur – but the God of Abraham, Isaac and Jacob refers to the end of time: "The days are coming, declares the LORD, when I will raise up to David a righteous Branch, a King who will reign wisely and do what is just and right in the land In His days Judah will be saved and Israel will live in safety. This is the name by which He will be called: The LORD Our Righteousness" (Jer. 23: 5 f.). This righteous branch that will be called "our righteousness" is no one other than Jeshua. Some chapters later in the book of Jeremiah we come across the following statement: "In those days Judah will be saved and Jerusalem will live in safety. This is the name by which it will be called: The LORD Our Righteousness" (Jer. 33:16). That is not a misprint. The Hebrew text confirms it: Jesus and Jerusalem are given the same name!

Again and again we come across phrases in the Scriptures such as "the time will come" or "days are coming when…", for instance concerning the repatriation into the Promised Land (Jer. 30:3), the gathering from all nations (Jer. 16:14-15), the expansion and restoration (Jer. 31:27; Am. 9:13 f.) and the promise of a new covenant (Jer. 31:31). For all these special events "the LORD set a time…" (Ex. 9:5). What is written about the birth of Jesus? "When the time had fully come, God sent His Son" (Gal. 4:4).

When Solomon prays that God may answer *"according to each day's need"*, he understood: "There is a time for everything" (Ecc. 3:1). What can we learn from that? Sometimes it is like this with us: we would like God to show us not only the next step but the further ones as well. And are we not inclined to wait impatiently for immediate answer to our prayers? We must learn to persevere, trusting in the grace of our faithful Father in heaven, grace that is new day by day. He knows best what is right for us at any given moment. "The eyes of all look to You, and You give them their food at the proper time" (Ps. 145:15). And we should not be worried. "Therefore do not worry about tomorrow, for tomorrow will worry about itself. Each day has enough trouble of its own" (Mt. 6:34).

We can learn something further from Solomon's prayer: His concern is *"that all the peoples of the earth may know that the LORD is God and that there is no other" (v. 60).*

Shabbat Shekalim

2 Kings 11:17 - 12:17

At the new moon of the Hebrew month of Adar (usually in February), in addition to the weekly portion, we will also read verses about the poll tax of half a Shekel that every Israeli above the age of twenty had to pay for the maintenance of the temple (Ex. 30:11–16). The supplementary text also deals among other things with money (Shekalim) for the restoration of the temple.

1) Cleansing

"Jehoiada then made a covenant between the LORD and the king and people that they would be the LORD´s people. He also made a covenant between the king and the people. All the people of the land went to the temple of Baal and tore it down. They smashed the altars and idols to pieces and killed Mattan the priest of Baal in front of the altars" (11:17 f.)
"And the city was quiet because Athaliah had been slain with the sword at the palace" (11:20).

The covenant that the Almighty God made with Israel lasts forever. God promises His beloved people: "…My unfailing love for you will not be shaken nor My covenant of peace be removed…" (Is. 54:10). "He provided redemption for His people; He ordained His covenant forever…" (Ps. 111:9).

But as the Israelites repeatedly broke this covenant and as we human beings far too often want to go our own way, then from the human side it's clear that a decision for renewal of the covenant is needed again and again. This is why Moses confronts the people of Israel before crossing the Jordan River with these words: "This day I call heaven and earth as witnesses against you that I have set before you life and death, blessings and curses. Now choose life...!" (Deut. 30:19). Later Joshua orders the people: "...Choose for yourselves this day whom you will serve", and after they answer "we will serve the LORD our God and obey Him" Joshua makes a covenant for the people and sets up a stone as a "witness against you if you are untrue to your God" (Josh. 24:15 + 24 + 27). And in the Haftarah we read that Jehoiada, the priest makes a new covenant between God and the king and the people following the wicked reign of the self appointed Athaliah who served the idols.

In our lives, too, it is not sufficient to make just one decision to live with God. Satan is lying in wait. "So, if you think you are standing firm, be careful that you don't fall" (1 Cor. 10:12). It can happen too easily that we succumb to temptation. But we are privileged to turn again to our LORD and Saviour, just as we are, to pray for forgiveness – and to receive forgiveness. "For though a righteous man falls seven times, he rises again..." (Prov. 24:16). Jesus Christ said once and for all "yes" to us; we should express our "yes" to Him again and again and also in "presence" of the unseen world confirm our decision for a life with God. This is stated in many different ways; in Ps. 119, for example, we read: "I have chosen the way of truth, I have set my heart on Your laws" (Ps. 119:30).

But from the behaviour of Jehoiada we also learn that the renewal of the covenant with God has concrete consequences. As the Israelites under Jehoiada pull down all of their idols and cult places according to the instructions of their LORD, so we should ask ourselves: What needs to be erased from our lives? Who and what enjoys priority with us? Do we still have our secret "altars"? "...Flee from idolatry" 1 Cor.10:14 shouts to us. Have we "renounced secret and shameful ways?" (2 Cor. 4:2) "No one can serve two masters...", our LORD Jesus warns us (Mt. 6:24). And Paul adds: We are either "...slaves to sin, which leads to death, or to obedience, which leads to righteousness" (Rom. 6:16).

2)   Administering of money

"Joash said to the priests: `Collect all the money that is brought as sacred offerings to the temple of the LORD... Let every priest receive the money from one of the treasurers, and let it be used to repair whatever damage is found in the temple. But by the twenty-third year of King Joash the priests still had not repaired the temple (12:4–6).
"The priests agreed that they would not collect any more money from the people and that they would not repair the temple themselves" (12:8).

It is written about King Joash of Judah, that he "did what was right in the eyes of the LORD all the years Jehoiadah the priest instructed him". He intends to press for the restoration of the House of God. Therefore the priests and Levites are asked to go into the Judean cities in order to collect money. Joash specifically emphasizes: "Do it now!" as we read in 2 Chr. 24:5. But then Jehoiadah has to explain why he didn't require the Levites to collect the tax imposed by Moses. The priests are released from this task, and this led to the birth of the offertory (12:10) so to speak, which is also used at the time of Jesus (Mk. 12:41). The money collected in this way is given to the men appointed to supervise the work and by them to the workers for the repairs of the House of God. Astonishingly enough, they*"did not require an accounting from those to* *whom they gave the money to pay the workers, because they acted with complete honesty" (12:15).*

What can we learn from these texts ? Number one: We find the distinction between (1) the contributions that the Israelites were obligated to make: the poll tax according to the census on the one hand and (2) *"the money brought voluntarily to the temple"* on the other hand (12:4). Translated into our setting this could mean that even insofar as we are assessed for the church tax prescribed by the government, we need to ask: Is there still room in our hearts for voluntary offerings?

Number two: What priority does the advancement of the congregation have for us compared to our personal affairs? "Is it a time for you yourselves to be living in your panelled houses, while this house remains a ruin?" (Haggai 1:4).

Number three: "Now it is required that those who have been given a trust must prove faithful" (1 Cor. 4:2).

Shabbat Sachor

1 Samuel 15: 1 – 34

In the four weeks before the Feast of Pessach one reads special sections on Shabbat. Shabbat Sachor (Shabbat of remembrance) is just before Purim, the commemorative feast of the rescue of the Jewish people from the fatal threat by the atrocious Haman. Haman, an Agagite (Esther 3:1), comes from the Amalekite lineage, as Agag is reported to be king of the Amalekites. Therefore the Haftarah on Shabbat Sachor deals with Saul´s victory over Amalek.

1) The LORD judges Israel´s enemies

"This is what the LORD Almighty says: ´I will punish the Amalekites for what they did to Israel when they waylaid them as they came up from Egypt. Now go, attack the Amalekites and totally destroy everything that belongs to them" (v. 2 f.)

What do we know about Amalek? He fights against the Israelites when they come out of Egypt, but Joshua wins, supported by the impressive way Moses, Aaron and Hur intercede for him in prayer. (Notice that the enemy appears just when the people are grumbling and doubting the grace of God – certainly an admonition for us.) Again and again the Israelites have to battle against Amalek: At the time of the Judges (Judges 3:13; 6:3 f.), of Saul (1 Sam. 15), and of David (1 Sam. 27:8; 1 Sam. 30:1 ff.). The last remnant of the Amalekites is killed only by the sons of Simeon (1 Chr. 4:42 f.). But why does it say in Ex. 17:16: "…The LORD will be at war against the Amalekites from generation to generation"? It could mean that the mind of Amalek is still present, the spirit of anti-Semitism.

In the Haftarah of today we learn the reason that Amalek should be defeated with a crushing blow: The God of Abraham, Isaac and Jacob did not forget how the cowardice with which Amalek attacked the Israelites, especially the weak stragglers who were no longer fit for action at the time of Israel´s long march through the desert. So we read in Deut. 25:17 ff: "Remember what the Amalekites did to you along the way when you came out of Egypt. When you were weary and worn out, they met you on your journey and cut off all who were lagging behind; they had no fear of God. When the LORD your God gives you rest from all the enemies around you in the land He is giving you to possess as an inheritance, you shall blot out the memory of Amalek from under heaven. Do not forget!"

Because the Almighty One bound Himself to His beloved people Israel by the holiness of His name, He time and again competes against Israel´s enemies by judging them – as they are actually His own enemies. That is why the Psalmist prays: "O God, do not keep silent; be not quiet, O God, be not still. See how Your enemies are astir, how Your foes rear their heads. With cunning they conspire against Your people…" (Ps. 83: 1 – 3). The attacks of the nations against the Jewish people arise from the same cause through all history: rebellion against God´s choice and God´s plan to glorify Himself with Israel. But the manner by which they become guilty is often quite different.

The judgment on Moab reads: "Moab´s horn is cut off; her arm is broken, declares the LORD. Make her drunk, for she has defied the LORD … Was not Israel the object of your ridicule?

Was she caught among thieves, that you shake your head in scorn whenever you speak of her?" (Jer. 48:25 ff.) The Ammonites must hear: "...Because you said ´Aha!´ over My sanctuary when it was desecrated and over the land of Israel when it was laid waste and over the people of Judah when they went into exile ... Because you have clapped your hands and stamped your feet, rejoicing with all the malice of your heart against the land of Israel, therefore I will stretch out My hand against you and give you as plunder to the nations" (Ezek. 25:3 + 6 f.). In the book of Zephaniah this judgment is confirmed once more: "I have heard the insults of Moab and the taunts of the Ammonites, who insulted My people and made threats against their land. Therefore, as surely as I live, declares the LORD Almighty, the God of Israel, surely Moab will become like Sodom, the Ammonites like Gomorrah" (Zeph. 2:8 f.). (See also Ezek. 35:14 f.).

As the LORD so clearly turns against scorn and contempt, it is quite natural that He also announces punishment to Gaza and Tyre because they even "...took captive whole communities" and sold them to Edom (Am. 1:6 + 9). He promises to "...throw down the horns of the nations who lifted up their horns against the land of Judah to scatter its people"(Zech. 1:21). "I will gather all nations and bring them down to the Valley of Jehoshaphat. There I will enter into judgment against them concerning My inheritance, My people Israel, for they scattered My people among the nations and divided up My land. They cast lots for My people ..." (Joel 3:2 f.). How relevant a warning this is to our politicians and to those with similar intentions in our day! And when we read "you sold the people of Judah and Jerusalem to the Greeks, that you might send them far from their homeland" (Joel 3:6), should we not feel uneasy about similar attempts to send the Jews to Uganda or wherever instead of to the Promised Land?

How awful the controversy of Non-Jews against Israel is in the eyes of God, is made especially clear by the following verses: "Israel is a scattered flock that lions have chased away. The first to devour him was the king of Assyria; the last to crush his bones was Nebuchadnezzar king of Babylon. Therefore this is what the LORD Almighty , the God of Israel, says: I will punish the king of Babylon and his land as I punished the king of Assyria" (Jer. 50:17 f.). It is against Edom that His threats come out: "Because you harboured an ancient hostility and delivered the Israelites over to the sword at the time of their calamity, the time their punishment reached its climax, therefore as surely as I live, declares the Sovereign LORD, I will give you over to bloodshed and it will pursue you" (Ezek. 35:5 f.). Yes, punishment applies also to those who "only" stood by, sat back and watched or looked away: "On the day you stood aloof while strangers carried off his (= Jacob's) wealth and foreigners entered his gates and cast lots for Jerusalem, you were like one of them ... Your deeds will return upon your own head" (Ob. 11 + 15). Even assistance for Israel that is only pretentious or superficial (as in the case of Egypt in those days – and today as well?) gets punished by God: "...You have been a staff of weed for the house of Israel. When they grasped you with their hands, you splintered and you tore open their shoulders; when they leaned on you, you broke and their backs were wrenched" (Ezek. 29:6 ff.)

Furthermore the Holy One of Israel proclaims: "...O mountains of Israel, hear the word of the LORD. This is what the Sovereign LORD says: The enemy said of you: ´Aha! The ancient heights have become our possession´... In My burning zeal I spoken against the rest of the nations, and against all Edom, for with glee and with malice in their hearts they made My land their own possession so that they might plunder its pastureland" (Ezek. 36:1 – 5; see also Jer. 49:1 ff.).

But taking possession is not confined to the physical land; it happened also in the spiritual sphere! "Son of man, because Tyre has said of Jerusalem, ´Aha! The gate to the nations is broken, and its doors have swung open to me; now that she lies in ruins I will prosper´, therefore this is what the Sovereign LORD says: I am against you ..." (Ezek. 26:2 f.). How many churches and congregations in many countries succumbed to such views and disseminate the false doctrine that the church is the "new Israel" and the only one to "prosper"! Let us listen with a respectful shudder to the words of the Holy One of Israel: "I am against you"!

So the LORD says in very plain and manifold terms that He punishes Israel´s enemies consistently because He is so serious about His love of the Jewish people. As in a light-focusing lens He sums this up in the following words: "...I am very jealous for Jerusalem and Zion, but I am very angry with the nations that feel secure". And He continues: "I was only a little angry, but they added to the calamity" (Zech. 1:14 f.). This might well be an answer to those who think the Holocaust "was from God"...

At the end of times the God of 'Abraham, Isaac and Jacob promises: "On that day I will set out to destroy all the nations that attack Jerusalem. And I will pour out on the house of David and the inhabitants of Jerusalem a spirit of grace and supplication" (Zech. 12:9 f.).

2) No things by halves!

"Now go, attack the Amalekites and totally destroy everything that belongs to them. Do not spare them..." (v. 3)
"To obey is better than sacrifice, and to heed is better than the fat of rams. For rebellion is like the sin of divination, and arrogance like the evil of idolatry" (v. 22 f.).

God´s instruction is clear and precise. But notice how Saul ignores it coldly. (Can it be that – after sincere scrutiny - we find ourselves mirroring some of his attitudes?) Saul spares the leader of the enemies. Let us apply this to us! Immanuel, David´s Son, admonishes us: Even when an evil spirit comes out, seven other spirits more wicked will return with it, if we do things by halves with God (Mt. 12:43 ff.). Therefore Paul writes: "...Don´t you know that a little yeast works through the whole batch of dough? Get rid of the old yeast..." (1 Cor. 5:6 f.).

"...the best of the sheep and cattle, the fat calves and lambs – everything that was good. These they were unwilling to destroy completely" (v. 9). What do we hold on to? Jeshua orders us: "Store up for yourselves treasures in heaven ... For where your treasure is, there your heart will be also" (Mt. 6:20 f.).

"When Samuel reached him, Saul said: The LORD bless you! I have carried out the LORD´s instructions" (v.13). In Proverbs we find clear words concerning such a hypocrisy: "The way of a fool seems right to him" (Prov. 12:15). Do you recall how Moses warned the people? There should be nobody who "...invokes a blessing on himself and therefore thinks, ´I will be safe, even though I persist in going my own way..." (Deut. 29:19).

When Samuel takes Saul to task for the bleating of sheep and lowing of cattle, Saul answers: *"The soldiers ...spared the best of the sheep and cattle to sacrifice to the LORD our God ...But I did obey the LORD...The soldiers took sheep and cattle from the plunder" (v.15 + 20 f.).* Although in the position of leadership, Saul uses the people as an excuse. Here we recognize an age-old behavioural pattern that goes all the way back to Adam and Eve: to off-load guilt onto someone else.

"I was afraid of the people and so I gave in to them", admits Saul (v. 24). The LORD asks us: "...Who are you that you fear mortal men, the sons of men, who are but grass?" (Isa. 51:12). David can confess: "The LORD is my light and my salvation – whom shall I fear?" (Ps. 27:1). And from Paul's letter to the Romans we know: "...those who are led by the Spirit of God are sons of God. For you did not receive a spirit that makes you a slave again to fear, but you received the Spirit of sonship. And by him we cry, ´Abba, Father" (Rom. 8:14 f.).

3) Interceding action of atonement

"And Samuel put Agag to death before the LORD at Gilgal" (v.33).

Since Saul spared the hostile king Agag against the strict order of God, Samuel finds himself compelled to take command in Saul's place in order to avert a curse from the people of Israel.

What a privilege it is for us to know the interceding sacrifice of our LORD Jeshua who blotted out our iniquity!
"When you were dead in your sins and in the uncircumcision of your sinful nature, God made you alive with Christ. He forgave us all our sins, having cancelled the written code, with its regulations, that was against us and that stood opposed to us; He took it away, nailing it to the cross" (Col. 2:13 f.). He "gave Himself for us to redeem us from all wickedness and to

purify for Himself a people that are His very own, eager to do what is good" (Titus 2:14).

Praise and glory to our Heavenly Father for sending us His only Son! "God made Him who had no sin to be sin for us, so that in Him we might become the righteousness of God" (2 Cor. 5:21). "For He has rescued us from the dominion of darkness and brought us into the kingdom of the Son He loves, in whom we have redemption, the forgiveness of sin" (Col. 1:13 f.). "Therefore there is no condemnation for those who are in Christ Jesus" (Rom. 8:1).

And how precious is this: We, who were once "...excluded from citizenship in Israel and foreigners to the covenants of the promise" now know that "...He Himself is our peace, who has made the two one and has destroyed the barrier, the dividing wall of hostility" (Eph. 2:12 – 14).

Shabbat Para

Ezekiel 36:16 – 38

One of the four Haftarah readings that precede the Feast of Pessach is "Shabbat Para". It refers to the Torah section dealing with the offering of a red cow and with the water of cleansing (Numbers 19:1–22). "Para" is the Hebrew word for cow.

1) The desecrated name of the Most High

"Son of man, when the people of Israel were living in their own land, they defiled it by their conduct and their actions. Their conduct was like a woman's monthly uncleanness in My sight. So I poured out My wrath on them because they had shed blood in the land and because they had defiled it with their idols. And I dispersed them among the nations ... And wherever they went among the nations they profaned My holy name..." (v.16–20).

These first verses can easily be grist for the mill of those who don't want to see anything good about Israel anyway. (That makes it all the more important to read the second part.) Yes, the Bible does not conceal guilt and wrong ways. Reading about the failure and disobedience of the Jewish people should be a severe warning to us, since we have no cause at all for turning up our noses or pointing our fingers at the Jews. "Do not judge, or you too will be judged" (Mt. 7:1).

At the very beginning of our reflections we should listen to God's promise: "As you have been an object of cursing among the nations, O Judah and Israel, so will I save you, and you will be a blessing" (Zech. 8:13). So uncompromising is the LORD in His faithfulness and love towards the Jewish people that He names the guilt, He punishes for offences, He keeps His promises, and finally He determines His beloved Israel to be a blessing in the world in spite of all her failures!

Israel gets punished for her bloodshed. What kind of bloodshed is it? It is not what some people may assume with regard to the recent history of Israel, the bloodshed of war. Why not? In the days of the Old Testament Israel went to war according to God´s strict order, so that the idolatry of the pagans should be eliminated. (And nowadays Israel is urged to wage defensive wars in order to protect their citizens.) No, it is about another kind of blood: "…Since you eat meat with the blood still in it and look to your idols and shed blood…" (Ezek. 33:25). Idolatry entails terrible offences: "They did not destroy the peoples as the LORD had commanded them, but they mingled with the nations and adopted their customs. They worshiped their idols, which became a snare to them. They sacrificed their sons and their daughters to demons. They shed innocent blood, the blood of their sons and daughters, whom they sacrificed to the idols of Canaan, and the land was desecrated by their blood" (Ps. 106:34–38).

This was of course a horror in God´s view. His holy name must not be desecrated. The world should recognize that the God of Israel is the Holy One. The Jewish people received the calling to bear witness to that. But *"wherever they went among the nations they profaned My holy name, for it was said of them, 'These are the LORD´s people, and yet they had to leave His land"* (v.20).
What about us? May it also be that those around us recognize that our behaviour does not fit our calling? How often may we have profaned the name of our LORD Jesus whereas we should be "…a letter from Christ, the result of our ministry" (2 Cor.

3:3). Live "good lives among the pagans" Paul calls out to us (1 Peter 2:12). "Just as He who called you is holy, so be holy in all you do" (1 Peter 1:15).I pray to the Heavenly Father: "May those who hope in You not be disgraced because of me, O LORD, the LORD Almighty; may those who seek You not be put to shame because of me, O God of Israel" (Ps. 69:6).

2) God´s promises for the sake of His name

"I had concern for My holy name, which the house of Israel profaned among the nations where they had gone. Therefore say to the house of Israel, 'This is what the Sovereign LORD says: It is not for your sake, O house if Israel, ... but for the sake of My holy name... I will show the holiness of My great name, which has been profaned among the nations" (v. 21-23).

We read in the following verses how the Holy One of Israel intends to and will treat His people so that the world will recognize Him as the Almighty God. He bestows on them a multitude of blessings. We should realize that as we read it here, God takes action only towards Israel. Nevertheless we want to ask whether and in what ways, concerning several gifts of God there are similarities for us as Christians.

a)"The nations will know that I am the LORD, declares the Sovereign LORD, when I show Myself holy through you before their eyes" (v. 23)
Israel has such a pre-eminence in God´s plan of salvation and the changes for good will be so enormous after all the dramatic changes in history, that all the world will realize the acting one as the Sovereign. "Israel will be saved by the LORD with an everlasting salvation... Gather together and come, assemble, you fugitives from the nations, ...There is no God apart from Me, a righteous God and a Saviour, there is none but Me. ...

Before Me every knee will bow, by Me every tongue will swear. They will say of Me, 'In the LORD alone are righteousness and strength" (Isa. 45:17–24).

God has set aside Israel for a certain while so that the pagans should also have a chance to recognize Him. "Because of their transgression, salvation has come to the Gentiles..." (Rom. 11:11). But it is always individuals who are added to the first chosen people, never a whole nation or an entire people. Through the way in which God is at work in the lives of believers, those who are still far from Him shall recognize Him as Saviour.

b) "I will take you out of the nations; I will gather you from all the countries..." (v. 24)

The Creator gathers believers from all corners of the earth "...until the full number of the Gentiles has come in" (Rom. 11:25). God "wants all men to be saved and to come to a knowledge of the truth" (1 Tim. 2:4). "For God so loved the world that He gave His one and only Son, that whoever believes in Him shall not perish but have eternal life" (John 3:16).

The Jewish people, too, is being gathered from all four directions by the LORD, but only this people exactly at one place.

c) "... and bring you back into your own land" (v. 24).

After nearly 2000 years the Jewish people returned (and continue to return) to the same land they were expelled from and that the LORD had named specifically. This miracle is unique in world history.

Is there also a land promised to us? There is a German chorus „Take possession of he good land God gives to you" (Nimm ein das gute Land; das Gott dir gibt!). Our good Shepherd Jeshua says: "In My Father´s house are many rooms; if it were not so, I would have told you. .I am going there to prepare a place for you" (John 14:2 f.).

d) "I will sprinkle clean water on you, and you will be clean" (v. 25)

Unfortunately we have grown accustomed to relating these words first of all to us, and we easily disregard that they are explicitly spoken to Israel. But there is this enormous, nearly incomprehensible promise for the end of the times: "In those days, at that time, declares the LORD, search will be made for Israel´s guilt, but there will be none, and for the sins of Judah, but none will be found, for I will forgive the remnant I spare" (Jer. 50:20). We don´t find such a promise of a national movement of repentance (Zech. 12:10) and national atonement for any other nation.

Nevertheless: we can rejoice that we are cleansed "...by the washing with water through the word" (Eph. 5:26) and to know the precious promise of Jesus: "Whoever drinks the water I give him will never thirst. Indeed, the water I give him will become in him a spring of water welling up to eternal life" (John 4:14).

e) "I will give you a new heart and put a new spirit in you; I will remove from you your heart of stone and give you a heart of flesh" (v. 26)

First of all we need to have this in mind again: These words are spoken to the Jewish people. God swore everlasting faithfulness towards Israel. Therefore He does not abandon them in spite of their failure. We to can hope for this grace. "Create in me a pure heart, O God, and renew a steadfast spirit within me!" (Ps. 51:10). When this is granted to us it can be that we are "...a letter from Christ, the result of our ministry, written not with ink but with the Spirit of the living God, not on tablets of stone but on tablets of human hearts" (2 Cor. 3:3).

f) "I will move you to follow My decrees and be careful to keep My laws" (v. 27).
The LORD will do it! He alone can do it! Neither Jews nor Christians can keep His commandments by their own strength. Therefore "let us fix our eyes on Jesus, the author and perfecter of our faith" (Hebr. 12: 2).

g) "You will be My people, and I will be your God" (v. 28).
Here we are reminded of the words in 1 Peter 2:9: "You are a chosen people , a royal priesthood, a holy nation, a people belonging to God". Indeed, this is valid for the congregation of the New Covenant, which consists of believers from many nations. But this precious promise does not in any case substitute for the promise given to Israel. The congregation, the church, is added alongside Israel and does not replace the first beloved people. (See Rom. 11:1-21)

h) "And I will increase the fruit of the trees and the crops of the field" (v. 30).
The God of Israel not only guides His people back into the Promised Land, but He faithfully supplies their needs in great abundance.
Among Christians there is a so called "Welfare Theology" proclaiming it is a sign of true faith to be blessed in an exceptional way with earthly goods, culminating in the theory that the more you believe, the wealthier you will be. This is a false doctrine. But of course we can trust that our loving Father knows quite well all that we need and that He gives us beyond our immediate needs. "God is able to make all grace abound to you, so that in all things at all times, having all that you need, you will abound in every good work" (2 Cor. 9:8).Everything depends on God´s grace and not on the amount of our faith.

i) "I will resettle your towns, and the ruins will be rebuilt... They will say: `This land that was laid waste has become like the garden of Eden" (v. 33–35).

Mark Twain is often cited as the one who, when visiting Palestine at the end of the nineteenth century, stated that the land was totally deserted and inhospitable. What a contrast to how Israel appears nowadays! There are large forests, nice parks, luxuriant splendour of flowers (even in the desert after the rainy season!), flourishing agriculture and attractive towns. The LORD gave success to the diligent and imperturbable people of Israel and let His promise come true.

Is there a parallel in the life of Christians? We know from experience that our LORD can encourage, comfort and strengthen us again and again, if something is broken within us or through us. What a wonderful perspective we have is illustrated by the following verses for example! "The righteous will flourish like a palm tree , they will grow like a cedar of Lebanon; planted in the house of the LORD, they will flourish in the courts of our God" (Ps. 92:12 f.).

j) "Once again I will yield to the plea of the house of Israel and do this for them: I will make their people as numerous as sheep" (v. 37).

God answers prayers. We too may ask Him for the growth of our congregations and for the spreading of the Gospel in the world.

k) "I want you to know that I am not doing this for your sake, declares the Sovereign LORD. Be ashamed and disgraced for your conduct, O house of Israel!" (v. 32).

Although the God of Abraham, Isaac and Jacob loves His people with an everlasting love, He says that His miraculous deeds are not because of Israel. Why? He calls Israel "…My people, who are called by My name" (2 Chr. 7:14). Everything concerns the honour of His holy name which has to be re-established. In the LORD´s Prayer we pray "Hallowed be Your name!" This has to be the central concern of our lives.

Recalling the inconceivable grace God has granted to each of us innumerable times, we can only be ashamed of our failures and decide to bring them to Him again and again. "Or do you show contempt for the riches of His kindness, tolerance and patience, not realizing that God´s kindness leads you towards repentance?" (Rom. 2:4).

Shabbat Hagadol

Malachi 3:4 – 4: 6

The Shabbat preceding Pessach is called "the great Shabbat". (There are several different explanations for that name. One refers to Malachi, who speaks of a "great and dreadful day of the LORD", Mal. 4:5). Malachi speaks to the Jewish people in a period when they are not only unfaithful but even carelessly ask "Where is the God of justice?" (Mal. 2:17). Therefore he calls them to repent and announces the day of the Last Judgement. Why is this text read just before Pessach? While Pessach is celebrated as feast of release in the past, the Haftara speaks of a future salvation.

1) The tithe

"Return to Me, and I will return to you, says the LORD Almighty. But you ask, 'How are we to return?' Will a man rob God? ... Bring the whole tithe into the storehouse, that there may be food in My house. Test Me in this, says the LORD Almighty, and see if I will not throw open the floodgates of heaven and pour out so much blessing that you will not have room enough for it" (v. 7-10).

The first time we read about the tithe in the Bible is in connection with Melchizedek, king of Salem and "priest of God Most High", to whom Abram gave "a tenth of everything" after being rescued from his enemies (Gen. 14:18 ff.). And Jacob makes a vow: If God brings him safely back from Haran and provides for him, "...of all that You give me I will give You a tenth" (Gen. 28:22). Several times in the five books of Moses the tithe is prescribed as an offering. Differences in details are not important enough to be described here (Lev. 27:30 ff.; Num. 18:25 ff: Deut. 14:22 ff.). But statements like these are important: "A tithe of everything ... belongs to the LORD; it is holy to the LORD" (Lev. 27:30). And: "Be sure to set aside a tenth of all..." (Deut. 14:22). When we withhold something from the LORD it is out of selfishness. In Haggai we read: "These people say: 'The time has not yet come for the LORD's house to be built.' ...Is it a time for you yourselves to be living in your panelled houses, while this house remains a ruin?" (Haggai 1:2-4). *"Will a man rob God?"*

But our attention is also drawn to some other dangers. Amos exposes the failure to bring "tithes every three years" only (Am. 4:4). This could be a warning for us not to wait with our financial offering to see whether there are still some leftovers after our purchases or to donate quickly by the end of the year so that it has a favourable tax deduction.

But does the commandment to give the tithe to the LORD apply to the New Testament also? Yes, we know that Jesus Christ never revoked this rule. He only opposes undesirable ways of carrying it out practically. In one of Jesus' parables, a complacent Pharisee insists on his achievement: "I fast twice a week and give the tenth of all I get" (Luk. 18:12). We certainly cannot buy anything with our tithe! "Woe to you, teachers of the law and Pharisees, you hypocrites! You give a tenth of your spices – mint, dill and cumin. But you have neglected the more important matters of the law – justice, mercy and faithfulness" (Mt. 23:23). Luke writes in this context: "...you neglect ... the love of God" (Luk. 11:42).
The words of Paul also can be applied to the tithe offering: "If I give all I possess to the poor and surrender my body to the flames, but have not love, I gain nothing" (1 Cor. 13:3). How

should we be disposed while giving? "...not reluctantly or under compulsion, for God loves a cheerful giver" (2 Cor. 9:7).

What a wonderful promise we have concerning the blessing we receive if we give the tithe toward His kingdom in faithfulness and obedience! He will *"open the floodgates of heaven"* and pour out blessings in abundance (v. 10). The Israelites experience that in the days of Hezekiah when they once again begin to observe the sacrificial laws after abolishing the idols: "Since the people began to bring their contributions to the temple of the LORD, we have had enough to eat and plenty to spare, because the LORD has blessed His people..." (2 Chr. 31:10).

2) The scroll of remembrance

"A scroll of remembrance was written in His presence concerning those who feared the LORD and honoured His name. They will be Mine, says the LORD Almighty, in the day when I make up My treasured possession" (v.16 f.)
"And you will again see the distinction between the righteous and the wicked, between those who serve God and those who do not" (v.18).
"But for you who revere My name, the sun of righteousness will rise with healing in its wings" (4:2)

From Psalm 139:16 we can conclude that the name of every human being is written in a book that belongs to God, which the Bible speaks of "the Book of Life: "All the days ordained for me were written in Your book before one of them came to be". But then there are two different fates: to remain inscribed in the book or to be deleted from it.
Moses is well aware of this when he intercedes for the people who were guilty of creating and worshipping a golden calf.

"But now, please forgive their sin – but if not, then blot me out of the book You have written. The LORD replied to Moses, 'Whoever has sinned against Me I will blot out of My book" (Ex. 32:32 f.). So it may be understandable that David prays with regard to Israel's enemies who were guilty before God: "May they be blotted out of the book of life and not be listed with the righteous!" (Ps. 69:28).

In Revelation we read about those worshipping the blaspheming beast instead of the exalted LORD: "All inhabitants of the earth will worship the beast – all whose names have not been written in the book of life belonging to the Lamb that was slain from the creation of the world" (Rev. 13:8; see Rev. 17:8). "If anyone's name was not found written in the book of life, he was thrown into the lake of fire" (Rev. 20:15). So only those will become citizens of the New Jerusalem whose names were not blotted out from the book: "Nothing impure will ever enter it, nor will anyone who does what is shameful or deceitful, but only those whose names are written in the Lamb's book of life" (Rev. 21:27).

Now the question is: Who will have their names written in the book of life? We find several clues in the Holy Scripture: Paul speaks of those "…who have contended at my side in the cause of the gospel … whose names are in the book of life" (Phil. 4:3). In the letter to the church in Sardis, the LORD speaks of people "…who have not soiled their clothes. They will walk with Me, dressed in white, for they are worthy. He who overcomes will, like them, be dressed in white. I will never blot out his name from the book of life, but will acknowledge his name before My Father and His angels" (Rev. 3:4 f.)

Is it then true that only the names of born-again Christians are written in the book of life? Far from it! "In that day the Branch of the LORD will be beautiful and glorious, and the fruit of the land will be the pride and glory of the survivors in Israel. Those who are left in Zion, who remain in Jerusalem, will be called holy, all who are recorded among the living in Jerusalem" (Isa. 4:2 f.). The author of the letter to the Hebrews turns to the followers of Jesus with these words: "You have come to Mount Zion, to the heavenly Jerusalem, the city of the living God. You have come to thousands upon thousands of angels in joyful assembly, to the church of the firstborn, whose names are written in heaven. You have come to God, the judge of all men, to the spirits of righteous men made perfect, to Jesus the mediator of a new covenant" (Hebr. 12:22–24). Interpreters of the Bible say the "righteous men made perfect" are the saints of the First Covenant, justified through their faith.

Furthermore, the vision of Daniel makes very clear the importance that the book of life has also for the Jews: "At that time Michael, the great prince who protects your people, will arise. There will be a time of distress such as has not happened from the beginning of nations until then. But at that time your people – everyone whose name is found written in the book – will be delivered. Multitudes who sleep in the dust of the earth will awake: some to everlasting life, others to shame and everlasting contempt. Those who are wise will shine like the brightness of the heavens, and those who lead many to righteousness, like the stars for ever and ever" (Dan. 12:1-3).
What do we read in the Haftarah? *"And you will again see the distinction between the righteous and the wicked, between those who serve God and those who do not... But for you who revere My name, the sun of righteousness will rise with healing in its wings. And you will go out and leap like calves released from the stall" (3:18 + 4:2).*

Indeed, what a reason for rejoicing! The LORD Jesus explains this also to His seventy disciples when they return joyfully from their missions: "Do not rejoice that the spirits submit to you, but rejoice that your names are written in heaven" (Luk. 10:20).

By the way, Jews greet each other on Yom Kippur wishing: "May you be enrolled and sealed to a good and long life, together with all the righteous of Israel!"

Pessach[22]

Joshua 5:2 – 6:1,27

Each day of the feast of Pessach we read another section of the books of Moses. On the first day it is Ex. 12:21–51. The supplementary text is about the people of Israel celebrating Passah for the first time in the Promised Land, after being circumcised.

1) Circumcision

"In that time the LORD said to Joshua, 'Make flint knives and circumcise the Israelites again" (5:2)
"Now this is why he did so: All those who came out of Egypt – all the men of military age – died in the desert on the way after leaving Egypt. All the people that came out had been circumcised, but all the people born in the desert during the journey from Egypt had not" 5:4 f.)
"And after the whole nation had been circumcised... Then the LORD said to Joshua: Today I have rolled away the reproach of Egypt from you" (5:8 f.)

Concerning circumcision, we read in Gen. 17:10 ff: "This is My covenant with you and your descendants after you, the covenant you are to keep: Every male among you shall be circumcised... For the generations to come every male among you who is eight days old must be circumcised" (See Gen. 21:4) That is why Jesus too was circumcised on the eighth day (Luk. 1:59).

---

[22] The Haftarah is read on the first day of Pessach.

After crossing the Jordan the whole people of Israel is circumcised irrespective of their age, because the LORD wants to roll away the disgrace from the whole people.

What does the term "circumcision" mean to us? To begin with, we should be aware that the LORD speaks about circumcision as a metaphor for inner cleansing: ""Circumcise your hearts and do not be stiff-necked any longer" (Deut. 10:16). "Break up your unplowed ground and do not sow among thorns. Circumcise yourself to the LORD, circumcise your hearts" (Jer. 4:3 f.). Since these words apply both to Israel and us, it is obviously up to us men to act. We can and we must decide not to be rebellious against God any more, but to humbly submit to His wise guidance.

But on the other hand we read also what the New Tesatament says about our circumcision in Christ: "In Him you were also circumcised, in the putting off of the sinful nature, not with a circumcision done by hands of men but with the circumcision done by Christ, having been buried with Him in baptism and raised with Him ... When you were dead in your sins and in the uncircumcision of your sinful nature, God made you alive with Christ. He forgave us all our sins" (Col. 2:11–13). For such "heart surgery" both are needed: We need to say yes to it and the Great Physician needs to take action. Also in the book of Moses we find both next to each other: "When you and your children return to the LORD your God," then the promise: "The LORD your God will circumcise your hearts and the hearts of your descendants, so that you may love Him with all your heart and with all your soul, and live" (Deut. 30:2 + 6).

In the early history of the church a controversy arose as to whether physical circumcision is also required for the followers of Jesus. A council invoked to address this issue rejected the need for physical circumcision and decided: "It seemed good to the Holy Spirit and to us not to burden you with anything beyond the following requirements: You are to abstain from food sacrificed to idols, from blood, from the meat of strangled animals and from sexual immorality" (Acts 15:28 f.). Paul takes up this decision with the following words: "Was a man already circumcised when he was called? He should not become uncircumcised. Was a man uncircumcised when he was called? He should not be circumcised. Circumcision is nothing and uncircumcision is nothing. Keeping God´s commandments is what counts" (1 Cor. 7:18 f.). "Circumcision has value if you observe the law, but if you break the law, you have become as though you had not been circumcised" (Rom. 2:25; see Gal. 5:2 f.).

Concerning the connection between circumcision and faith Paul points out: Abraham "received the sign of circumcision, a seal of the righteousness that he had by faith while he was still uncircumcised" (Rom. 4:11). Faith and obedience in faith are crucial. "For in Christ Jesus neither circumcision nor uncircumcision has any value. The only thing that counts is faith expressing itself through love" (Gal. 5:6). "For it is we who are the circumcision, we who worship by the Spirit of God" (Phil. 3:3). To summarize the importance of circumcision for Jews and Christians, Pauls says in a concise way: There is only one God, who will "…justify the circumcision b y faith and uncircumcision t h r o u g h faith" (Rom 3:30; King James Version).

2)   Gilgal

"Then the LORD said to Joshua: 'Today I have rolled away the reproach of Egypt from you.' So the place has been called Gilgal to this day" (5:9).

This is a day of a new beginning. The burdens of the past have no meaning any more. We are reminded what our Saviour Jeshua has done for us: "Surely He took up our infirmities and carried our sorrows ... The punishment that brought us peace was upon Him, and by His wounds we are healed" (Isa. 53:4 f). "He forgave us all our sins, having cancelled the written code, with the regulations, that was against us and that stood opposed to us; He took it away, nailing it to the cross" (Col. 2:13 f.). The reproach is rolled away!

Now what does the LORD mean by the "reproach of Egypt" concerning Israel? Is it the "reproach" that the Jewish people have not been circumcised throughout the long journey in the desert? Did the disgrace still cling to them that they were oppressed by the Egyptians for forty years? It is decisive to know that the reproach was rolled away!

The name of the place "Gilgal" is derived from the Hebrew word "gilgel, what means "to roll, to turn something over". Gilgal is the place where Joshua set up twelve stones in memory of the crossing of the river Jordan (Josh. 4:19 ff.), a place of new beginning. Elsewhere in the Scripture we read again of Gilgal in connection with a new beginning. It is from Gilgal that an angel comes with a threat of punishment from the LORD after Israel made an alliance with foreign people, and he brings about a new approach to the LORD in tears (Judges 2:1 ff.). When after the anointing of Saul some do not acknowledge him as king, we're told: "Then Samuel said to the people, ´Come, let us go to Gilgal and there reaffirm the kingship!´ So all the people went to Gilgal and confirmed Saul as king in the presence of the LORD" (1 Sam. 11:14 f.). In Gilgal Samuel put Agag to death, the king of the Amalekites who has been falsely spared by Saul. Because of that the punishment of God is averted from Israel (1 Sam. 15:33). The people of Judah come to Gilgal to meet David who fled from Absalom and to call him back as king (2 Sam. 19:16). And when the sons of the prophets nearly eat something poisonous it is again in Gilgal that Elisha is able to counter succcessfully the concern that "...there is death in the pot" (2 Kings 4:38 ff.). But it is also in Gilgal that Saul is deprived of royal dignity because of his premature and unauthorized offering (1 Sam. 13:8 ff.). So the place of Gilgal is often connected with some kind of turning point. And at the time of Joshua the *"reproach is rolled away"* from Israel after their renewed circumcision. After that, the Israelites celebrate the Passover in the Promised Land for the first time (Joshua 5:10).

3) Stages of supply

"On the evening of the fourteenth day of the month, while camped at Gilgal on the plains of Jericho, the Israelites celebrated the Passover. The day after the Passover, that very day, they ate some of the produce of the land: unleavened bread and roasted grain. The manna stopped the day after they ate this food from the land; there was no longer any manna for the Israelites, but that year they ate of the produce of Canaan" (5:10–12).

Keep in mind this amazing report: "Then the LORD said to Moses: I will rain down bread from heaven for you. The people are to go out each day and gather enough for that day. In this way I will test them and see whether they will follow My instructions. On the sixth day they are to prepare what they bring in, and that is to be twice as much as they gather on the other days" (Ex. 16:4 f.). The Sabbath shall be free from work of gathering.

This is a marvellous example of how the LORD faithfully provides. Jeshua admonishes us: "Do not worry, saying, ´What shall we eat?´ or ´What shall we drink?´ or ´What shall we wear?´ For the pagans run after all these things, and your Heavenly Father knows that you need them" (Mt. 6:31 f.).

During all the journey through the drought of the desert God provided for His people in great faithfulness : "The Israelites ate manna forty years, until they came to a land that was settled; they ate manna until they reached the border of Canaan" (Ex. 16:35). *"The manna stopped the day after ..."* Why is that? By entry into the Promised Land "of milk and honey" God no longer needs to rain down food directly from heaven, because the Jewish people are meant to meet their need for food on their own from now on and to enjoy the yield of the land.

Shawuot[23]

Habakkuk 2:20 – 3:19

On Shawuot the people of Israel remember that they received the Law on Mount Sinai. In addition, the "Feast of Weeks" is celebrated as "Feast of the Firstfruits of the Wheat Harvest". In Exodus 34, where we learn about this festival, God reveals Himself as "the compassionate and gracious God, slow to anger, abounding in love and faithfulness(v. 6). And He speaks to Moses: "Before all your people I will do wonders never before done in any nation in all the world" (v. 10). The Haftarah text, too, speaks about mercy and miraculous salvation.

1) Wrath and mercy

"In wrath remember mercy!" (3:2)
"In wrath You strode through the earth and in anger You threshed the nations" (v. 12).
"You came out to deliver Your people, to save Your anointed one" (v. 13).

Sometimes it is said that the "God of the Old Testament" was a God of wrath, but the "God of the New Testament" is a God of mercy. This is simply not true, however. Consider the following words of God from the Old Testament, for example: "As a mother comforts her child, so will I comfort you" (Isa. 66:13) or of the words mentioned above from Exodus 34:6. On the other hand we read in the New Testament: "It is a dreadful thing to fall into the hands of the living God" (Hebr. 10:31).

---

[23] The Haftarah is read on the second day of Shawuot.

Both are true about God: wrath as well as mercy. We believe in the one true God who says of Himself: "I AM WHO I AM" (Ex. 3:14), "who does not change like shifting shadows" (James 1:17).

When Habakkuk asks the LORD *"In wrath remember mercy" he* tacitly admits: Yes indeed, Your wrath is justified. The Bible does not conceal or excuse the fact that the Israelites were guilty. "They have rejected the law of the LORD Almighty and spurned the word of the Holy One of Israel, Therefore the LORD´s anger burns against His people; His hand is raised and He strikes them down" (Isa. 5:24 f.). That is why Israel was sent into exile and dispersed among the nations, and that is why the Temple was destroyed. (But we have no reason at all to point with our fingers towards the failure of others.)

We read also that Isaiah can pass on the good news to the people of Israel: "The LORD longs to be gracious to you; He rises to show you compassion. For the LORD is a God of justice. Blessed are all who wait for Him! O people of Zion, who live in Jerusalem, you will weep no more. How gracious He will be when you cry for help! As soon as He hears, He will answer you" (Isa. 30:18 f.). God says: "Though in anger I struck you, in favour I will show you compassion" (Isa. 60:10).

As mentioned before, we also read of an angry Got in the New Testament, and because we are all guilty of sin, we deserve God´s wrath. How is it possible for us "...to flee from the coming wrath? Produce fruit in keeping with repentance", Jesus says (Mt. 3:7 f.). "Or do you show contempt for the riches of His kindness, tolerance and patience, not realizing that God´s kindness leads you towards repentance?" (Rom. 2:4). It is Jesus "...who rescues us from the coming wrath" (1

Thess. 1:10). "Since we have now been justified by His blood, how much more shall we be saved from God´s wrath through Him!" (Rom. 5:9). This is our incomprehensible privilege": Whoever believes in the Son has eternal life, but whoever rejects the Son will not see life, for God´s wrath remains on him" (John 3:36).

2)   Yet I will ...

"Though the fig tree does not bud and there are no grapes on the vines, though the olive crop fails and the fields produce no food, though there are no sheep in the pen and no cattle in the stalls, yet I will rejoice in the LORD, I will be joyful in God my Saviour. The Sovereign LORD is my strength..." (3:17 f.)

Despite the hopelessness all around him, Habakkuk nevertheless decides to rejoice and be cheerful. Are we not reminded of Job? "I know that my redeemer lives, and that in the end He will stand upon the earth.... I myself will see Him with my own eyes – I, and not another" (Job 19:25 and 27). Obviously both Job and Habakkuk have a perspective that reaches far beyond their present misery.

"Yet I will", that is an act of volition. One needs strength for that. Where does such strength from? *"The Sovereign LORD is my strength"*. From the book of Isaiah come these well-known verses: "Even youths grow tired and weary, and young men stumble and fall; but those who hope in the LORD will renew their strength..." (Isa. 40:30 f.). Here we come across the same "but, yet", as in 1 Sam. 30:6: "David was greatly distressed because the men were talking of stoning him ...But David found strength in the LORD his God". We read of how Jonathan, the son of Saul, strengthened David´s hand in God (1

Sam. 23: 16). But how can we find strength in the LORD? The letter to the Ephesians gives us a hint: "Be strong in the LORD and in His mighty power. Put on the full armour of God ..." (t Eph. 6:10-17).

Isaiah confesses: "Surely God is my salvation; I will trust and not be afraid. The LORD, the LORD is my strength and my song; He has become my salvation" (Isa. 12:2). By the way, in Hebrew, the phrase "God is my salvation" is "El jeshuati" – revealing the word for Jeshua, our Saviour. Just as Job hopes to see the LORD with his own eyes, so we can await in amazement: "We shall see Him as He is" (1 John 3:2). In anticipation we may rejoice like Habakkuk: *"He makes my feet like the feet of a deer, He enables me to go on the heights" (3:19).*

Tisha b´Av

Jeremiah 8:13 – 9:24

Tisha b´Av is a day of mourning as a reminder that on this very day, the ninth of the month Av (about July) not only the first temple in 587 BC but also the second temple in 70 AD was destroyed. In Israel these events make us aware of the punishment of God.

The Parasha (Deut. 4:25-40) also comprises a warning against disobedience followed by the dispersion among the nations, as well as the promise that the LORD will be found by those who seek Him earnestly and sincerely. "Has any god ever tried to take for himself one nation out of another nation, by testings, by miraculous signs and wonders, by war, by a mighty hand and an outstretched arm, or by great and awesome deeds, like all the things the LORD your God did for you in Egypt before your very eyes? You were shown these things so that you might know that the LORD is God; besides Him there is no other" (verse 34 f.).

In addition to the entire book of Lamentations, the supplementary text on Tisha b´Av is a paragraph that clearly names and laments Israel´s failure but also calls for seeing the God of Abraham, Isaac and Jacob in His mercy and justice.

1) Sorrow and need for comfort

"O my Comforter in sorrow, my heart is faint within me" (8:18)
"Since my people are crushed, I am crushed; I mourn, and horror grips me... Oh, that my head were a spring of water and my eyes a fountain of tears! I would weep day and night for the slain of my people" (8:21 – 9:1)

In the book of Nehemiah we read that from afar he asks about the situation of the Jews and the condition of Jerusalem. When he hears of the devastation of the wall in Jerusalem and of great disaster, he says: "I sat down and wept. For some days I mourned and fasted and prayed before the God of heaven" (Neh. 1:4). What about us when we think back to the dreadful occurrences of the Holocaust and when we witness the current hostilities to the Jews and horror in Israel? Are we touched by this or do we just go on doing whatever the day holds? "Who will have pity on you, O Jerusalem? Who will mourn for you? Who will stop to ask how you are?" (Jer. 15:5). "No one is near to comfort me, no one to restore my spirit" (Lam. 1:16; similar: Lam. 1:2 and 21). The LORD knows about this need and therefore once said of Jerusalem "O afflicted city, lashed by storms and not comforted" (Isa. 54:11). David cries: "I looked for sympathy, but there was none, for comforters, but I found none" (Ps. 69:20).

It is therefore all the more important to hear what the LORD instructs us to do: "Comfort, comfort My people, says your God. Speak tenderly to Jerusalem…" (Isa. 40:1). It is certainly proper to be "sympathetic, love as brothers, be compassionate" (1 Pt. 3:8). We are brothers who in former times were "excluded from citizenship in Israel" – but now are reconciled to God through the blood of Christ as "one body" with the Jews and are "fellow citizens with God´s people and members of God´s household" (Eph. 2:11–19). And because we are members of one body with the Jews, what we read in 1 Cor. 12:26 applies to us: "If one part suffers, every part suffers with it."

2) The process of melting

"I will take away their harvest, declares the LORD. There will be no grapes on the vine. There will be no figs on the tree, and their leaves will wither. What I have given them will be taken from them" (8:13).
"We hoped for peace but no good has come, for a time of healing but there was only terror" (8:15).
"See I will refine and test them, for what else can I do because of the sin of My people?" (9:7).

Jeremiah laments a multitude of sins -- which are also found among us and with us, alas! These include idolatry – as if there were no Almighty God ("Is the LORD not in Zion?", 8:19) -- adultery, lies, insidiousness, and fraud.

But miraculously the LORD carries out a purification instead of final rejection. It is an act of His mercy, even when it is painful, "because the LORD disciplines those He loves..." (Hebr. 12:6). That is why it says in Proverbs: "My son, do not despise the LORD´s discipline and do not resent His rebuke!" (Prov. 3:11). "No discipline seems pleasant at the time, but painful. Later on, however, it produces a harvest of righteousness and peace for those who have been trained by it" (Hebr. 12:11). To ensure that such fruit can come about, the LORD resorts to a process that He compares to the melting of silver and gold. He says to Israel: "See, I have refined you, though not as silver; I have tested you in the furnace of affliction" (Isa. 48:10; see Ezek. 22:17 ff.)

Through how much misery the people of Israel had to go! But nevertheless God emphasizes: "I will not completely destroy you. I will discipline you but only with justice; I will not let you go entirely unpunished" (Jer. 46:28; The King James

Version reads: "I will not make a full end of thee, but correct thee in measure"; See also Jer. 30:11). This process of purification is the expression of divine mercy. There is still a chance! And notice what is written in Lamentations that is read on Tisha b´Av, too: "For men are not cast off by the LORD forever. Though He brings grief, He will show compassion, so great is His unfailing love. For He does not willingly bring affliction or grief to the children of men" (Lam. 3:31 ff.; see also Jer. 3:12). Our loving Father in Heaven wants to rebuke and correct us. We already read about the "fruit of justice". As Isaiah puts it: "When Your judgments come upon the earth, the people of the world learn righteousness" (Isa. 26:9). Every one of us needs this process of learning and refining again and again. "Repent and live!" (Ezek. 18:32). Our LORD Jesus turns to Peter saying: "Unless I wash you, you have no part with Me" (John 13:8).

This purification is for our healing, as our conversion is just the beginning of a life-long training of our hearts in God´s school! "So I tell you this, and insist on it in the LORD, that you must no longer live as the Gentiles do, in the futility of their thinking… You, however, did not come to know Christ that way. Surely you heard of Him and were taught in Him in accordance with the truth that is in Jesus. You were taught, with regard to your former way of life, to put off your old self …" (Eph. 4:17 and 20 ff.). Then we shall gain the attitude Paul identifies in Phil. 3:7 f.: "Whatever was to my profit I now consider loss for the sake of Christ. What is more, I consider everything a loss compared to the surpassing greatness of knowing Christ Jesus my LORD…"

We shall honour and love God as our merciful and just LORD, just as is expressed in the last verses of our Haftarah text: *"This is what the LORD says: 'Let not the wise man boast of his wisdom or the strong man boast of his strength or the rich man boast of his riches, but let him who boasts boast about this: that he understands and knows Me, that I am the LORD, who exercises kindness, justice and righteousness on earth, for in these I delight´, declares the LORD" (9:23 f.)*

Why is the LORD so merciful in spite of Israel´s failure and our failure? He lets us know: "For My own name´s sake I delay My wrath; for the sake of My praise I hold it back from you, so as not to cut you off. See, I have refined you, though not as silver; I have tested you in the furnace of affliction. For My own sake, for My own sake, I do this. How can I let Myself be defamed? I will not yield My glory to another" (Isa. 48:9 ff.).

Ultimately everything is about glorifying God´s name. And so these verses are a precious and powerful closing to this exegesis of the Haftarot.

Table of Contents

Haftarot concerning Genesis page 12

1	Isaiah 42:5 – 43:10
2	Isaiah 54:1 – 55:5
3	Isaiah 40:27 - 41:16
4	2 Kings 4:1 – 37
5	1 Kings 1:1 – 31
6	Malachi 1:1 – 2:7
7	Hosea 12:13 – 14:10
8	Obadiah 1:1 – 21
9	Amos 2:6 – 3:8
10	1 Kings 3:15 – 4:1
11	Ezekiel 37:15 – 28
12	1 Kings 2:1 – 12

Haftarot concerning Exodus page 70

13	Isaiah 27:6 – 28:13 and 29:22 – 24
14	Ezekiel 28:25 – 29:21
15	Jeremiah 46:13 – 28
16	Judges 4:4 – 5:31
17	Isaiah 6:1 – 7:6 and 9:6 - 7
18	Jeremiah 34:8 – 22 and 33:25 – 26
19	1 Kings 5:12 – 6:13
20	Ezekiel 43:10 – 27
21	1 Kings 18:1 – 39
22	1 Kings 7:13 – 26
23	1 Kings 7:51 – 8:21

Haftarot concerning Leviticus page 129

24	Isaiah 43:21 – 44:23
25	Jeremiah 7:21 – 8:3 and 9:22 – 23
26	2 Samuel 6:1 – 7:17
27	2 Kings 4:42 – 5:19
28	2 Kings 7:3 – 20
29	Ezekiel 22:1 – 19
30	Amos 9:7 – 15
31	Ezekiel 44:15 – 31
32	Jeremiah 32:6 – 27
33	Jeremiah 16:19 – 17:14

Haftarot concerning Numbers page 182

34	Hosea 1:10 – 2:20
35	Judges 13:2 – 25
36	Zechariah 2:14 – 4:7
37	Joshua 2:1 – 24
38	1 Samuel 11:14 – 12:22
39	Judges 11:1 – 33
40	Micah 5:6 – 6:8
41	1 Kings 18:46 – 19:21
42a	Jeremiah 1:1 – 2:3
42b	Jeremiah 2:4 – 28

Haftarot concerning Deuteronomy page 239

43	Isaiah 1:1 - 27
44	Isaiah 40:1 – 26
45	Isaiah 49:14 – 51:3
46	Isaiah 54:11 – 55:5
47	Isaiah 51:12 – 52:12
48	Isaiah 54:1 – 10

49	Isaiah 60:1 – 22	
50a	Isaiah 61:10 – 63:9	
50b	Hosea 14:2 – 10; Joel 2:15 – 27; Micah 7:18 – 20	
51	2 Samuel 22:1 - 51	
52	Joshua 1:1 – 18	

Some Haftarot concerning special occasions   page 293

Rosh Hashana	1 Samuel 1:1 – 2:10	p. 293
Yom Kippur	Isaiah 57:14 – 58:14	p. 299
Sukkot (eighth day)	1 Kings 8:54 – 66	p. 304
Simchat Torah	Joshua 1 (Week 52)	
Chanukka	Zechariah 2:14 – 4:7 (Week 36)	
Shabbat Shekalim	2 Kings 11:17 – 12:17	p. 309
Shabbat Sachor	1 Samuel 15:1 – 34	p. 313
Shabbat Para	Ezekiel 36:16 – 38	p. 321
Shabbat Hagadol	Malachi 3:4 – 4:6	p. 329
Pessach (first day)	Joshua 5:2 – 6:1,27	p. 335
Shawuot (second day)	Habakkuk 2:20 – 3:19	p. 341
Tisha B´Av	Jeremiah 8:13 – 9:24	p. 345